A 2000 HOMETOWN COLLECTION

America's Best Recipes

Oxmoor House®

©2000 by Oxmoor House, Inc.
Book Division of Southern Progress Corporation
P.O. Box 2463, Birmingham, Alabama 35201

ISBN: 0-8487-1949-2
ISSN: 0898-9982

Printed in the United States of America
First Printing 2000

Editor-in-Chief: Nancy Fitzpatrick Wyatt
Senior Foods Editor: Susan Carlisle Payne
Senior Editor, Copy and Homes: Olivia Kindig Wells
Art Director: James Boone

America's Best Recipes: A 2000 Hometown Collection

Editor: Kelly Hooper Troiano
Senior Copy Editor: Keri Bradford Anderson
Copy Editor: Donna Baldone
Editorial Assistants: Allison Long Lowery, Suzanne Powell
Director, Test Kitchens: Elizabeth Tyler Luckett
Assistant Director, Test Kitchens: Julie Christopher
Recipe Editor: Gayle Hays Sadler
Test Kitchens Staff: Donna Baldone; Gretchen Feldtman, R.D.;
    Natalie E. King; Rebecca Mohr Boggan; Jan A. Smith
Senior Photographer: Jim Bathie
Photographer: Brit Huckabay
Senior Photo Stylist: Kay E. Clarke
Photo Stylist: Virginia R. Cravens
Director, Production and Distribution: Phillip Lee
Book Production Manager: Larry Hunter
Production Assistant: Faye Porter Bonner
Publishing Systems Administrator: Rick Tucker

CONTRIBUTORS
Designer: Rita Yerby
Test Kitchens: Leigh Mullinax; Kathleen Royal Phillips;
    Kate M. Wheeler, R.D.
Recipe Consultant: Janice Krahn Hanby
Copy Editor and Indexer: Mary Ann Laurens
Project Consultants: Meryle Evans, Jean Wickstrom Liles
Photo Stylist: Cathy Harris

Cover: Flourless Chocolate Cake *(page 107)*

WE'RE HERE FOR YOU!
    We at Oxmoor House are dedicated to serving you with
reliable information that expands your imagination and
enriches your life. We welcome your comments and
suggestions. Please write to us at:
    Oxmoor House, Inc.
    Editor, *America's Best Recipes*
    2100 Lakeshore Drive
    Birmingham, AL 35209

To order additional publications, call 1-205-877-6560.

Contents

Introduction

We invite you to a sampling of "America's best" in this extraordinary collection of recipes from community cookbooks across our nation. *America's Best Recipes–A 2000 Hometown Collection* offers recipes that represent the best of regional cuisine as well as tried-and-true family favorites. Each recipe is tested and rated by our Test Kitchens staff to ensure the quality of recipes you receive. Any minor changes from the originals reflect an update on can and package sizes and cooking techniques.

The beginner cook will appreciate the easy-to-use style of our recipes. *America's Best Recipes* also appeals to the experienced cook who will enjoy the creative and distinctive recipes found throughout the regions of our country. In today's busy world we can all relate to demands on our time. With this in mind, we offer the "Quick and Easy Recipes" chapter plus a special "What's for Supper?" chapter. These two chapters help you get a terrific meal on the table in a hurry. In them, you'll find:

• recipes that can be prepared and cooked in 45 minutes or less
• recipes that focus on easy family-friendly main dishes and one-dish meals. Some recipes include ingredients that can marinate during the day, while others can be made ahead and chilled overnight—all enabling the busy cook to prepare great family meals in less time and with great ease.

As a bonus, *America's Best Recipes* introduces you to wonderful charitable organizations across America. We invite you to find out more about these groups and their efforts to lend a helping hand to their communities. On page 320 you'll find addresses to contact the organizations to place an order for their cookbooks. Your purchase of their publications provides you with family-pleasing recipes as well as the satisfaction of knowing you've helped support the local communities and their charitable causes.

The Editors

What's for Supper?

Cantonese Shrimp and Pea Pods, page 31

What's For Supper?

If you're like most people, you want to serve nutritious and flavorful meals but a busy schedule doesn't leave you with much time to cook. Throughout this chapter, you'll find main dishes, one-dish meals, and slow cooker recipes that will allow you to enjoy great taste with little effort. To aid in your dinner preparation, peruse these quick tips to help get you in and out of the kitchen *fast*!

Shopping Savvy

- Prepare your grocery list in categories to match the aisles in the supermarket—you'll be surprised by how fast you can shop.

- Keep an ongoing grocery list to jot down items you need.

- Purchase ready-to-use bags of spinach, broccoli flowerets, carrots, and mixed greens for easy salads and side dishes.

- Have your grocer peel, devein, and steam shrimp for you.

- Use refrigerated or fresh pasta—it cooks in a fraction of the time of dried. And boil-in-bag rice cooks in half the time of regular rice.

- Buy deli-roasted chicken to use in recipes calling for cooked chicken. One roasted chicken yields about 2½ cups chopped cooked chicken.

Be a Kitchen Magician

- Use kitchen shears to chop canned tomatoes right in the can, trim fat from raw meat, snip fresh herbs, and cut up mini pizzas or pita bread.

- Chop extra onions and peppers to freeze in plastic bags for later.

- Brown a pound of ground beef, with onion if desired, and freeze in 1-cup containers. Then just thaw a portion for a head start on dinner.

- Freeze extra tomato sauce, gravy, or broth in ice cube trays to reheat as needed in soups and main dishes.

- Save butter wrappers in your refrigerator to grease cooking pans.

- Keep a container of cut-up brownies in your freezer for an instant dessert. Just pop brownies in the microwave, and top with ice cream.

Tricks for Easy Cleanup

- Marinate ingredients in zip-top plastic bags to eliminate cleanup.

- Line your broiler pan with aluminum foil for instant cleanup.

- Spray a grater with cooking spray before shredding cheese to make the grater easy to clean. Freeze extra cheese for quick use.

- Save cleanup time and avoid a huge stack of dishes in the sink later by cleaning as you go.

Save Time with Appliances

- Invest in a gas grill; it heats up instantly, and cleanup is simple.

- Dust off your slow cooker. By producing a low temperature, the slow cooker safely simmers food for hours, giving you a home-cooked meal at the end of the day.

- Make the most of your microwave by using it for these shortcuts:

Microwave Shortcuts

FOOD	TEMPERATURE	AMOUNT	TIME
Melting Chocolate Morsels	Cook at MEDIUM (50% power)	½ to 1 cup 1½ cups 2 cups	2 to 3 minutes 3 to 3½ minutes 3½ to 4 minutes
Place chocolate in a bowl; microwave at MEDIUM until melted, stirring once.			
Melting Chocolate Squares	Cook at MEDIUM (50% power)	1 to 3 squares 4 to 5 squares 6 squares	1½ to 2 minutes 2 to 2½ minutes 2½ to 3 minutes
Place chocolate in a bowl; microwave at MEDIUM until melted, stirring once.			
Melting Butter	Cook at HIGH	1 to 2 tablespoons ¼ to ½ cup 1 cup	35 to 45 seconds 1 minute 1½ to 2 minutes
Place butter in a 2-cup liquid measure; microwave at HIGH until melted.			
Softening Butter	Cook at LOW (10% power)	1 to 2 tablespoons ¼ to ½ cup 1 cup	15 to 30 seconds 1 to 1¼ minutes 1½ to 1¾ minutes
Place butter on a microwave-safe plate; microwave at LOW until softened.			
Baking Potatoes	Cook at HIGH	1 medium (6 to 7 oz.) 2 medium 4 medium	4 to 6 minutes 7 to 8 minutes 12 to 14 minutes
Rinse potatoes, and pat dry; prick several times with a fork. Arrange in microwave, leaving 1-inch space between potatoes. (Arrange in a circle if microwaving more that 2 potatoes.) Microwave at HIGH until done, turning and rearranging once. Let stand 5 minutes to complete cooking.			
Cooking Bacon	Cook at HIGH	1 slice 2 slices 4 slices 6 slices	1 to 2 minutes 2 to 3 minutes 3½ to 4½ minutes 5 to 7 minutes
Place bacon on a microwave-safe rack in an 11- x 7- x 1½ -inch baking dish; cover with paper towels. Microwave at HIGH until bacon is crisp; drain.			

These times are based on a 700-watt microwave oven. Your times may vary if your oven is a different wattage.

Three-Cheese Enchiladas

Cheese lovers will delight over these enchiladas loaded with Monterey Jack, Cheddar, and cream cheese.

Vegetable cooking spray
1½ cups (6 ounces) shredded
  Monterey Jack cheese,
  divided
1½ cups (6 ounces) shredded
  Cheddar cheese, divided
1 (3-ounce) package cream
  cheese, softened
1 cup picante sauce,
  divided

1 medium-size sweet red or
  green pepper, diced
1½ cups chopped onion
½ teaspoon ground cumin
8 (8-inch) flour tortillas
Shredded lettuce
Chopped tomato
Sliced ripe olives
Additional picante sauce
  (optional)

Lightly coat a 13- x 9- x 2-inch baking dish with cooking spray; set aside. Combine 1 cup Monterey Jack cheese, 1 cup Cheddar cheese, cream cheese, ¼ cup picante sauce, pepper, onion, and cumin; stir well. Spoon ½ cup cheese mixture down center of each tortilla. Roll up tortillas; place tortillas, seam side down, in prepared dish. Spoon remaining ¾ cup picante sauce over tortillas; sprinkle with remaining cheeses.

Bake, uncovered, at 350° for 20 minutes or until enchiladas are thoroughly heated. Top with lettuce, tomato, and olives. Serve with additional picante sauce, if desired. Yield: 4 servings.   Dorothy Bullard

Morrisonville's 125th Anniversary Cookbook
Morrisonville Historical Society & Museum
Morrisonville, Illinois

Greek Pizza

1 (3-ounce) package dried
  tomatoes
1 (16-ounce) Italian bread crust
  (we tested with Boboli)
1 tablespoon olive oil
1 cup pizza sauce
1 tablespoon chopped fresh
  basil or 1 teaspoon dried
  basil

1 (2¼-ounce) can sliced ripe
  olives, drained
1 (4-ounce) package crumbled
  feta cheese
¾ cup freshly grated Parmesan
  cheese

Pour enough boiling water over tomatoes to cover; let stand 10 minutes. Drain and slice tomatoes; set aside.

Place pizza on a baking sheet; brush olive oil over pizza crust. Spread pizza sauce over crust. Sprinkle basil over sauce. Add olives and chopped tomatoes. Sprinkle cheeses evenly over pizza. Bake at 400° for 10 to 12 minutes or until cheeses melt. Yield: 2 to 4 servings.   Jean Dobson

Food for the Soul
Matt Talbot Kitchen
Lincoln, Nebraska

Boeuf Bourguignon (Beef Burgundy)

1 (3-pound) beef round or rump roast, cut into 1½-inch cubes	2 tablespoons tomato paste
3 tablespoons butter or margarine, melted	1 teaspoon dried thyme, crushed
1 large onion, sliced	1 bay leaf
1 clove garlic, minced	½ pound frozen pearl onions
¼ cup all-purpose flour	1 (8-ounce) package small fresh mushrooms
1 cup dry red wine	½ teaspoon salt
1 (10½-ounce) can condensed beef broth	¼ teaspoon pepper
	Hot cooked egg noodles

Brown beef in butter in a large skillet over medium heat. Transfer beef to a 3-quart electric slow cooker.

Cook sliced onion and garlic 5 minutes in drippings in skillet. Stir in flour; cook, stirring constantly, 1 minute. Slowly stir in wine, broth, and tomato paste; cook until sauce thickens. Add thyme and next 5 ingredients; pour over beef in slow cooker. Cover and cook on LOW setting 8 hours. Discard bay leaf before serving. Serve over noodles. Yield: 6 servings.   Barb Teske

Kenwood Lutheran Church Cookbook
Kenwood Women of the Evangelical Lutheran Church in America
Duluth, Minnesota

Melt-in-Your-Mouth Roast

This roast really lives up to its name. Its rich flavor is achieved by just a few simple ingredients. Be sure to cut roast in half before placing in the slow cooker—this ensures even cooking for large cuts of meat.

1 large onion, sliced
2 teaspoons salt
½ teaspoon pepper
1 (3- to 4-pound) rump roast,
   cut in half

1 tablespoon vegetable oil
2 tablespoons Worcestershire
   sauce
3 tablespoons all-purpose flour
¼ cup water

Place onion in a 4-quart electric slow cooker. Combine salt and pepper, and rub on all sides of roast. Cook roast in hot oil in a large skillet over medium-high heat until browned on all sides. Remove roast from skillet, and place on top of onion in slow cooker. Add Worcestershire sauce to skillet, deglazing skillet by scraping particles that cling to bottom. Pour Worcestershire sauce mixture over meat and onion.

Cover and cook on HIGH setting 1 hour. Reduce to LOW setting, and cook 7 hours or until meat is very tender. Remove meat and onion to a platter; cover and keep warm. Combine flour and water, stirring until smooth. Stir flour mixture into drippings in cooker. Cook on HIGH 10 minutes or until thickened and bubbly, stirring occasionally. Yield: 8 servings.

Stephanie Hightower Kraft

Savory Secrets
Runnels School
Baton Rouge, Louisiana

Mushroom Beef Patties

These patties are comfort food at its best! Be sure to serve with plenty of mashed potatoes to soak up every bit of the Mushroom Sauce.

1 pound ground round
1 cup chopped fresh
  mushrooms
1 large egg, lightly beaten
⅛ teaspoon salt
⅛ teaspoon pepper
2 green onions, finely chopped

1 tablespoon cornstarch
⅓ cup half-and-half
2 tablespoons butter or
  margarine, melted
Mushroom Sauce
2 tablespoons minced fresh
  parsley

Combine first 8 ingredients in a large bowl; shape into 6 patties. Cook patties in butter in a large skillet over medium heat 5 to 6 minutes on each side or until done.

While patties cook, prepare Mushroom Sauce. Spoon warm sauce over patties, and sprinkle with parsley. Yield: 6 servings.

Mushroom Sauce

1½ cups sliced fresh
  mushrooms
1 tablespoon butter or
  margarine, melted

2 tablespoons all-purpose flour
1⅓ cups half-and-half
⅛ teaspoon salt
⅛ teaspoon pepper

Sauté sliced mushrooms in melted butter in a medium saucepan over medium heat until tender. Sprinkle flour over mushrooms, stirring gently until blended; gradually add half-and-half. Cook, stirring constantly, until sauce is thickened and bubbly; add salt and pepper. Yield: 1¾ cups.

Susan Knight

Cookin' in the Canyon
Jarbidge Community Hall
Jarbidge, Nevada

Quick Chili-Rice Dinner

Quick-cooking rice adds to the ease of this one-dish meal. Top it off with cornbread from the deli counter of your local supermarket, and you'll have dinner ready in a snap! An iron skillet works well for cooking and serving this home-style dinner.

1 pound ground beef
⅓ cup chopped onion
1 (15¼-ounce) can whole
    kernel corn
1 (15-ounce) can tomato sauce
1 large green pepper, chopped
½ cup water

1 teaspoon chili powder
½ teaspoon dry mustard
1 cup uncooked instant rice
    (we tested with Minute Rice)
½ cup (2 ounces) shredded
    Cheddar cheese

Brown beef and onion in a large skillet over medium-high heat, stirring until beef crumbles. Drain meat mixture, and return to skillet. Add corn and next 5 ingredients. Cover and bring to a boil, stirring often. Stir in rice; cover, reduce heat, and simmer 5 minutes. Sprinkle with cheese before serving. Yield: 4 servings. Val Boone

The Great Delights Cookbook
Genoa Serbart United Methodist Churches
Genoa, Colorado

Corn Moussaka

1 (15¼-ounce) can whole
    kernel corn, drained
Vegetable cooking spray
1 pound ground beef
1 small onion, chopped
2 tablespoons all-purpose flour
½ (6-ounce) can tomato paste
1 teaspoon garlic salt
1 teaspoon ground cinnamon
1 (12-ounce) carton cottage
    cheese

1 tablespoon chopped fresh
    chives
2 large eggs, lightly beaten
2 cups (8 ounces) shredded
    mozzarella cheese
¼ cup freshly grated Parmesan
    cheese
½ cup slivered almonds

Spread corn on bottom of an 11- x 7- x 1½-inch baking dish coated with cooking spray; set aside.

Brown ground beef and onion in a large skillet over medium-high heat, stirring until beef crumbles; drain. Return meat to skillet. Reduce heat to low; stir in flour. Cook 2 minutes. Stir in tomato paste, garlic salt, and cinnamon. Spread meat mixture over corn, pressing firmly. Bake at 350° for 15 minutes.

Combine cottage cheese, chives, and eggs; spread over meat mixture. Top with mozzarella cheese, Parmesan cheese, and almonds. Bake, uncovered, 30 more minutes or until topping is set and cheese browns. Yield: 6 servings. The Wade Family

From Home Plate to Home Cooking
The Atlanta Braves
Atlanta, Georgia

Olive Mexican Fiesta

1 **pound ground beef**
1 **small onion, chopped**
1 **(14.5-ounce) can diced tomatoes**
1 **(8-ounce) can tomato sauce**
1 **(1.25-ounce) package chili sauce mix**
1 **(15-ounce) can kidney beans, drained**
1 **(11-ounce) can whole kernel corn, drained**

1 **(4.5-ounce) can chopped green chiles**
1 **cup pitted ripe olives, cut in half lengthwise**
½ **(10-ounce) package tortilla chips**
1 **cup (4 ounces) shredded Cheddar cheese**
Additional tortilla chips (optional)

Brown beef and onion in a large skillet over medium-high heat, stirring until beef crumbles; drain. Return meat to skillet. Stir in tomatoes, tomato sauce, and chili sauce mix. Bring to a boil; reduce heat, and simmer, uncovered, 5 minutes. Add beans and next 3 ingredients.

Arrange half of tortilla chips in bottom of a greased 13- x 9- x 2-inch baking dish. Spoon half of meat mixture over chips. Repeat layers with remaining half of chips and meat mixture. Top with cheese; arrange additional tortilla chips around edges of dish, if desired. Bake, uncovered, at 400° for 15 minutes. Yield: 6 servings. Charline Poulan

Shared Treasures
First Baptist Church
Monroe, Louisiana

One-Skillet Spaghetti

Serve this spaghetti straight from the skillet. During preparation, be sure to add spaghetti to the skillet before tomatoes, vegetables, and seasonings to ensure pasta cooks evenly.

1 pound ground beef
2 medium onions, chopped
1 (7-ounce) package spaghetti
1 (28-ounce) can diced
  tomatoes, undrained
¾ cup chopped green peppers
½ cup water
1 (8-ounce) can sliced
  mushrooms, drained

1 teaspoon sugar
1 teaspoon salt
1 teaspoon chili powder
1 teaspoon dried oregano
1 cup (4 ounces) shredded
  Cheddar cheese

Brown beef and onion in a heavy 12-inch skillet, stirring until beef crumbles; drain. Return meat to skillet. Break spaghetti in half; add spaghetti, tomatoes, and next 7 ingredients to skillet, stirring well. Bring mixture to a boil. Cover, reduce heat, and simmer 30 minutes or until spaghetti is tender. Sprinkle with cheese; cover and let stand 3 minutes or until cheese melts. Yield: 4 servings.

Culinary Classics
Hoffman Estates Medical Center Service League
Hoffman Estates, Illinois

Sweet-and-Sour Meatballs with Pineapple and Pepper over Rice

1 pound ground beef
1 large egg, beaten
2 tablespoons chopped
  onion
1 tablespoon cornstarch
1 teaspoon salt
¼ teaspoon pepper
1 tablespoon vegetable oil
1 (8-ounce) can sliced
  pineapple, undrained

1 (6-ounce) can pineapple
  juice
3 tablespoons cornstarch
1 tablespoon soy sauce
3 tablespoons white vinegar
¼ cup plus 2 tablespoons water
⅓ cup sugar
3 medium-size green peppers,
  cut into strips
Hot cooked rice

Combine first 6 ingredients; shape into 40 (1-inch) balls. Cook meatballs in hot oil in a large skillet over medium-high heat until browned; drain.

Drain pineapple, reserving juice; cut pineapple slices into sixths, and set aside. Combine reserved juice, pineapple juice, and next 5 ingredients, stirring well with a wire whisk.

Add juice mixture to skillet. Bring to a boil over medium-high heat, deglazing skillet by scraping particles that cling to bottom. Stir in green pepper. Reduce heat, and simmer, stirring constantly, 2 minutes or until thickened. Add meatballs and reserved pineapple. Cook just until thoroughly heated. Serve over rice. Yield: 4 to 5 servings.   Carol Porter

Cooking from the Heart
Girl Scout Troop 669
Metairie, Louisiana

Pinky's Soup

1 pound ground chuck
2 carrots, scraped and finely chopped
2 stalks celery, finely chopped
1 medium onion, chopped
1 (1.25-ounce) package spaghetti sauce mix

1 (6-ounce) can tomato paste
6 cups water
½ cup instant mashed potato flakes (we tested with Idahoan)
Salt and pepper to taste

Cook first 4 ingredients in a Dutch oven over medium-high heat, stirring until beef crumbles and vegetables are crisp-tender; drain. Return mixture to Dutch oven.

Add sauce mix, tomato paste, and water to Dutch oven. Bring to a boil; cover, reduce heat, and simmer 30 minutes, stirring occasionally. Stir in potato flakes, and cook 5 more minutes. Stir in salt and pepper. Yield: 9 cups.   Margaret Peterson

Barnard's 'Beary' Best Cookbook
Barnard United Methodist Youth Department
Barnard, Kansas

Veal Stew with Roquefort

1½ pounds veal for stew
¼ cup all-purpose flour
1 tablespoon butter, melted
1 tablespoon olive oil
1½ quarts hot water
1½ teaspoons salt
¼ teaspoon pepper
4 medium baking potatoes,
   sliced
4 medium carrots, scraped and
   sliced
2 medium onions, sliced
¼ cup chopped fresh parsley
¼ cup crumbled Roquefort
   cheese
½ cup dry white wine

Place veal in a heavy-duty, zip-top plastic bag; add flour. Close bag, and shake until veal is coated.

Brown veal in butter and oil in a large Dutch oven. Add water, salt, and pepper; bring to a boil. Cover, reduce heat, and simmer 1 hour or until tender. Add potato, carrot, onion, and parsley. Bring to a boil; cover, reduce heat, and simmer 30 more minutes or until vegetables are tender.

Remove meat and vegetables from Dutch oven to a serving dish; keep warm. Add cheese and wine to remaining sauce; cook until cheese melts. Serve sauce with meat and vegetables. Yield: 12 cups.

Eat Your Dessert or You Won't Get Any Broccoli
Sea Pines Montessori School
Hilton Head Island, South Carolina

Lamb and White Bean Chili

1 cup dried navy beans
12¾ cups water, divided
4 (1-ounce) slices smoked slab
  bacon
4 dried hot New Mexico chiles
1 dried chipotle chile
3 cups hot water
1½ pounds trimmed boneless
  lamb
1½ teaspoons salt
¼ teaspoon pepper
2 tablespoons olive oil
1 medium onion, finely
  chopped

3 cloves garlic, minced
1½ tablespoons ground cumin
2 tablespoons coarsely
  chopped fresh thyme
1 tablespoon coarsely chopped
  fresh oregano
1 (28-ounce) can crushed
  tomatoes, undrained
1 (6-ounce) can tomato paste
2 tablespoons sugar
3 bay leaves
3 cups hot cooked rice

Sort and rinse beans; place beans in a medium saucepan. Add 6 cups water. Bring to a boil over high heat; boil, uncovered, 3 minutes. Cover, remove from heat, and let stand 1 hour. Drain beans, and return to saucepan. Add bacon and another 6 cups water; bring to a boil. Cover, reduce heat, and simmer 30 minutes or until beans are tender. Coarsely chop bacon, and return to bean mixture.

Using rubber gloves, remove and discard stems and seeds from chiles. Place chiles in a medium bowl; add 3 cups hot water, and let stand 20 minutes. Process mixture in container of an electric blender until smooth, stopping once to scrape down sides; set aside.

Season lamb with salt and pepper. Brown lamb in olive oil in a large Dutch oven over medium-high heat. Remove lamb from pan, reserving drippings in pan; set lamb aside.

Add onion and garlic to drippings in Dutch oven; cook, stirring constantly, until onion is tender. Stir in cumin, thyme, and oregano; cook 1 minute, stirring constantly.

Return lamb to Dutch oven. Add chile mixture, tomatoes, tomato paste, sugar, bay leaves, and remaining ¾ cup water. Bring to a boil; partially cover, reduce heat, and simmer 1 hour and 30 minutes, stirring occasionally. Discard bay leaves.

Add beans to lamb mixture, and serve over rice. Yield: 8 cups.

International Home Cooking
The United Nations International School Parents Association
New York, New York

Fantastic Pork Fajitas

1 pound lean boneless pork (we tested with pork tenderloin)
2 cloves garlic, minced
1 teaspoon dried oregano
1 teaspoon seasoned salt
½ teaspoon ground cumin
2 tablespoons orange juice
2 tablespoons cider vinegar
Dash of vinegar-pepper sauce
1 tablespoon vegetable oil
1 medium onion, sliced
1 medium-size green pepper, sliced
4 (8-inch) flour tortillas
Shredded lettuce
Sliced green onions
Salsa

Slice pork into ⅛-inch-thick strips. Combine garlic and next 6 ingredients in a large heavy-duty, zip-top plastic bag; add pork. Seal bag, tossing to coat pork; marinate in refrigerator 10 minutes.

Heat oil in a large skillet over medium-high heat until hot. Add pork mixture; sauté until pork is no longer pink. Add onion and green pepper; sauté 8 minutes or until onion is golden.

Heat tortillas according to package directions, if desired. Divide pork mixture evenly among tortillas. Top with lettuce, green onions, and salsa. Roll up tortillas. Yield: 4 servings.   Ann Martens

Scent from P.E.O. Sisterhood
Philanthropic Educational Organization, Chapter AG
Newcastle, Wyoming

Basque Bean Cassoulet

This classic French dish is cooked slowly in the oven, allowing the flavors to blend. The result is a hearty one-dish meal guaranteed to warm you up on a winter's night.

1 pound navy beans
3 cups water
¼ pound salt pork
1 pound mild or hot Italian sausage, cut into ½-inch slices
2 medium leeks, thinly sliced
2 cups chopped onion
6 whole cloves
1 medium onion
1 bay leaf

6 whole peppercorns
1 (14½-ounce) can chicken broth
5 carrots, scraped and cut into 1-inch slices
5 cloves garlic, minced
1 teaspoon dried thyme
1 teaspoon dried marjoram
2 teaspoons hot sauce
1 (14.5-ounce) can diced tomatoes, undrained

Sort and rinse beans; place in an ovenproof Dutch oven, and add water. Let soak 2 hours; do not drain.

Brown salt pork and sausage in a large skillet over medium-high heat. Remove salt pork, and discard. Drain sausage, reserving drippings in skillet. Add leeks and chopped onion to skillet; sauté over medium-high heat 5 minutes or until tender.

Press cloves firmly into 1 side of whole onion.

Place bay leaf and peppercorns on a square of cheesecloth; tie with string.

Add leek mixture to beans, stirring well; add sausage, clove-studded onion, cheesecloth bag, chicken broth, and remaining ingredients. Cover and bake at 350° for 1½ hours. Uncover and bake 30 more minutes or until beans are tender. Discard clove-studded onion and cheesecloth bag before serving. Yield: 11 cups.

Simply Divine
Second-Ponce de Leon Baptist Church
Atlanta, Georgia

Baked Salsa Pork Chops

These jazzy chops make plenty of extra sauce—perfect for topping mashed potatoes.

8 (6-ounce) rib pork chops
   (½ to ¾ inch thick)
8 (¼-inch-thick) onion slices
⅔ cup medium salsa
3 tablespoons lemon juice

⅔ cup firmly packed brown
   sugar
1¼ teaspoons salt
¼ teaspoon pepper

Arrange pork chops in a single layer in a 13- x 9- x 2-inch baking dish. Top each pork chop with 1 onion slice.

Combine salsa and remaining 4 ingredients; stir well. Pour salsa mixture evenly over pork chops.

Cover and bake at 350° for 30 minutes. Uncover and bake 1 more hour. Yield: 8 servings.

June E. Albert

St. Paul's 50th Anniversary Cookbook
St. Paul's Lutheran Church
Erie, Pennsylvania

Bubble-Up Pizza

Here's a one-dish meal the whole family will enjoy. Just add a green salad, if desired, and forget the pizza deliveryman.

2 (7.5-ounce) cans buttermilk
   biscuits (we tested with
   Pillsbury)
1 (14-ounce) jar pizza sauce or
   spaghetti sauce (about 1⅓
   cups), divided (we tested with
   Ragu Pizza Quick)
1 pound ground pork sausage,
   cooked and drained

1 (2¼-ounce) can sliced ripe
   olives, drained
1 (8-ounce) package sliced
   fresh mushrooms
3 cups (12 ounces) shredded
   Cheddar cheese, divided
½ to 1 (8-ounce) package sliced
   pepperoni

Tear biscuit dough into quarters; place in a large bowl. Add 1 cup pizza sauce, sausage, olives, mushrooms, and 1½ cups cheese; stir well. Spread in a greased 13- x 9- x 2-inch pan. Layer pepperoni as desired over biscuit mixture; spread remaining pizza sauce over pepperoni. Sprinkle with remaining cheese. Bake, uncovered, at 375° for 35 to 40 minutes or until biscuits are done. Yield: 8 servings. Ann Linn

The Flavors of Mackinac
Mackinac Island Medical Center
Mackinac Island, Michigan

Ham and Cheese Stromboli

Stuffed with savory ham, mozzarella, and spaghetti sauce, this "sand-wich" makes a family-pleasing supper.

1 (32-ounce) package frozen bread dough, thawed and divided (we tested with Rich's)	1 cup (4 ounces) shredded mozzarella cheese
2 cups diced cooked ham	1 (4.5-ounce) can sliced mushrooms, drained
1 cup grated Parmesan cheese	⅓ cup spaghetti sauce
	Butter or margarine, melted

Place 1 loaf bread dough on a lightly floured surface; roll dough into a 15- x 8-inch rectangle. Layer half each of ham, Parmesan cheese, mozzarella cheese, sliced mushrooms, and spaghetti sauce lengthwise down 1 side of dough, leaving a ½-inch border at top and bottom of dough. Fold plain half of dough over filling; pinch seam and ends to seal. Repeat with remaining loaf dough and filling ingredients.

Transfer loaves to lightly greased baking sheets; cut 5 small slits in top of each loaf. Brush loaves with melted butter. Bake at 375° for 35 minutes or until loaves are lightly browned. Slice loaves to serve. Yield: 8 servings. Hedy Nagel

Plummer House Museum
Traill County Historical Society
Hillsboro, North Dakota

Chef Elizabeth Ware's Arroz con Pollo

¼ cup vegetable oil
1 medium onion, chopped
1 large green pepper, chopped
2 cloves garlic, minced
¼ cup tomato sauce
1 teaspoon bijol or ¾ teaspoon saffron threads
1 (3-pound) chicken, cut up and skinned

1 tablespoon salt
½ teaspoon pepper
1 (12-ounce) can beer
1 cup water
2 cups uncooked long-grain rice
1 (8½-ounce) can English peas, drained
1 (4-ounce) jar diced pimientos, drained

Heat oil in a large straight-sided ovenproof skillet over medium-high heat. Add onion, green pepper, and garlic; sauté 2 minutes. Stir in tomato sauce and bijol.

Sprinkle chicken with salt and pepper; arrange chicken in skillet with vegetables. Cook 2 minutes on each side. Add beer and next 3 ingredients. Set aside 1 tablespoon pimiento; add remaining pimiento to skillet.

Cover and bake at 325° for 30 to 35 minutes or until chicken is done, rice is tender, and liquid is absorbed. Garnish with reserved pimiento. Yield: 4 to 6 servings.

Tested by Time
Porter Gaud Parents Guild
Charleston, South Carolina

Chicken Pontarelli

Mix these ingredients the night before, and you can pop this dish in the oven as soon as you get home from work.

1 (8-ounce) package vermicelli
Vegetable cooking spray
1 (8-ounce) package sliced fresh mushrooms
1 pound skinned and boned chicken breast halves, cut into bite-size pieces
1 (8-ounce) can sliced water chestnuts, drained

2 (10¾-ounce) cans cream of chicken soup, undiluted
½ cup mayonnaise
1 cup (4 ounces) shredded Cheddar cheese
¾ cup shredded Parmesan cheese

Cook vermicelli according to package directions; drain and rinse with cold water. Drain well.

Meanwhile, coat a large skillet with cooking spray. Cook mushrooms in skillet over medium-high heat, stirring constantly, until tender.

Place vermicelli in a 13- x 9- x 2-inch baking dish coated with cooking spray. Top evenly with chicken pieces, mushrooms, and water chestnuts.

Combine soup, mayonnaise, and Cheddar cheese; stir well. Spoon evenly over chicken mixture. Sprinkle with Parmesan cheese. Cover and chill overnight, if desired.

Remove from refrigerator 10 minutes before baking. Cover and bake at 350° for 1 hour. Uncover and bake 20 more minutes; let stand 10 minutes before serving. Yield: 6 servings.   Karen Stensrud

Our Favorite Recipes
Lutheran Church of the Good Shepherd
Billings, Montana

Crock-Pot® Chicken Dinner

Toast rice in a little oil for a nutty flavor before adding water.

5 **large skinned and boned chicken breast halves**	1 **(4.5-ounce) can chopped green chiles, undrained**
1 **(14½-ounce) can ready-to-serve chicken broth**	1 **medium onion, chopped**
1 **(10¾-ounce) can cream of chicken soup, undiluted**	1 **tablespoon vegetable oil**
	1 **cup uncooked long-grain rice**
	2 **cups water**

Place chicken in a 4- or 5-quart electric slow cooker. Combine broth, soup, chiles, and onion; stir well. Pour over chicken. Cook on HIGH setting 1 hour; reduce to LOW setting, and cook 7 hours.

Pour oil into a medium saucepan; heat over medium-high heat until hot. Add rice, and cook, stirring constantly, until rice is lightly browned. Gradually add water; bring to a boil. Cover, reduce heat, and simmer 20 minutes or until liquid is absorbed and rice is tender. Serve chicken and sauce over rice. Yield: 5 servings.   Heidi Cave

Cooking with Pride
Madison Park/Camelview PTO
Phoenix, Arizona

Adobe Chicken Casserole

This is a great make-ahead dish. But if you prefer to serve it the same day, just cover and bake at 350° for 40 minutes; then uncover and bake 5 more minutes or until bubbly. Don't worry if you don't have brown rice on hand, simply double the amount of white rice–or vice versa!

1 medium onion, chopped
3 cloves garlic, minced
2 tablespoons vegetable oil
3 cups chopped cooked chicken
2 cups cooked long-grain rice
2 cups cooked brown rice
1 (14½-ounce) can whole tomatoes, drained and chopped

½ teaspoon salt
½ teaspoon pepper
1 (16-ounce) carton sour cream
2 (4-ounce) cans whole green chiles, drained and cut into strips
3 cups (12 ounces) shredded Monterey Jack cheese
1 (2¼-ounce) can sliced ripe olives, drained

Cook onion and garlic in hot oil in a medium skillet, stirring constantly, until tender. Combine onion mixture, chicken, and next 5 ingredients in a large bowl; stir well.

Spoon half of chicken mixture into a greased deep 3-quart casserole. Spoon half of sour cream over chicken mixture; top with half of chiles, half of cheese, and olives. Repeat layers, ending with cheese. Cover and chill overnight.

Remove casserole from refrigerator; let stand at room temperature 20 minutes. Cover and bake at 350° for 45 minutes. Uncover and bake 15 more minutes or until thoroughly heated and bubbly. Let stand 10 minutes before serving. Yield: 6 servings. Ethel Ihrig

Culinary Tastes of Blue Mountain Cooks
Grand Terrace Branch Library: Friends
Grand Terrace, California

Deluxe Chicken Casserole

If this recipe reminds you of similar recipes you had growing up, then you'll enjoy this comforting casserole as much as we did. The chopped nuts are an added pleasure to this classic chicken dish.

1½ cups diced cooked chicken
1½ cups cooked rice
1 cup chopped celery
½ cup chopped walnuts or pecans
1 (10¾-ounce) can cream of chicken soup, undiluted
2 teaspoons finely chopped onion
½ teaspoon salt
½ teaspoon black pepper
¼ teaspoon ground red pepper
1 tablespoon lemon juice
¾ cup mayonnaise
¼ cup water
3 hard-cooked eggs, sliced
2 cups coarsely crumbled potato chips

Combine first 10 ingredients in a large bowl. Combine mayonnaise and water; stir with a wire whisk until smooth. Add mayonnaise mixture to chicken mixture. Gently fold in egg slices.

Spoon mixture into a greased 11- x 7- x 1½-inch baking dish; top with potato chips. Bake, uncovered at 400° for 15 minutes or until bubbly. Yield: 6 servings.   Selina Lyman

'Pon Top Edisto
Trinity Episcopal Church
Edisto Island, South Carolina

Green Enchiladas

Stuffed with cheese, sour cream, chicken, spinach, and chiles, these savory enchiladas received our highest rating. For extra zip, substitute Monterey Jack cheese with peppers for regular Jack cheese. If you'd like to get a jumpstart on this recipe using leftover chicken, you'll need 6 cups shredded.

4 cups water
2 pounds skinned and boned chicken breast halves
1 medium onion, finely chopped
¼ cup butter or margarine
1 (10-ounce) package frozen chopped spinach, thawed and drained
1 (16-ounce) carton sour cream
1 (8-ounce) carton sour cream
1 (4.5-ounce) can chopped green chiles, drained
¾ cup milk
1 teaspoon ground cumin
¼ teaspoon salt
¼ teaspoon pepper
12 (6-inch) flour tortillas
1 (16-ounce) package Monterey Jack cheese, shredded

Bring water to a boil in a large nonstick skillet over medium heat. Add chicken; cover, reduce heat, and simmer 15 minutes or until tender. Remove chicken, and shred; set aside.

Sauté onion in butter in a large skillet over medium-high heat until tender. Remove from heat; add spinach and next 7 ingredients, stirring well.

Combine half of spinach mixture with chicken; stir well. Spoon one-third cup chicken mixture evenly down center of each tortilla; roll up tortillas, jellyroll fashion. Place tortillas, seam side down, in two lightly greased 11- x 7- x 1½-inch baking dishes. Sprinkle one-fourth of cheese evenly over each casserole. Spoon remaining spinach mixture over cheese; sprinkle with remaining cheese. Bake, uncovered, at 350° for 30 minutes. Yield: 6 servings. Pamela Hamza

Somethin's Cookin' with Married Young Adults
Houston's First Baptist Church
Houston, Texas

Chicken Fajita Potatoes

4 large baking potatoes
1 medium-size sweet red or green pepper, chopped
1 small onion, chopped
2 tablespoons butter or margarine, melted
1 tablespoon taco seasoning mix
1½ cups shredded cooked chicken breast (about 6 ounces)
½ cup (2 ounces) shredded Cheddar cheese

½ cup (2 ounces) shredded Monterey Jack cheese
1 (2¼-ounce) can sliced ripe olives, drained
2 tablespoons diced green chiles
1 cup salsa
Sour cream (optional)
Guacamole (optional)
Additional salsa (optional)

Scrub potatoes; pat dry. Wrap in aluminum foil, and bake at 400° for 1 hour or until tender. Cook pepper and onion in butter in a medium saucepan until tender. Add taco seasoning mix. Cook 1 minute, stirring constantly; remove from heat. Stir in chicken, cheeses, olives, and chiles.

Cut a lengthwise slit in top of each potato. Press each potato open. Spoon chicken mixture into potatoes. Spoon ¼ cup salsa over each potato. If desired, serve with sour cream, guacamole, and additional salsa. Yield: 4 servings.

Debbie Yagoda

Doggone Good Cookin'
Support Dogs, Inc.
St. Louis, Missouri

Oriental Chicken Salad

This easy one-dish meal makes good use of leftover chicken. If you prefer a meatless entrée, just omit the chicken—either way, you'll enjoy the crunchy creation.

1 (3-ounce) package oriental-flavored ramen noodles
½ cup slivered almonds
½ cup sunflower kernels
½ cup canola or vegetable oil
2 tablespoons sugar
2 tablespoons cider vinegar
2 roasted chicken breast halves, chopped (about 2⅓ cups)
1 (16-ounce) package coleslaw or salad mix

Crumble uncooked noodles; set seasoning packet aside. Combine noodles, almonds, and sunflower kernels on a baking sheet. Bake at 350° for 7 to 8 minutes or until golden, stirring occasionally.

Combine seasoning packet, oil, sugar, and vinegar in a jar. Cover tightly, and shake vigorously. Combine chicken, coleslaw mix, toasted noodles, almonds, sunflower kernels, and dressing; toss well. Serve immediately. Yield: 4 to 6 servings.   Marsha Taylor

Somethin's Cookin' with Married Young Adults
Houston's First Baptist Church
Houston, Texas

Cornish Hens Succotash

Corn and limas, traditional Succotash ingredients, cook in the pot with cornish hens for a colorful dinner.

2 (1½- to 2-pound) Cornish hens
¼ teaspoon salt
¼ teaspoon pepper
3 slices thickly sliced bacon
1 (10-ounce) package frozen lima beans
1 (10-ounce) package frozen whole kernel corn
1 (14.5-ounce) can whole tomatoes, undrained and chopped
1 tablespoon minced fresh parsley
1 teaspoon dried sage

Remove giblets from hens; reserve for another use. Rinse hens thoroughly under cold water, and pat dry with paper towels. Halve hens, and remove backbones. Sprinkle salt and pepper over hens.

Cook bacon in a Dutch oven until crisp; remove bacon, reserving drippings in Dutch oven. Crumble bacon, and set aside.

Cook hens in drippings 15 minutes or until browned; drain, reserving hens and 1 tablespoon drippings in pan. Add lima beans and remaining 4 ingredients. Cover and cook 25 minutes or until hens and vegetables are done; sprinkle with bacon. Yield: 4 servings.

Perennial Palette
Southborough Gardeners
Southborough, Massachusetts

Crock-Pot® Turkey Breast

This slow cooker recipe yields a deliciously moist turkey breast. For convenience, have the butcher cut the turkey breast in half to ensure even cooking.

1 (5-pound) bone-in turkey breast, cut in half	2 tablespoons all-purpose flour
2 teaspoons lemon pepper	3 tablespoons water

Sprinkle turkey evenly with lemon-pepper seasoning. Place turkey meaty side down, in a 4-quart electric slow cooker. Cook on HIGH setting 1 hour; reduce to LOW setting, and cook 7 to 9 hours.

Remove turkey from cooker. Combine flour and water with a wire whisk. Add to juices in slow cooker. Cook, uncovered, on HIGH setting 15 minutes or until gravy is thickened and bubbly, stirring often. Serve gravy with hot cooked rice and over turkey breast. Yield: 10 servings.

Eileen deHaro

Spice It Up!
Baton Rouge Branch of American Association
of University Women
Baton Rouge, Louisiana

Easy Salmon and Vegetables in Foil

Substitute any favorite fresh herb, such as basil, thyme, or parsley, for dill in this easy and tasty salmon dish.

2 small round red potatoes
1 cup fresh snow pea pods
2 medium carrots, scraped and thinly sliced
4 (6-ounce) salmon fillets (½ inch thick)
1 tablespoon plus 1 teaspoon fresh lemon juice
2 teaspoons minced fresh ginger

¼ teaspoon salt
⅛ teaspoon ground pepper
2 tablespoons extra-virgin olive oil
1 small fennel bulb
½ cup sliced zucchini
1 tablespoon plus 1 teaspoon chopped fresh dill, divided

Cook potatoes in boiling water to cover 15 minutes or just until tender; slice and set aside. Blanch snow peas in boiling water 30 seconds or until crisp-tender; drain and set aside. Blanch sliced carrots in boiling water 1 minute or until crisp-tender; drain and set aside.

Prepare four 16- x 10-inch sheets aluminum foil. Place 1 fish fillet slightly left of center on each sheet. Sprinkle each with 1 teaspoon lemon juice and ½ teaspoon ginger. Sprinkle fillets evenly with salt and pepper. Drizzle each with 1½ teaspoons olive oil.

Rinse fennel thoroughly. Trim stalks to within 1 inch of bulb. Discard hard outside stalks; reserve leaves for another use. Cut a slice off bottom of bulb. Cut out tough core from bottom of bulb. Starting at 1 side, cut one-fourth bulb lengthwise into ¼-inch julienne slices, reserve remaining fennel for another use.

Divide potatoes, snow peas, carrot, zucchini, and fennel evenly among fillets. Fold foil over to form a rectangle. Crimp edges tightly.

Place foil packets on a baking sheet. Bake at 400° for 20 to 25 minutes or until fish flakes easily when tested with a fork. Make an X in foil to open, and sprinkle 1 teaspoon dill over each serving. Yield: 4 servings.

I'll Cook when Pigs Fly
The Junior League of Cincinnati, Ohio

Cantonese Shrimp and Pea Pods

To complete this one-dish meal, serve over rice or Asian noodles.

1½ pounds unpeeled medium-
    size fresh shrimp
1 small onion, thinly sliced
1 clove garlic, minced
1 tablespoon vegetable oil
1 cup boiling water
1½ teaspoons chicken-flavored
    bouillon granules

½ teaspoon ground ginger
Dash of pepper
2 tablespoons cornstarch
2 tablespoons water
1 (8-ounce) package frozen
    snow pea pods, thawed
½ teaspoon salt

Peel shrimp, and devein, if desired. Set aside.

Combine sliced onion, minced garlic, and oil in a deep 3-quart casserole. Microwave, uncovered, at HIGH 2 to 3 minutes or until onion is tender.

Combine 1 cup boiling water and chicken bouillon granules; stir well. Add bouillon mixture, shrimp, ginger, and pepper to onion mixture. Cover tightly with heavy-duty plastic wrap; fold back a small corner of wrap to allow steam to escape. Microwave at MEDIUM (50% power) 3 minutes. Combine cornstarch and 2 tablespoons water; stir well. Add to shrimp mixture. Cover and microwave at MEDIUM 4 to 5 minutes. Add pea pods and salt; microwave at MEDIUM 5 to 6 minutes or until sauce thickens, stirring after 4 minutes. Stir well before serving. Yield: 4 servings.

Classically Kiawah
The Alternatives
Kiawah Island, South Carolina

Kathleen Argiroff's Seafood Lasagna

3 tablespoons olive oil
1 large onion, chopped
4 cloves garlic, minced
1 (28-ounce) can whole tomatoes, drained and chopped
1 (14.5-ounce) can whole tomatoes, drained and chopped
½ cup dry white wine
1 cup chopped fresh basil, divided
2 teaspoons fennel seeds
¾ teaspoon salt, divided
¾ teaspoon pepper, divided
1 cup heavy whipping cream
2 tablespoons Pernod
½ pound cooked, peeled, and deveined shrimp (start with 1 pound uncooked in the shell)
1 pound bay scallops, poached
9 dried lasagna noodles
1 (15-ounce) carton ricotta cheese
1 (8-ounce) package cream cheese, softened
2 large eggs
1 (10-ounce) package frozen chopped spinach, thawed and drained
1 pound fresh lump crabmeat, drained
1 medium-size sweet red pepper, chopped
1 bunch green onions, sliced
1 pound mozzarella cheese, thinly sliced

Heat oil in a large skillet over medium heat. Add onion and garlic; sauté 5 minutes. Add tomatoes; cook 5 minutes. Stir in wine, ½ cup basil, fennel seeds, ½ teaspoon salt, and ½ teaspoon pepper. Bring to a boil; reduce heat, and simmer, uncovered, 40 minutes or until sauce thickens, stirring occasionally. Stir in cream and Pernod; cook 5 minutes. Add shrimp and scallops; simmer 1 minute. Remove from heat.

Cook noodles according to package directions; drain and set aside.

Combine ricotta cheese, cream cheese, and eggs. Add spinach, crabmeat, sweet red pepper, green onions, remaining ½ cup basil, ¼ teaspoon salt, and ¼ teaspoon pepper.

Spread about ½ cup seafood sauce in a greased 15- x 10- x 2-inch baking dish. Top with 3 noodles, half of cheese filling, half of seafood sauce, and one-third of cheese slices. Cover with 3 noodles, remaining cheese filling, half of remaining cheese slices, remaining 3 noodles, remaining seafood sauce, and remaining cheese slices. Bake, uncovered, at 350° for 50 minutes or until bubbly. Let stand 10 minutes before serving. Yield: 10 to 12 servings.   Marguerite Morris

Expressions
National League of American Pen Women, Chester County
Coatesville, Pennsylvania

Quick & Easy Recipes

Streusel Shortcake, page 47

Quick Baba Ghanoujh

Eggplant, garlic, and tahini are key ingredients in this Middle Eastern puree. Serve it as a spread or a dip with pita bread.

1 large eggplant (about 1 to 1½ pounds)
3 cloves garlic, minced
3 tablespoons tahini
2 tablespoons lemon juice
½ teaspoon salt
⅛ teaspoon ground cumin
2 tablespoons olive oil
Garnishes: kalamata olives, chopped fresh parsley

Remove and discard ends of eggplant (do not peel). Prick eggplant with a fork. Microwave at HIGH 7 to 10 minutes or until eggplant is tender; cool completely.

Cut eggplant in half lengthwise, and scrape out soft cooked pulp; discard shell. Process pulp, garlic, tahini, lemon juice, salt, and cumin in a food processor until smooth. Add water to reach desired consistency, if necessary. Place mixture in a shallow serving dish; drizzle with olive oil. Garnish, if desired. Serve with pita bread. Yield: 1⅓ cups.

Classically Kiawah
The Alternatives
Kiawah Island, South Carolina

Cinco de Mayo Bean Dip

Any celebration calls for this tasty bean dip. It's easy and can be prepared in about 15 minutes.

1 (16-ounce) can refried beans
1 cup (4 ounces) shredded sharp Cheddar cheese
1 cup chunky salsa
⅔ cup (2.6 ounces) shredded Monterey Jack cheese
1 (4.25-ounce) can chopped ripe olives, drained
¼ cup sliced green onions
1½ tablespoons minced fresh cilantro
¼ teaspoon garlic powder
¼ teaspoon salt (optional)

Combine all ingredients; stir well. Spoon into a shallow 1-quart microwave-safe dish. Cover tightly with heavy-duty plastic wrap; fold back a small corner of wrap to allow steam to escape. Microwave at

HIGH 4 to 5 minutes or until cheese melts, stirring after 3 minutes. Serve with tortilla chips. Yield: 3 cups. Jerry Mitchell

Meet Me in the Kitchen
Northside Church of Christ
Waco, Texas

Coffee Liqueur-Cinnamon Fruit Dip

2 (3-ounce) packages cream
  cheese, softened
¼ cup plus 2 tablespoons
  sifted powdered sugar
¼ cup plus 2 tablespoons sour
  cream

3 tablespoons Kahlúa or other
  coffee-flavored liqueur
½ teaspoon ground cinnamon

Beat cream cheese at medium speed of an electric mixer until creamy. Add sugar, sour cream, Kahlúa, and cinnamon; beat well. Serve with fresh fruit. Yield: 1½ cups.

Have You Heard . . . A Tasteful Medley of Memphis
Subsidium, Inc.
Memphis, Tennessee

Goat Cheese Log with Cranberry-Pecan Crust

This elegant appetizer is a grand starter to a festive holiday evening.

½ cup finely chopped dried
  cranberries
¼ cup finely chopped pecans

¼ teaspoon salt
1 (11-ounce) log soft goat
  cheese

Combine first 3 ingredients. Roll goat cheese in cranberry mixture, pressing firmly. Wrap in plastic wrap; chill. Serve with assorted crackers. Yield: 8 to 10 appetizer servings.

A Capital Affair
The Junior League of Harrisburg, Pennsylvania

Havarti en Croûte

1 sheet frozen puff pastry,
  thawed
1 teaspoon Dijon mustard

1 (8-ounce) oblong Havarti
  cheese with dillweed
1 large egg, lightly beaten

Cut pastry sheet into a 7-inch square; reserve remaining pastry for another use.

Spread mustard lightly over pastry sheet; place cheese in center. Enclose cheese with pastry, sealing top and ends; brush with egg. Place in a greased 8-inch square pan; cover and chill 1 hour. Chill remaining beaten egg.

Brush again with remaining beaten egg, and bake at 400° for 15 to 20 minutes or until golden. Serve warm with fresh fruit or crudités. Yield: 4 to 8 appetizer servings.   Lisa Paul

Noel Bluffin' We're Still Cookin'
Noel Area Chamber of Commerce
Noel, Missouri

Fruit Balls

½ cup whole pitted dates
½ cup dried apricot halves
½ cup golden raisins
½ cup chopped pecans or
  walnuts

½ teaspoon grated lemon rind
½ teaspoon grated orange rind
Powdered sugar

Process all ingredients except powdered sugar in a food processor 1 minute or until mixture is ground, stopping once to scrape down sides. Shape mixture into 1-inch balls; roll in powdered sugar. Yield: 21 balls.   Mamie Merick

Generations of Good Food
Jeannette Public Library
Jeannette, Pennsylvania

Frozen Mango Daiquiri

This frozen beverage is a refreshing treat year-round. Because the sweetness of mangoes will vary with each season, you may need to increase or decrease the amount of sugar.

2 small ripe mangoes (about 1 pound), peeled and cut into chunks
½ cup dark or light rum
¼ to ½ cup sugar

¼ cup fresh lime juice
¼ teaspoon ground ginger
Ice cubes
Garnish: lime slices

Process first 5 ingredients in container of an electric blender until smooth, stopping once to scrape down sides. Add ice to 4¾ cup level on blender container; process until mixture is thick and slushy. Garnish, if desired. Yield: 5 cups.   Sheri M. Creasy

Nun Better: Tastes and Tales from Around a Cajun Table
St. Cecilia School
Broussard, Louisiana

Winey French Bread

1 (1-pound) loaf French bread
½ cup butter, softened
½ cup freshly grated Parmesan cheese
¼ cup dry red wine

2 teaspoons dried Italian seasoning
1 clove garlic, pressed

Cut bread into 1-inch slices, cutting to, but not through, bottom of loaf; place loaf on a baking sheet.

Combine butter and remaining 4 ingredients in a small bowl; stir well (wine may not blend completely). Spread mixture evenly on each side of bread slices. Bake loaf, uncovered, at 400° for 10 minutes. Yield: 1 loaf.   Nancy Krebs

Savory Secrets
P.E.O. Chapter LR
St. Charles, Missouri

Beignets

Frozen rolls provide a quick start for these New Orleans pastries. Whether serving beignets for breakfast or as a late-night dessert, be liberal when dusting with powdered sugar–and don't forget the café au lait!

1 (16-ounce) package frozen rolls, thawed (we tested with Rich's)

Vegetable oil
Powdered sugar

Flatten and stretch each roll slightly.

Pour oil to depth of 2 inches into a Dutch oven; heat to 375°. Fry beignets, 4 at a time, in hot oil 1 to 2 minutes or until golden, turning often. Drain on paper towels. Sprinkle with powdered sugar; serve immediately. Yield: 21 beignets.   Debbie and Lucille Landry

Nun Better: Tastes and Tales from Around a Cajun Table
St. Cecilia School
Broussard, Louisiana

Pecan Mini-Muffins

These muffins taste like pecan tassies but are easier to prepare because there's no separate crust.

1 cup firmly packed brown sugar
½ cup butter or margarine, melted
2 large eggs

1 teaspoon vanilla extract
1 cup chopped pecans
½ cup all-purpose flour
Vegetable cooking spray

Combine first 4 ingredients in a bowl, beating with a wire whisk until smooth. Stir in pecans and flour. Spoon batter into miniature (1¾-inch) muffin pans coated with cooking spray, filling to within ⅛ inch from top. Bake at 375° for 12 minutes or until lightly browned. Cool in pans on wire racks 1 minute. Remove from pans; cool completely on wire racks. Yield: 40 muffins.   Caroline Rippee

First Baptist Church Centennial Cookbook
First Baptist Church
Cushing, Oklahoma

German Skillet Dinner

1 tablespoon butter or margarine
1 (14-ounce) can sauerkraut, undrained
½ cup uncooked long-grain rice
½ cup water
1 medium onion, chopped
1 pound ground round
½ teaspoon salt
¼ teaspoon pepper
1 (8-ounce) can tomato sauce

Melt butter in a large skillet over medium heat. Spread sauerkraut evenly in skillet; layer rice, water, onion, and ground round evenly on top of sauerkraut. Sprinkle with salt and pepper; top with tomato sauce. Cover and cook over medium heat 35 minutes. Serve from skillet. Yield: 8 cups. Colleen Prough

Cooking from the Heart
Pleasant View Mennonite Church
Goshen, Indiana

Sloppy Joes

1 pound ground chuck
1 medium onion, chopped
½ cup ketchup
3 tablespoons sweet pickle relish
1 tablespoon brown sugar
1 tablespoon prepared mustard
¼ teaspoon salt
¼ teaspoon pepper
5 hamburger buns, toasted

Brown ground chuck and onion in a large nonstick skillet, stirring until meat crumbles; drain. Stir in ketchup and next 5 ingredients. Bring to a boil; cover, reduce heat, and simmer 5 minutes, stirring occasionally. Spoon meat mixture over bottom halves of buns; top with remaining halves. Yield: 5 servings. Nena Moon

Bread from the Brook
The Church at Brook Hills
Birmingham, Alabama

Swiss-Ham Kabobs

Turn leftover ham into a feast. These kabobs are grilled with chunks of pineapple and Swiss cheese and topped with a tangy orange marmalade sauce.

1 (20-ounce) can pineapple chunks in juice, undrained
½ cup orange marmalade
1 tablespoon prepared mustard
¼ teaspoon ground cloves

1 pound cooked ham, cut into 1-inch cubes
8 ounces Swiss cheese, cut into 1-inch cubes

Drain pineapple, reserving 2 tablespoons juice. Combine reserved juice, marmalade, mustard, and cloves; stir well with a wire whisk. Set mixture aside.

Alternately thread ham, cheese, ham, and pineapple chunks on six 12-inch skewers. (Cheese cubes must be between and touching ham to prevent rapid melting.) Place kabobs on grill rack. Brush with marmalade mixture.

Grill, uncovered, over medium-hot coals (350° to 400°) 3 to 4 minutes or until cheese is partially melted and ham is lightly browned, brushing often with juice mixture. Serve kabobs immediately. Yield: 6 servings.   Adrienne Thomas

Carolina Cuisine: Nothin' Could Be Finer
The Junior Charity League of Marlboro County
Bennettsville, South Carolina

Chicken Fast & Fancy

Mushroom soup and wine are mixed together, creating a savory sauce that's spooned over cheese-topped chicken breasts and drizzled with melted butter before baking.

8 skinned and boned chicken breast halves
8 (1-ounce) slices Swiss cheese
1¼ cups sliced fresh mushrooms
1 (10¾-ounce) can cream of mushroom soup

¼ cup dry white wine
2 cups seasoned stuffing mix (we tested with Pepperidge Farm)
¼ cup butter or margarine, melted

Place chicken breasts in a single layer in a lightly greased 13- x 9- x 2-inch baking dish. Top each chicken breast with a cheese slice, and sprinkle with mushrooms. Combine soup and wine in a small bowl, and pour over chicken. Sprinkle with stuffing mix, and drizzle with butter. Bake, uncovered, at 350° for 35 minutes or until chicken is done. Yield: 8 servings.   Ann Livers

Green Thumbs in the Kitchen
Green Thumb, Inc.
Arlington, Virginia

Easy Chicken Pot Pie

Deli-roasted chicken, frozen vegetables, and refrigerated biscuits make assembling this chicken classic a breeze.

2 (10¾-ounce) cans cream of broccoli soup or cream of chicken soup
1 cup milk
¼ teaspoon dried thyme
¼ teaspoon pepper
1 (16-ounce) package frozen chopped mixed vegetables (broccoli, cauliflower, and carrots)

2 cups cubed cooked chicken
1 (12-ounce) can refrigerated biscuits

Combine first 4 ingredients in an ungreased 13- x 9- x 2-inch baking dish. Add vegetables and chicken. Bake at 350° for 15 minutes. Remove from oven. Cut each biscuit into fourths, and arrange over chicken. Bake 22 more minutes or until biscuits are golden. Yield: 6 servings.

When Kiwanis Cooks
Wisconsin-Upper Michigan District of Kiwanis International
Plover, Wisconsin

Turkey Breast Cutlets

1 pound turkey breast cutlets
½ teaspoon salt
½ teaspoon ground white
  pepper
¼ cup vegetable oil
¾ cup all-purpose flour

2 large eggs, lightly beaten
1 avocado, peeled and sliced
1 tomato, sliced
1 (6-ounce) package sliced
  mozzarella cheese

Sprinkle turkey cutlets with salt and pepper. Place oil in a large skillet over medium-high heat until hot. Dredge cutlets in flour; dip in egg, and dredge again in flour. Add cutlets to skillet, and cook until browned.

Remove turkey cutlets from skillet, and place on a rack in a broiler pan. Arrange avocado and tomato slices evenly on top of cutlets. Top evenly with cheese slices. Broil 5½ inches from heat (with electric oven door partially opened) 5 minutes or until cheese melts. Yield: 4 to 6 servings.   Michael Chase

Rave Reviews
Ogunquit Playhouse
Ogunquit, Maine

Fish Florentine

2 (6-ounce) sea bass or other
  firm white fish fillets
1 (12-ounce) package frozen
  spinach soufflé, thawed

⅓ cup cracker crumbs (we
  tested with saltines)
3 tablespoons freshly grated
  Parmesan cheese

Place fish in a greased 11- x 7- x 1½-inch baking dish. Cover with spinach soufflé.

Combine cracker crumbs and cheese; sprinkle over fish. Bake, uncovered, at 400° for 25 minutes or until fish flakes easily when tested with a fork. Yield: 2 servings.   Suzanne S. Dixon

Fishing for Compliments
Shedd Aquarium Society
Chicago, Illinois

Oriental Baked Salmon

Fresh ginger and teriyaki sauce lend a taste of the Orient to this baked salmon.

2 (6-ounce) salmon fillets
2 tablespoons sliced green onions
1 teaspoon teriyaki sauce

¼ teaspoon grated fresh ginger
1 tablespoon butter or margarine
1 navel orange, sliced

Place salmon, skin side down, in a microwave-safe baking dish. Sprinkle each fillet evenly with green onions, teriyaki sauce, and ginger; dot with butter. Place orange slices over fillets.

Cover dish with heavy-duty plastic wrap; fold back a small corner of wrap to allow steam to escape. Microwave at HIGH 3 to 4 minutes or until fish flakes easily when tested with a fork, turning dish once. Yield: 2 servings.   Jacqueline Spink

Recipes for Reading
New Hampshire Council on Literacy
Concord, New Hampshire

Tasty Fish Bake

1 pound (½-inch-thick) flounder fillets
2 tablespoons cream sherry
¼ cup stone-ground mustard

½ cup soft breadcrumbs (homemade), toasted
2 tablespoons butter or margarine

Place fish fillets in a lightly greased 13- x 9- x 2-inch baking dish. Combine sherry and mustard; spread evenly over each fish fillet. Top with breadcrumbs, and dot with butter. Bake, uncovered, at 400° for 30 minutes or until fish flakes easily when tested with a fork. Yield: 4 servings.   Mark Wilson

Chautauqua Porches–A Centennial Cookbook
Colorado Chautauqua Cottagers, Inc.
Boulder, Colorado

Shrimp with Jalapeño-Orange Sauce

Add more zip to this dish by using two jalapeños instead of one.

¼ cup butter or margarine
24 large fresh shrimp, peeled
   and deveined (about 1
   pound)
2 tablespoons minced shallots
1 to 2 small jalapeño peppers,
   seeded and finely chopped

½ cup dry white wine
1½ cups orange juice
¾ cup heavy whipping cream
¼ teaspoon salt

Melt butter in a large skillet over medium-high heat. Add shrimp, and cook just until shrimp turn pink. Remove shrimp from skillet; set aside, and keep warm.

Add shallot and jalapeño pepper to skillet; cook over medium-high heat 1 minute, stirring constantly. Add wine, and bring to a boil. Stir in orange juice and cream; return to a boil. Cook over high heat about 10 minutes or until thickened, stirring occasionally; stir in salt. Return shrimp to sauce, and cook just until thoroughly heated. Serve with rice or pasta. Yield: 4 servings.

Special Selections of Ocala
Ocala Royal Dames for Cancer Research, Inc.
Ocala, Florida

Asparagus with Blue Cheese and Chive Vinaigrette

Blue cheese fans will love this crumbled goody combined with minced chives for a zesty vinaigrette that tops hot asparagus.

1 pound fresh asparagus
2 tablespoons olive oil
2 teaspoons red wine vinegar
¼ cup crumbled blue cheese

2 tablespoons minced fresh
   chives
Ground white pepper

Snap off tough ends of asparagus; remove scales from stalks with a vegetable peeler, if desired. Add water to a medium skillet to depth of 1 inch, and bring to a boil. Add asparagus in a single layer; cook 6 to

8 minutes or until crisp-tender. Drain asparagus, and arrange on a serving plate.

Combine oil and vinegar in a small bowl; stir well with a wire whisk. Add cheese and chives; stir well. Pour vinegar mixture over hot asparagus. Sprinkle with pepper. Yield: 4 servings.

Our Sunrise Family Cookbook
Sunrise Drive Elementary School
Tucson, Arizona

Garlic Mashed Potatoes

4 **medium baking potatoes (about 2½ pounds)**	1¼ **cups milk**
2 **tablespoons butter or margarine**	¼ **teaspoon salt**
2 **to 3 medium cloves garlic, minced**	⅛ **teaspoon pepper**

Scrub potatoes, and prick several times with a fork. Place potatoes, 1 inch apart, on a microwave-safe rack or on paper towels. Microwave at HIGH 15 to 17 minutes or until potatoes are tender; let stand 5 minutes. Peel potatoes, and mash.

Microwave butter and garlic in a 2-cup liquid measuring cup at HIGH 30 seconds to 1 minute; add milk, and microwave at HIGH 2 minutes.

Pour milk mixture into mashed potatoes, stirring to blend. Add salt and pepper. Microwave at HIGH 1 to 2 minutes or until thoroughly heated. Yield: 5 servings.

Beyond Chicken Soup
Jewish Home of Rochester Auxiliary
Rochester, New York

Rice-Cheese Casserole

This recipe tasted grand with the full 16 ounces of cheese per the original recipe, but we found it equally rich and wonderful with half that amount, if you're inclined to cut corners. Either way, this dish is a nice accompaniment with any simple meat or poultry entrée or any Mexican main dish.

2 cups cooked rice
1 (8-ounce) carton sour cream
1 (4.5-ounce) can chopped green chiles, undrained

2 to 4 cups (8 to 16 ounces) shredded Monterey Jack cheese

Combine first 3 ingredients in a large bowl. Spoon half of rice mixture into a lightly greased 11- x 7- x 1½-inch baking dish. Cover with half of cheese. Spoon remaining half of rice mixture over cheese, and sprinkle with remaining cheese. Bake, uncovered, at 350° for 25 minutes. Yield: 8 to 10 servings.   Paige Swiggart

Somethin's Cookin' with Married Young Adults
Houston's First Baptist Church
Houston, Texas

Risotto in the Microwave

Microwave risotto takes about the same amount of time to prepare as traditional risotto, and most of its preparation is hands off, giving you more time for preparing the rest of your dinner.

2 tablespoons butter or margarine
2 tablespoons olive oil
½ cup minced onion
1 cup Arborio rice

3 cups reduced-sodium chicken broth
½ cup freshly grated Parmesan cheese
¼ teaspoon pepper

Heat butter and oil in a microwave-safe 1½-quart glass or ceramic dish, uncovered, at HIGH 1 minute and 15 seconds to 2 minutes. Add onion; stir well. Cover and cook at HIGH 45 seconds to 1 minute. Add rice, stirring well. Cover and cook at HIGH 3 to 4 minutes. Stir in chicken broth, and cook, uncovered, at HIGH 9 minutes. Stir well, and cook, uncovered, at HIGH 7 to 9 minutes. Remove from microwave oven, and let stand 5 minutes. Stir in Parmesan cheese and pepper. Yield: 3½ cups. Susan Reiss

A Gardener Cooks
Danbury Garden Club
New Milford, Connecticut

Streusel Shortcake

3 cups biscuit mix	½ cup chopped walnuts
⅔ cup milk	¼ cup butter or margarine
¼ cup butter or margarine, melted	1 (8-ounce) container frozen whipped topping, thawed
½ cup firmly packed brown sugar	2 pints fresh strawberries, sliced

Combine first 3 ingredients in a large bowl; stir until a soft dough forms. Spread dough evenly in two greased 8-inch square pans.

Combine sugar and walnuts; cut in ¼ cup butter with a pastry blender until mixture is crumbly. Sprinkle nut mixture over dough.

Bake, uncovered, at 400° for 18 minutes or until a wooden pick inserted in center comes out clean. Cool in pans on wire racks 10 minutes; remove from pans, and cool completely on wire racks.

Place 1 cake layer on a serving plate. Spread half of whipped topping over layer, and arrange half of sliced strawberries on top. Repeat procedure with remaining layer, whipped topping, and strawberries. Chill until ready to serve. Yield: one 8-inch cake. Pat Trzaskos

Just Desserts
Amsterdam Free Library
Amsterdam, New York

Toffee Temptation

1 (3.4-ounce) package vanilla
  instant pudding mix
2 cups milk
1 (12.75-ounce) package cream-
  filled sponge cakes (we tested
  with Twinkies)

1 (8.4-ounce) package English
  toffee-flavored candy bars,
  crushed
½ (8-ounce) container frozen
  whipped topping, thawed

Prepare pudding with milk according to package directions.

Slice cakes in half horizontally. Line an 11- x 7- x 1½-inch dish with bottom halves of cakes, cut side up. Sprinkle with ½ cup candy. Spoon pudding over candy. Arrange top of cakes over pudding, cut side down. Spread with whipped topping; sprinkle with remaining candy. Cover and chill 2 hours. Yield: 10 servings.   Jeri Young

Love for Others
Our Shepherd Lutheran Church
Birmingham, Michigan

Blueberry Icebox Pie

Blueberries make a nice variation from the traditional lemon icebox pie. The recipe makes 2 pies—one to keep and one to give away.

2 (14-ounce) cans sweetened
  condensed milk
⅔ cup fresh lemon juice
1 teaspoon vanilla extract
1 teaspoon almond extract
1 (12-ounce) container frozen
  whipped topping, thawed

1 (15½-ounce) can blueberries
  in syrup, drained
2 (6-ounce) graham cracker
  crusts

Combine first 4 ingredients in a large bowl; stir well. Fold in whipped topping. Gently fold in blueberries.

Spoon mixture evenly into crusts. Cover and chill at least 3 hours. Yield: two 9-inch pies.   Robbie Boshart

The Fruit of the Spirit
Sumrall United Methodist Women's Circle
Sumrall, Mississippi

Easy Peanut Butter Cookies

These cookies are good with or without chocolate kisses–either way you have a winner.

1 (14-ounce) can sweetened
   condensed milk
¾ cup creamy peanut butter
2 cups biscuit mix (we tested
   with Bisquick)

1 teaspoon vanilla extract
Sugar
66 milk chocolate kisses,
   unwrapped (optional)

Combine sweetened condensed milk and peanut butter in a large mixing bowl. Beat at medium speed of an electric mixer until well blended. Add biscuit mix and vanilla; beat well.

Shape mixture into 1-inch balls; roll in sugar. Place 2 inches apart on ungreased cookie sheets. Dip a fork in sugar; flatten cookies in a crisscross design. Bake at 375° for 6 to 7 minutes. Immediately press a chocolate kiss in center of each cookie after removing from oven, if desired. Remove cookies to wire racks to cool completely. Yield: 5½ dozen.

Mike Stillwell

Praise the Lord and Pass the Gravy
Stanley United Methodist Church
Stanley, Virginia

Cranberry-Macadamia Bark

8 (2-ounce) vanilla-flavored
   candy coating squares,
   chopped

½ cup dried cranberries
1 (3.5-ounce) jar lightly salted
   macadamia nuts

Place coating in a heavy saucepan; cook over medium-low heat until coating is melted and smooth, stirring often. Stir in cranberries and nuts. Pour mixture onto an aluminum foil-lined baking sheet; spread into a ¼-inch-thick layer. Cool completely; break into pieces. Yield: 1¼ pounds.

Sweet Memories
Holy Covenant United Methodist Women
Katy, Texas

Easy Gift Candy

2 cups (12 ounces) semisweet
  chocolate morsels
1 (11-ounce) package
  butterscotch morsels

1 (16-ounce) jar unsalted
  roasted peanuts
1 (5-ounce) can chow mein
  noodles

Lightly grease a baking sheet or an aluminum foil-lined baking sheet. Combine chocolate and butterscotch morsels in a large microwave-safe bowl. Microwave at HIGH 2½ to 3½ minutes or until morsels melt; stir well. Add peanuts to melted mixture, stirring to coat. Add noodles, gently stirring to coat.

Pour mixture onto prepared baking sheet. Spread mixture evenly on baking sheet. Cover and chill at least 8 hours. Break into pieces. Yield: 2½ pounds. Maureen Bard

White Clay Creek Presbyterian Church 275th Anniversary Cookbook
White Clay Creek Presbyterian Church
Newark, Delaware

Microwave Pralines

Pralines are easy to make using this microwave recipe. If your oven is 1000 watts, use the lower time option.

2 cups sugar
2 cups pecans, chopped
1 (5-ounce) can evaporated
  milk

¼ cup butter or margarine
1 tablespoon vanilla extract

Combine all ingredients in a 2-quart microwave-safe liquid measuring cup. Microwave at HIGH 5 to 6 minutes, stirring well. Microwave 5 to 6 more minutes, stirring well. Working rapidly, drop by tablespoonfuls onto wax paper; let stand until firm. Yield: about 2½ dozen. Jesse Messex

Somethin' to Smile About
St. Martin, Iberia, Lafayette Community Action Agency
Lafayette, Louisiana

Appetizers & Beverages

Pine Nut-Pesto-Tomato Torte, page 58

Roasted Herbed Nuts with Sesame Seeds

1 egg white
¼ teaspoon cream of tartar
2¼ cups pecan halves (about 8 ounces)
1⅔ cups salted whole cashews (about 8 ounces)
1½ cups whole almonds (about 8 ounces)

¼ cup sesame seeds
2 teaspoons dried thyme or dried rosemary
½ teaspoon freshly ground pepper
Salt (optional)

Beat egg white and cream of tartar at medium speed of an electric mixer until soft peaks form. Add nuts, sesame seeds, thyme, and pepper, tossing until nuts are evenly coated. Pour nut mixture into a lightly oiled 15- x 10- x 1-inch jellyroll pan; arrange nuts in a single layer.

Bake at 325° for 35 to 40 minutes or until nuts are golden, turning nuts with a spatula every 10 minutes. Let cool 15 minutes in jellyroll pan; transfer nuts to paper towels, and let cool completely. Sprinkle with salt, if desired. Store roasted nuts in airtight containers. Yield: 5½ cups.   Kathy Vockins and Hans Hallundbaek

Katonah Cooks!
Katonah Village Improvement Society, Katonah Village Library
Katonah, New York

Blue Chip White Salsa

Cilantro lovers will fancy this salsa mixed with 1½ cups of the pungent herb. The salsa is also good as an accompaniment with grilled fish.

1 cup mayonnaise
1 (8-ounce) carton sour cream
¼ cup fresh lime juice
4 cloves garlic, minced
1½ cups finely chopped fresh cilantro

1 (4.25-ounce) can chopped ripe olives
1½ cups chopped green onions
½ teaspoon hot sauce
⅛ teaspoon salt
⅛ teaspoon pepper
Blue corn chips

Combine mayonnaise and sour cream in a medium bowl, stirring well with a wire whisk; stir in lime juice and next 7 ingredients. Cover and chill at least 6 hours; serve salsa with blue corn chips. Yield: 4 cups.

Simply Divine
Second-Ponce de Leon Baptist Church
Atlanta, Georgia

Cranberry-Amaretto Chutney With Cream Cheese

This spiked chutney is great for gift giving or for keeping on hand when unexpected guests drop by. If time is tight, just spoon the rosy mixture over softened cream cheese.

2 (8-ounce) packages cream
  cheese, softened
2 tablespoons milk
1 (12-ounce) bag fresh
  cranberries (3 cups)
1½ cups sugar

2 tablespoons fresh lemon
  juice
¾ teaspoon grated lemon rind
⅓ cup amaretto
1 tablespoon orange
  marmalade

Combine cream cheese and milk in a small bowl; beat at medium speed of an electric mixer until smooth.

Line a 2-cup mold with cheesecloth, letting cloth hang over edge. Firmly press cream cheese mixture, 1 spoonful at a time, into mold. Fold cheesecloth over top; cover and chill 8 hours.

Combine cranberries, sugar, and lemon juice in a small saucepan. Bring to a boil over medium heat, stirring constantly. Reduce heat, and simmer 20 minutes. Remove from heat; stir in lemon rind, amaretto, and marmalade. Cool to room temperature.

Unmold cheese onto a serving platter; remove cheesecloth. Spoon cranberry sauce over cheese. Serve with crackers. Yield: 16 appetizer servings.

Jacqueline Underwood

Savory Secrets
P.E.O. Chapter LR
St. Charles, Missouri

Jan's Herbed Cheese Fondue

Fondue is back! Serve this savory appetizer with large chunks of bread and fruit to soak up every delicious bite.

1 clove garlic, halved
¾ cup dry white wine
2 (7-ounce) packages Gouda cheese, shredded
1½ tablespoons cornstarch
1½ teaspoons dried parsley flakes

¾ teaspoon dried tarragon
⅛ teaspoon ground nutmeg
⅛ teaspoon pepper
3 tablespoons kirsch or water

Rub inside of a heavy saucepan or fondue pot with cut sides of garlic; discard garlic. Add wine, and heat 2 minutes over medium heat. Gradually add shredded cheese, stirring until cheese melts and mixture begins to bubble.

Combine cornstarch and next 4 ingredients; stir well. Add cornstarch mixture and kirsch to cheese mixture; stir until thickened and smooth. To serve, pour mixture into fondue pot, and keep warm over a small flame. Serve with French bread cubes or apple or pear slices. Yield: 3 cups.

Soni Bickmore

What's Cooking in Hampton
Friends of Hampton Community Library
Allison Park, Pennsylvania

Red Pepper Dip with Walnuts

Scoop up this colorful and flavorful dip with lightly toasted pita wedges or raw vegetables.

1 small onion, chopped
2 large cloves garlic, sliced
¼ cup olive oil
1 (12-ounce) jar roasted red peppers, drained and rinsed

½ cup walnut pieces, toasted
⅓ cup packed fresh basil leaves
1 slice white bread (crust removed), torn into pieces
2 tablespoons lemon juice
¼ teaspoon salt

Sauté onion and garlic in oil in a medium skillet over medium-high heat until tender.

Process roasted red peppers and remaining 5 ingredients in a food processor until walnuts are finely chopped. With processor running, add onion mixture through food chute. Serve dip with toasted pita wedges or assorted raw vegetables. Yield: 2 cups.

Food Fabulous Food
Women's Board to Cooper Hospital/University Medical Center
Camden, New Jersey

Tropical Guacamole Dip

This dip is spicy. For a milder version, substitute a jalapeño in place of the Scotch bonnet pepper, and seed the pepper.

1 small purple onion, chopped (about 1 cup)
1 medium papaya, coarsely chopped
2 ripe avocados, coarsely chopped
1 medium tomato, peeled and coarsely chopped
2 green onions, chopped
3 tablespoons chopped fresh cilantro
2 cloves garlic, minced
½ Scotch bonnet pepper, minced
¼ cup lime juice
1 tablespoon ground cumin
1 teaspoon hot sauce
⅛ teaspoon salt
⅛ teaspoon pepper

Combine first 8 ingredients in a large bowl, and mix well. Add lime juice and remaining ingredients, mixing well. Serve with tortilla chips or plantain chips. Yield: 4 cups.

Made in the Shade
The Junior League of Greater Fort Lauderdale, Florida

Hot Spinach Dip

Here's a spicy twist on the traditional spinach dip that will delight a hungry crowd. Halve the recipe if you're serving just a few.

2 (10-ounce) packages frozen chopped spinach, thawed
2 (8-ounce) packages cream cheese, softened
2 cups (8 ounces) shredded Monterey Jack cheese
1 cup freshly grated Parmesan cheese
1 small onion, chopped
1 (14-ounce) can artichoke hearts, drained and chopped
2 (10-ounce) cans diced tomatoes and green chiles
2 teaspoons ground cumin
2 teaspoons chili powder
1 teaspoon garlic powder

Drain spinach; press between layers of paper towels to remove excess moisture.

Combine spinach, cream cheese, and remaining ingredients, stirring well. Spoon mixture into a greased 2½-quart baking dish. Bake, uncovered, at 350° for 30 minutes or until bubbly. Serve with melba toast rounds or corn chips. Yield: 8 cups.   Debbie Robinson

Blessings
First Presbyterian Church
Pine Bluff, Arkansas

Cilantro Mousse

We suggest serving plain water crackers with this mousse to fully appreciate the cilantro flavor.

2 envelopes unflavored gelatin
½ cup cold water
1 cup mayonnaise
2 cups packed fresh cilantro leaves (about 1 bunch)
3 tablespoons half-and-half
½ medium onion, chopped
1 small serrano chile, seeded and chopped
1 teaspoon chicken-flavored bouillon granules

Soften gelatin in cold water in a small saucepan 1 minute. Cook over low heat, stirring until gelatin dissolves; set aside.

Process mayonnaise and remaining 5 ingredients in a food processor until blended. Add gelatin; process until well blended.

Spoon mixture into a lightly oiled 2½-cup mold. Cover and chill several hours until firm. Unmold mousse onto a serving platter. Serve with crackers. Yield: 2½ cups.

Savoring the Southwest Again
Roswell Symphony Guild
Roswell, New Mexico

Brandied Pâté

1 small onion, minced
2 tablespoons unsalted butter
1 cup brandy
3 cloves garlic, minced
2 teaspoons salt
1 teaspoon chopped fresh thyme
¾ teaspoon freshly ground pepper
½ teaspoon ground allspice
¾ pound ground pork
½ pound ground veal
¾ cup chopped pistachios
2 large eggs, beaten
1 bay leaf
8 slices bacon

Sauté onion in butter in a large skillet over medium heat 10 minutes or until onion is golden. Transfer onion mixture to a large bowl; set aside. Carefully pour brandy into skillet; simmer 6 minutes or until reduced to ¼ cup. Pour brandy over onion mixture; stir in garlic and next 4 ingredients. Add pork, veal, pistachios, and eggs, stirring until blended.

Place bay leaf in center of a 9- x 5- x 3-inch loafpan. Line pan crosswise with bacon slices, allowing ends to drape over sides. Spoon pork mixture into pan, smoothing top. Fold bacon ends over pork mixture.

Place loafpan in a 13- x 9- x 2-inch pan. Add hot water to pan to depth of 1½ inches. Bake at 350° for 1 hour and 15 minutes.

Remove loafpan from water; drain any liquid from pâté. Cover with aluminum foil. Place a smaller loafpan on top of pâté; fill with heavy objects to weigh down pâté. Chill at least 8 hours.

Remove foil; invert pâté onto a serving platter. Serve with baguette slices or assorted crackers. Yield: 12 to 15 servings.

Texas Ties
The Junior League of North Harris County
Spring, Texas

Pine Nut-Pesto-Tomato Torte

Store-bought pesto sauce keeps preparation time to a minimum for this elegant appetizer that sports ribbons of color and flavor.

2 (3-ounce) packages dried
  tomatoes
1 (8-ounce) package cream
  cheese, softened
½ cup plus 1 tablespoon
  butter, divided and softened

1 (8-ounce) package feta
  cheese
1½ cups pine nuts, divided
2 (3-ounce) jars pesto sauce

Soak tomatoes in hot water to cover 10 minutes; drain and pat dry with paper towels. Chop tomatoes, and set aside.

Beat cream cheese, ¼ cup plus 3 tablespoons butter, and feta cheese at medium speed of an electric mixer until smooth; set aside.

Process remaining 2 tablespoons butter and ⅔ cup pine nuts in a food processor until nuts are coarsely chopped. Stir in ½ cup whole pine nuts; set aside.

Remove excess oil from pesto sauce with a spoon.

Line an 8½- x 4½- x 3-inch loafpan with plastic wrap. Press pine nut mixture in bottom of pan. Spread one-third of cheese mixture over nut layer. Spread tomatoes over cheese mixture. Spread one-third of cheese mixture over tomatoes. Spoon pesto sauce over cheese mixture. Spread remaining cheese mixture over top. Cover and chill at least 8 hours. Unmold torte 30 minutes before serving. Remove plastic wrap; sprinkle remaining nuts over torte. Serve with unflavored water crackers. Yield: 20 appetizer servings.   Mary Alice Carpenter

Spice It Up!
Baton Rouge Branch of American Association
of University Women
Baton Rouge, Louisiana

Bruschetta

1 (3-ounce) package dried
  tomatoes
Perfect Pesto
1 baguette, cut into 24 (½-inch-
  thick) slices

1 (8-ounce) package feta
  cheese, crumbled

Soak tomatoes in hot water to cover 10 minutes; drain and pat dry with paper towels. Thinly slice tomatoes, and set aside.

Spread Perfect Pesto evenly over bread slices. Sprinkle evenly with feta. Top with dried tomato slices. Bake at 350° for 10 minutes or until bread is slightly crisp. Serve immediately. Yield: 2 dozen.

Perfect Pesto

2 cups packed fresh basil leaves, washed and patted dry	1 cup olive oil
	1 cup freshly grated Romano cheese
½ cup pine nuts	¼ teaspoon salt
4 large cloves garlic, peeled	¼ teaspoon pepper

Process basil, pine nuts, and garlic in a food processor until nuts are finely chopped. With processor running, pour oil through food chute, processing just until smooth. Add Romano cheese, salt, and pepper; pulse 2 times or just until blended. Yield: 1 cup.   Kerry Gilbert

Chautauqua Porches–A Centennial Cookbook
Colorado Chautauqua Cottagers, Inc.
Boulder, Colorado

Cayenne-Ginger Wafers

1 cup (4 ounces) shredded white Cheddar cheese	¼ teaspoon ground red pepper
	1 cup all-purpose flour
½ cup butter, softened	2 teaspoons crystallized ginger, finely chopped
1 teaspoon salt	

Beat first 4 ingredients at medium speed of an electric mixer until creamy; add flour, and mix thoroughly. Shape dough into a ball. Wrap in plastic wrap, and chill 30 minutes.

Shape dough into 30 balls. Place 1 piece of ginger in center of each ball; place 2 inches apart on ungreased cookie sheets, and flatten slightly with palm of hand. Bake at 350° for 15 minutes or until golden. Remove to wire racks to cool. Yield: 2½ dozen.

The Cook's Canvas
St. John's Museum of Art
Wilmington, North Carolina

Artichoke-Pepper Puffs

3 large shallots, chopped
2 cloves garlic, minced
3 tablespoons chopped fresh
  chives
2 tablespoons butter or
  margarine, melted
1 (14-ounce) can artichoke
  bottoms, drained and
  diced
6 slices bacon, cooked and
  crumbled
3 tablespoons chopped fresh
  basil
½ cup freshly grated Parmesan
  cheese

½ cup (2 ounces) shredded
  Jarlsberg cheese
½ cup mayonnaise
1 tablespoon lemon juice
¼ teaspoon sugar
¼ teaspoon salt
¼ teaspoon pepper
6 medium-size sweet red or
  yellow peppers
2 tablespoons olive oil
2 tablespoons red wine vinegar
¼ teaspoon salt
⅛ teaspoon pepper

Cook first 3 ingredients in butter in a medium skillet over medium-high heat, stirring constantly, 3 minutes or until tender. Transfer to a medium bowl. Add artichokes and next 9 ingredients, stirring well. Cover and chill.

Cut peppers into 2-inch squares; place in a 13- x 9- x 2-inch baking dish. Drizzle oil and vinegar over peppers; sprinkle with ¼ teaspoon salt and ⅛ teaspoon pepper, tossing well. Bake at 350° for 15 minutes, stirring after 7 minutes. Remove from oven, and let cool 10 minutes.

Spoon about 1 tablespoon artichoke mixture onto each pepper square; arrange pepper squares on ungreased baking sheets. Broil 5½ inches from heat 8 minutes or until lightly browned and bubbly. Yield: 4½ dozen.

I'll Cook When Pigs Fly
The Junior League of Cincinnati, Ohio

Petite Potato Hors d'Oeuvres

12 new potatoes, halved
1 tablespoon olive oil
Vegetable cooking
  spray

Choice of Smoked Salmon
  Filling, Sour Cream and
  Chive Filling, or Sour Cream
  and Caviar Filling

Combine potato and olive oil; toss well. Place potato, cut side down, on a 15- x 10- x 1-inch jellyroll pan coated with cooking spray. Bake, uncovered, at 350° for 25 minutes or until tender. Cool slightly.

Cut a small slice off rounded end of each potato half so potatoes will stand upright. Scoop out a small amount from center of each potato with a small spoon or melon baller. Spoon desired fillings into potato cavities. (Each filling yields enough to fill about 1 dozen potato halves. Choose two fillings or double one filling.) Yield: 2 dozen.

Smoked Salmon Filling

3½ ounces smoked salmon, finely chopped
2 tablespoons sour cream
2 tablespoons minced purple onion
1 teaspoon drained capers
½ teaspoon prepared horseradish
⅛ teaspoon pepper

Combine all ingredients in a small bowl; stir well. Yield: ½ cup.

Sour Cream and Chive Filling

½ cup sour cream
1 tablespoon prepared horseradish
3 tablespoons chopped ripe olives
2 tablespoons finely chopped chives

Combine all ingredients in a small bowl; stir well. Yield: ⅔ cup.

Sour Cream and Caviar Filling

1 tablespoon vodka
½ cup sour cream
2 tablespoons drained red or black caviar

Spoon ¼ teaspoon vodka into each potato cavity. Top with 2 teaspoons sour cream and ½ teaspoon caviar. Yield: about ⅔ cup.

Beyond Burlap, Idaho's Famous Potato Recipes
The Junior League of Boise, Idaho

Party Meatballs

1 small onion, quartered
⅓ cup water
1 large egg
1 tablespoon sugar
1¼ teaspoons salt
1 teaspoon dried marjoram
½ teaspoon curry powder
¼ teaspoon dried thyme
¼ teaspoon ground ginger
¼ teaspoon ground cloves
¼ teaspoon rubbed sage
Pinch of ground cinnamon
Pinch of ground nutmeg
1 pound ground beef
¾ cup herb-seasoned stuffing
   mix (we tested with
   Pepperidge Farm)
2 tablespoons all-purpose flour
1 tablespoon vegetable oil
½ cup prepared mustard
½ cup ketchup
½ cup molasses

Process first 13 ingredients in a food processor until blended. Add beef, stuffing mix, and flour; pulse until blended. Shape beef mixture into 32 balls.

Cook meatballs in 2 batches in hot oil in a large skillet over medium-high heat 7 minutes or until done. (Gently shake pan over burner often to turn and brown meatballs evenly.) Transfer meatballs to a chafing dish or electric slow cooker, and keep warm.

Combine mustard, ketchup, and molasses in a small saucepan. Cook over medium heat until warm. Pour sauce over meatballs. Serve warm. Yield: 8 appetizer servings.   Janet Shaffron

The Hallelujah Courses
Mayo United Methodist Church
Edgewater, Maryland

Tuscan Grilled Chicken Bites

This versatile dish is great spooned into a pita or piled atop a bed of greens for a hearty salad.

¾ cup vegetable oil
¾ cup chili oil
¾ cup red wine vinegar
½ cup soy sauce
¼ cup white wine
   Worcestershire sauce
1 tablespoon sweet red pepper
   flakes
1 tablespoon dried Italian
   seasoning
4 cloves garlic, minced
3 bay leaves

8 skinned and boned chicken
   breast halves (about 3½
   pounds)
2 (14-ounce) cans artichoke
   hearts, drained and
   quartered
1 cup oil-packed dried
   tomatoes, drained and
   chopped
1 bunch green onions,
   chopped
Pepper Vinegar Dressing

Combine first 9 ingredients in a large bowl; add chicken. Cover and marinate in refrigerator 8 hours. Remove chicken from marinade, discarding marinade.

Grill chicken, covered, over medium-hot coals (350° to 400°) 9 to 10 minutes on each side or until chicken is done. Let cool; cut into 2-inch pieces. Combine chicken, artichoke hearts, and remaining ingredients; toss gently. Yield: 8 to 10 servings.

Pepper Vinegar Dressing

¼ cup hot pepper-infused
   vinegar
½ cup vegetable oil
1 teaspoon Creole seasoning

1 teaspoon salt-free herb-and-
   spice blend
1 teaspoon salt

Combine all ingredients in a jar. Cover tightly, and shake vigorously. Yield: ¾ cup.

Susan Mitchell

The Art of Cooking
The Muscle Shoals District Service League
Sheffield, Alabama

Smoked Salmon with Wild Rice Pancakes

Make these pancakes ahead of time, and freeze them. To serve, just thaw, and reheat in a warm oven.

2 large eggs
2 cups buttermilk
2 cups all-purpose flour
1 teaspoon baking soda
1 teaspoon salt
¼ cup butter or margarine, melted
2 cups cooked wild rice

¾ pound thinly sliced smoked salmon
3 medium avocados, peeled and seeded
1 (8-ounce) carton sour cream
2 (2-ounce) jars caviar (optional)

Beat eggs at high speed of an electric mixer until thick and pale; stir in buttermilk. Set aside.

Stir together flour, soda, and salt. Gradually add flour mixture to buttermilk mixture, beating well. Stir in melted butter and wild rice; let stand 10 minutes.

Pour about 2 tablespoons batter for each pancake onto a hot, lightly oiled griddle. Cook pancakes until tops are covered with bubbles and edges look cooked; turn and cook other side. Remove to a serving platter, and keep warm.

Cut salmon into bite-size pieces (about 6½ dozen). Thinly slice each avocado half crosswise into about 14 slices. Cover each pancake with a salmon slice. Top with an avocado slice and about ½ teaspoon sour cream. Garnish each serving with caviar, if desired. Yield: about 6½ dozen.   Susan Odessa Froehlich

Note: This recipe can be divided in half easily to serve a smaller crowd.

A Taste of Tradition
Temple Emanu-El
Providence, Rhode Island

Prosciutto-Wrapped Shrimp with Garlic Dipping Sauce

Save time by skewering the shrimp, prosciutto, and basil the night before; then you'll be ready to grill the next day.

18 (6-inch) bamboo skewers
18 thin slices prosciutto
18 fresh basil leaves

18 jumbo shrimp, peeled and deveined

Soak bamboo skewers in water 30 minutes.

Place 1 slice prosciutto on work surface. Place a basil leaf at 1 end of prosciutto; place a shrimp over basil leaf. Roll shrimp in prosciutto, and thread onto a skewer. Repeat procedure with remaining prosciutto, basil, and shrimp.

Grill shrimp, covered, over medium-hot coals (350° to 400°) 3 minutes on each side or until shrimp turn pink. Serve hot or at room temperature with Garlic Dipping Sauce. Yield: 1½ dozen.

Garlic Dipping Sauce

⅓ cup red wine vinegar
2 tablespoons Dijon mustard
1 tablespoon minced garlic

¼ teaspoon salt
¼ teaspoon pepper
1 cup olive oil

Process first 5 ingredients in a blender. With blender on high, gradually add oil in a slow, steady stream. Yield: 1¼ cups.

Note: Use any leftover sauce as a salad dressing or as an accompaniment with chicken fingers.

Have You Heard . . . A Tasteful Medley of Memphis
Subsidium, Inc.
Memphis, Tennessee

Sparkling Summer Tea

1 quart boiling water
2 family-size tea bags
½ cup sugar
1 (12-ounce) can frozen
   lemonade concentrate,
   thawed and undiluted

1 quart water
1 (1-liter) bottle ginger ale,
   chilled
Garnishes: fresh mint sprigs,
   lemon slices, lime slices

Pour boiling water over tea bags; cover and steep 5 minutes. Remove tea bags from water, squeezing gently. Stir in sugar, lemonade concentrate, and 1 quart water; cover and chill.

Stir in chilled ginger ale just before serving. Serve over ice, and garnish, if desired. Yield: 14 cups.   Karen Walker Runnels

Savory Secrets
Runnels School
Baton Rouge, Louisiana

Blue Margaritas

For leftover margarita mix, recap the can of mix, and return it to the freezer for another batch in the future. Or go ahead and make a second batch of margaritas, and freeze it in a plastic pitcher. It will remain slushy; alcohol keeps it from freezing solid.

½ (10-ounce) can frozen
   margarita mix
¾ cup tequila

¼ cup blue curaçao
2 tablespoons lime juice

Combine all ingredients in a blender. Add ice to 5-cup level; process until smooth. Serve in glasses with salt-crusted rims, if desired. Yield: about 5 cups.

Note: To coat rims of glasses with salt, place coarse salt in a saucer; rub rims of glasses with lime wedges, and dip rims in salt.

Apron Springs: Ties to the Southern Tradition of Cooking
The Junior League of Little Rock, Arkansas

Sin-Free Sangría

This fruit-inspired refresher is quick and easy to prepare.

1 (12-ounce) can frozen white
   grape juice concentrate
1 (12-ounce) can frozen apple
   juice concentrate
1 (12-ounce) can frozen
   cranberry juice concentrate

1 (12-ounce) can frozen
   limeade concentrate
2 (2-liter) bottles lemon-lime
   carbonated beverage
Garnish: lemon or lime slices

Combine first 4 ingredients in a 6-quart punch bowl; beat with a wire whisk until smooth. Add lemon-lime beverage, stirring well. Garnish, if desired. Yield: 23 cups. Stephanie Guidry

In the Breaking of Bread
Catholic Committee on Scouting and Camp Fire
Lake Charles, Louisiana

Café del Rio

2 tablespoons chocolate syrup
1½ teaspoons ground
   cinnamon

3 cups strongly brewed coffee
2 tablespoons cinnamon-sugar
1 cup whipped cream

Pour 1 teaspoon chocolate syrup into each of 6 demitasse cups. Combine cinnamon and coffee; pour into demitasse cups.
   Stir cinnamon-sugar into whipped cream. Spoon a dollop of spiced cream on each serving. Yield: 6 (½-cup) servings. Elise Moir

The Parkway Palate
San Joaquin River Parkway & Conservation Trust
Fresno, California

Hot White Russian

White Russians are usually served over ice, but this warm version takes the chill off a winter night as an after-dinner drink.

2½ cups freshly brewed coffee
½ cup heavy cream
½ cup Kahlúa or other coffee-
   flavored liqueur

¼ cup vodka
Garnish: whipped cream

Combine first 4 ingredients in a medium saucepan; cook over medium heat until thoroughly heated.

Warm mugs or cups by rinsing with boiling water. Divide mixture evenly among mugs, and top each serving with a dollop of whipped cream. Serve immediately. Yield: 3¾ cups.   Joyce Donovan

Our Sunrise Family Cookbook
Sunrise Drive Elementary School
Tucson, Arizona

Breads

Sage Bread, page 80

Almond-Poppy Seed Bread

*Here's a clever takeoff on the ever-popular lemon poppy seed bread.
The essence of almond predominates, with highlights of orange provid-
ing a play on flavors.*

3 large eggs
1½ cups vegetable oil
2¼ cups sugar
1½ cups milk
1½ tablespoons poppy seeds
2 teaspoons almond extract
3 cups all-purpose flour

1½ teaspoons baking powder
1 teaspoon salt
¼ cup frozen orange juice
   concentrate, thawed
¾ cup sifted powdered sugar
1 teaspoon almond extract
½ teaspoon vanilla extract

Combine first 6 ingredients in a large bowl, beating with a wire
whisk until smooth. Add flour, baking powder, and salt, stirring just
until smooth.

Pour batter evenly into two greased and floured 8½- x 4½- x 3-inch
loafpans. Bake at 350° for 1 hour or until a wooden pick inserted in
center comes out clean. Cool in pans on a wire rack 10 minutes.
Remove from pans, and let cool completely on wire rack.

Combine orange juice concentrate and remaining 3 ingredients in
a small bowl, stirring until smooth. Drizzle glaze over cooled loaves.
Yield: 2 loaves.

Kelley Dow

Newport Cooks & Collects
Preservation Society of Newport County
Newport, Rhode Island

Pineapple-Nut Bread

1¾ cups all-purpose flour
2 teaspoons baking powder
¼ teaspoon baking soda
½ teaspoon salt
¾ cup chopped macadamia
   nuts
¾ cup firmly packed brown
   sugar

3 tablespoons butter or
   margarine, softened
2 large eggs, lightly beaten
1 cup crushed pineapple in
   juice, undrained
2 tablespoons sugar
½ teaspoon ground cinnamon

Combine first 5 ingredients in a bowl; make a well in center of mixture. Combine brown sugar, butter, and eggs. Add to dry ingredients, stirring just until moistened; stir in pineapple.

Spoon batter into a greased 9- x 5- x 3-inch loafpan. Combine sugar and cinnamon, and sprinkle over top. Bake at 350° for 1 hour or until a wooden pick inserted in center comes out clean. Cool in pan on a wire rack 10 minutes; remove from pan, and let cool completely on wire rack. Yield: 1 loaf.

The Tastes and Tales of Moiliili
Moiliili Community Center
Honolulu, Hawaii

Aunt Lucy's Irish Soda Bread

4 cups all-purpose flour
1½ teaspoons baking powder
1 teaspoon baking soda
1 teaspoon salt
¼ cup sugar
1 tablespoon caraway seeds
⅓ cup shortening
1 cup raisins
1⅓ cups buttermilk
1 large egg

Combine first 6 ingredients; cut in shortening with a pastry blender until mixture is crumbly. Stir in raisins.

Combine buttermilk and egg, stirring with a wire whisk. Gradually add milk mixture to flour mixture, stirring with a fork just until dry ingredients are moistened. Turn dough out onto a well-floured surface, and knead 3 or 4 times. Pat dough into a greased 9-inch round cakepan. Bake at 375° for 40 minutes. Remove to a wire rack, and let cool at least 5 minutes before slicing. Cut into wedges. Yield: one 9-inch round loaf.

The Many Tastes of Haverstraw Middle School
Home and Career Skills Department, Haverstraw Middle School
Haverstraw, New York

Herb Bread

Store-bought French bread gives you a head start when preparing this quick and easy recipe.

1 (16-ounce) loaf French bread
1 cup butter or margarine, softened
1 (2¼-ounce) can chopped ripe olives
½ cup chopped fresh parsley
⅓ cup chopped green onions
1½ teaspoons dried basil
½ teaspoon garlic powder
½ teaspoon dried tarragon
¼ teaspoon celery seeds

Slice bread in half horizontally; set aside.

Combine butter and remaining 7 ingredients; spread evenly over cut sides of bread. Place halves together; wrap in aluminum foil. Store in refrigerator until ready to bake.

Bake at 350° for 25 minutes or until thoroughly heated. Cut into slices to serve. Yield: 12 servings.   Annabelle Thomas

The Great Delights Cookbook
Genoa Serbart United Methodist Churches
Genoa, Colorado

Sun-Dried Tomato and Provolone Bread

⅓ cup oil-packed dried tomatoes
2 cloves garlic
2½ cups all-purpose flour
2 teaspoons baking powder
½ teaspoon baking soda
1¼ teaspoons salt
1 cup (4 ounces) shredded provolone cheese
½ cup finely chopped green onions
2 teaspoons minced fresh parsley
¾ teaspoon dried rosemary, crumbled
¾ teaspoon coarsely ground pepper
2 teaspoons shortening
2 teaspoons sugar
2 large eggs, lightly beaten
1¼ cups buttermilk
⅓ cup chopped pine nuts

Drain tomatoes, reserving 2 teaspoons oil; chop tomatoes, and set aside.

Cook garlic in small amount of boiling water 15 minutes; drain. Peel and mash garlic; set aside.

Combine flour, baking powder, soda, and salt; stir well. Add chopped tomatoes, cheese, and next 4 ingredients; stir well.

Combine reserved oil, shortening, and sugar; beat with a wire whisk until smooth. Add garlic, eggs, and buttermilk; stir well. Add chopped tomatoes, garlic mixture, and pine nuts to flour mixture, stirring just until blended.

Spread batter in a greased 8½- x 4½- x 3-inch loafpan; smooth top. Bake at 350° for 45 to 50 minutes or until golden. Cool in pan on a wire rack 5 minutes. Remove from pan; cool on wire rack. Yield: 1 loaf.

Special Selections of Ocala
Ocala Royal Dames for Cancer Research, Inc.
Ocala, Florida

Apple-Peach Puff Pancake

This puff pancake resembles a giant popover and will fall quickly after removing it from the oven. If using frozen peaches, add 1 tablespoon sugar to equal the sweetness of fresh peaches.

3 large eggs, lightly beaten
½ cup milk
1 tablespoon sugar
¼ teaspoon salt
½ cup all-purpose flour
2 tablespoons butter or
   margarine

1 cup chunky applesauce
1 cup sliced fresh or frozen
   peaches
½ teaspoon ground cinnamon
Powdered sugar

Combine first 4 ingredients in a large bowl. Gradually add flour, stirring with a wire whisk until blended. Place butter in a 10-inch cast-iron skillet, and place in a 425° oven for 2 minutes or until butter melts. Remove skillet from oven; immediately pour batter into hot skillet. Bake at 425° for 15 to 20 minutes.

Meanwhile, combine applesauce, peaches, and cinnamon in a saucepan; cook over low heat until heated. Spoon mixture on baked pancake immediately after removing from oven. Sprinkle with powdered sugar. Cut into wedges. Yield: 4 servings.   Maureen Johnstone

Culinary Classics
Hoffman Estates Medical Center Service League
Hoffman Estates, Illinois

Mocha Streusel Coffee Cake

A streusel topping laced with cinnamon, espresso granules, and chunks of chocolate transforms a simple sheet cake into a dreamy coffee cake suitable for serving any time of day.

Vegetable cooking spray
¼ cup firmly packed brown sugar
2 ounces milk chocolate, chopped (we tested with Hershey's)
1 tablespoon butter or margarine, cut into small pieces
2 teaspoons instant espresso granules (we tested with Ferrara)
2 teaspoons ground cinnamon
1¼ cups plus 1 tablespoon all-purpose flour, divided
2 teaspoons baking powder
½ teaspoon salt
½ cup sugar
½ cup milk
1 large egg
3 tablespoons butter or margarine, melted

Coat an 8-inch square pan with cooking spray; set aside.

Combine brown sugar, chocolate, 1 tablespoon butter, espresso, cinnamon, and 1 tablespoon flour in a small bowl, stirring well; set streusel mixture aside.

Combine remaining 1¼ cups flour, baking powder, salt, and sugar in a medium bowl. Combine milk, egg, and 3 tablespoons melted butter in a small bowl. Add to dry ingredients, and stir just until moistened.

Pour batter into prepared pan. Sprinkle streusel mixture evenly over batter. Bake at 375° for 20 to 25 minutes or until a wooden pick inserted in center comes out clean. Cool and cut into squares. Yield: 9 servings.

Kathleen Youse

Silver Spoons
Kaiser Rehabilitation Center
Tulsa, Oklahoma

Raspberry-Cream Cheese Coffee Cake

This attractive coffee cake coordinates well with any breakfast or brunch menu. You can vary the flavor and color of fillings by using preserves.

2¼ cups all-purpose flour
¾ cup sugar
¾ cup butter or margarine
½ teaspoon baking powder
½ teaspoon baking soda
¼ teaspoon salt
¾ cup sour cream
1 teaspoon almond extract

1 large egg, lightly beaten
1 (8-ounce) package cream cheese, softened
¼ cup sugar
1 large egg
½ cup raspberry preserves
½ cup sliced almonds
Fresh raspberries (optional)

Combine flour and ¾ cup sugar in a large bowl. Cut in butter with a pastry blender until mixture is crumbly; set aside 1 cup crumb mixture.

Add baking powder and next 5 ingredients to remaining crumb mixture; stir well. Spread dough in bottom and 2 inches up sides of a greased and floured 9-inch springform pan (dough should be about ¼ inch thick on sides).

Combine cream cheese, ¼ cup sugar, and 1 egg; beat at medium speed of an electric mixer until smooth. Pour batter into prepared pan. Spoon preserves evenly over cream cheese mixture.

Combine reserved 1 cup crumb mixture and sliced almonds; sprinkle over preserves.

Bake at 350° for 45 minutes or until filling is set and crust is lightly browned. Cool 15 minutes in pan; remove sides of pan. Serve warm or at room temperature. Garnish with fresh raspberries, if desired. Yield: 8 servings.

Susanne Voss

Scent from P.E.O. Sisterhood
Philanthropic Educational Organization, Chapter AG
Newcastle, Wyoming

Pumpkin-Pecan Biscuits

Serve these tasty biscuits hot with butter and honey or split, toasted, and topped with ham—either way is bound to please.

2 cups all-purpose flour
¼ cup sugar
1 tablespoon plus 1 teaspoon
  baking powder
½ teaspoon salt
½ teaspoon ground cinnamon

½ teaspoon ground nutmeg
½ cup butter or margarine, cut
  into pieces
⅓ cup chopped pecans, toasted
⅔ cup canned pumpkin
⅓ cup half-and-half

Combine first 6 ingredients in a large bowl. Cut in butter with a pastry blender until mixture is crumbly; stir in pecans. Combine pumpkin and half-and-half; add to flour mixture, stirring just until dry ingredients are moistened.

Turn dough out onto a lightly floured surface; knead 4 or 5 times. (Add more flour if dough is sticky.) Roll dough to ½-inch thickness; cut with a 2-inch biscuit cutter. Place on a lightly greased baking sheet. Bake at 400° for 12 to 14 minutes or until lightly browned. Yield: 20 biscuits.   Gene Crystal

Recipes from the Flock
Mandarin Senior Citizens Center
Jacksonville, Florida

Carrot-Zucchini Muffins

½ cup all-purpose flour
½ cup whole wheat flour
1 teaspoon baking powder
½ teaspoon baking soda
¼ teaspoon salt
1 teaspoon ground cinnamon
4 egg whites

⅔ cup sugar
¼ cup vegetable oil
½ teaspoon vanilla extract
¾ cup shredded zucchini
¾ cup shredded carrot
1 cup chopped walnuts
½ cup raisins

Combine first 6 ingredients in a large bowl; make a well in center of mixture. Combine egg whites, sugar, oil, and vanilla; add to dry ingredients, stirring just until moistened. Stir in zucchini, carrot, walnuts, and raisins.

Spoon batter into greased muffin pans, filling two-thirds full. Bake at 400° for 18 to 20 minutes or until a wooden pick inserted in center comes out clean. Remove from pans immediately, and let cool on a wire rack. Yield: 1 dozen.   Mary Contrucci

Great Expectations
The Assistance League of Southeast Michigan
Rochester Hills, Michigan

Cheddar and Bacon Muffins

For the perfect accompaniment with a hearty bowl of soup, you can't beat these savory muffins.

1 **pound bacon**
1 **cup finely chopped green onions**
1 **teaspoon salt**
1 **teaspoon freshly ground pepper**
1½ **teaspoons caraway seeds (optional)**
3 **cups all-purpose flour**
2 **teaspoons baking powder**

1 **teaspoon baking soda**
2 **tablespoons sugar**
2 **large eggs**
1½ **cups milk**
3 **tablespoons Dijon mustard**
3 **tablespoons shortening, melted and cooled**
2 **cups (8 ounces) shredded extra-sharp Cheddar cheese**

Cook bacon until crisp. Drain bacon, reserving 2 tablespoons drippings. Crumble bacon, and set aside.

Sauté green onions, salt, pepper, and, if desired, caraway seeds in reserved bacon drippings over medium heat until onion is tender; set aside.

Combine flour, baking powder, soda, and sugar; stir well.

Combine eggs, milk, mustard, shortening, and green onion mixture. Add to dry ingredients, stirring just until moistened. Stir in cheese and crumbled bacon.

Spoon batter into greased muffin pans. Bake at 375° for 20 minutes or until a wooden pick inserted in center comes out clean. Remove from pans immediately, and let cool on wire racks. Yield: 1½ dozen.

Call to Post
Lexington Hearing and Speech Center
Lexington, Kentucky

Peppercorn and Chive Cornbread

¾ cup yellow cornmeal
¾ cup all-purpose flour
1½ teaspoons cream of tartar
¾ teaspoon baking soda
¾ teaspoon salt
½ teaspoon coarsely ground
   pepper

1 tablespoon sugar
1 cup sour cream
¼ cup chopped fresh chives
3 tablespoons butter or
   margarine, melted
2 tablespoons milk
1 large egg, lightly beaten

Combine first 7 ingredients in a large bowl; stir well. Make a well in center of mixture. Combine sour cream and remaining 4 ingredients; add to dry ingredients, stirring just until moistened.

Spoon batter into a greased 8-inch square pan. Bake at 425° for 20 minutes or until golden. Cut into squares to serve. Yield: 8 servings.

Great Lake Effects
The Junior League of Buffalo, New York

Vegetable Bread

2 cups (8 ounces) shredded
   Swiss cheese
1 bunch green onions,
   chopped (1 cup)
3 tablespoons poppy seeds
⅓ cup butter or margarine,
   melted

⅛ teaspoon salt
1 (16-ounce) loaf frozen bread
   dough, thawed (we tested
   with Rich's)

Combine first 5 ingredients in a medium bowl; set aside.

Cut dough into 20 pieces. Place 10 pieces of dough in a heavily greased 12-cup Bundt pan. Spoon half of cheese mixture over dough to within ½ inch of sides. Layer with remaining dough, and top with remaining cheese mixture. Let rise in a warm place (85°), free from drafts, 1½ hours. Bake at 375° for 20 minutes or until golden. Yield: one 10-inch ring.

Cheryl Hirata-Dulas

Bridging the Generations
Japanese American Citizens League
Bloomington, Minnesota

Pumpernickel Bread

1½ cups bread flour
½ cup rye flour
1 tablespoon sugar
1 tablespoon cocoa
1 teaspoon salt
¾ cup brewed coffee, cooled
1 tablespoon butter or
  margarine
2 tablespoons molasses
1½ teaspoons bread-machine
  yeast or rapid-rise yeast

Combine all ingredients in bread machine according to manufacturer's instructions. Select bake cycle; start machine. Remove bread from pan; cool on a wire rack. Yield: 1 loaf.   Marie Evans

White Clay Creek Presbyterian Church 275th Anniversary Cookbook
White Clay Creek Presbyterian Church
Newark, Delaware

Hearty Oat and Walnut Bread

Be sure to check the instructions to your bread machine before adding walnuts. Some machines require adding them at mid-cycle.

1¼ cups very warm water (120°
  to 130°)
3 cups bread flour
1½ teaspoons salt
¼ cup firmly packed brown
  sugar
½ cup quick-cooking oats
1 tablespoon butter or
  margarine
1½ teaspoons bread-machine
  yeast or rapid-rise yeast
¾ cup chopped walnuts

Combine all ingredients in a bread machine according to manufacturer's instructions. Select bake cycle; start machine. Remove bread from pan; cool on a wire rack. Yield: 1 loaf.   Janice Funderburk

Morrisonville's 125th Anniversary Cookbook
Morrisonville Historical Society & Museum
Morrisonville, Illinois

Sage Bread

*Fresh sage sprigs top this savory bread, making an attractive presenta-
tion special enough for gift giving. We halved the recipe so it can be
mixed with a regular mixer. If you have a heavy-duty mixer, you can
double the recipe, if you'd like, and make three slightly larger loaves in
9- x 5- x 3-inch loafpans. They'll need a little more time to rise; bake
the loaves at 375° for 30 minutes or until they're golden.*

2¼ to 2½ cups all-purpose
    flour, divided
2 cups whole wheat flour
2 packages active dry yeast
1 tablespoon minced fresh
    sage
1¾ cups milk
¼ cup firmly packed brown
    sugar

2½ tablespoons butter or
    margarine
1 teaspoon salt
¼ cup plus 2 tablespoons
    yellow cornmeal, divided
1 large egg, lightly beaten
1 tablespoon water
Fresh sage sprigs

Combine 1 cup all-purpose flour, whole wheat flour, yeast, and
minced sage in a large mixing bowl; stir well.

Place milk, brown sugar, butter, and salt in a saucepan; cook over
low heat until butter melts, stirring often. Cool to 120° to 130°.

Gradually add milk mixture to flour mixture, beating 30 seconds at
low speed of an electric mixer. Beat 3 more minutes at medium-high
speed. Gradually stir in ¼ cup cornmeal and remaining 1¼ to 1½
cups all-purpose flour to make a soft dough.

Turn dough out onto a floured surface, and knead until smooth
and elastic (about 6 to 8 minutes). Shape into a ball. Place in a well-
greased bowl, turning to grease top. Cover and let rise in a warm place
(85°), free from drafts, 30 minutes or until doubled in bulk.

Punch dough down; turn out onto a lightly floured surface, and knead
lightly 4 or 5 times. Divide dough in half. Cover and let rest 10 minutes.

Lightly grease a baking sheet, and sprinkle with remaining 2 tablespoons cornmeal. Shape each half of dough into an 8½- x 4½-inch
loaf. Place on prepared baking sheet.

Combine egg and water, stirring well. Brush loaves with egg mixture. Place sage sprigs on top of loaves. Cover and let rise in a warm
place, free from drafts, 20 minutes or until doubled in bulk. Brush
again with egg mixture. (Do not brush sage leaves.)

Bake at 375° for 20 to 25 minutes or until golden, covering with
aluminum foil during last 15 minutes, if necessary, to prevent excessive

browning. Remove loaves from baking sheet, and let cool on a wire rack. Yield: 2 loaves.   Robin Westerick

Carnegie Hall Cookbook
Carnegie Hall, Inc.
Lewisburg, West Virginia

Swedish Limpa Bread with Fennel

Fennel seeds, anise seeds, and orange rind come together to create a fragrant rye bread.

2 packages active dry yeast
1½ cups warm water (105° to 115°)
½ cup raisins (optional)
⅓ cup sugar
¼ cup dark molasses
2 tablespoons corn oil

2 teaspoons grated orange rind
1 teaspoon fennel seeds
1 teaspoon anise seeds
1 teaspoon salt
2½ cups rye flour
3 cups all-purpose flour

Combine yeast and warm water in a 2-cup liquid measuring cup; let stand 5 minutes. Combine yeast mixture, raisins, if desired, and next 7 ingredients in a large bowl; stir well. Add rye flour; stir until thoroughly moistened. Add all-purpose flour; stir until a soft dough forms.

Turn dough out onto a floured surface; knead until smooth and elastic (6 to 8 minutes). Place dough in a well-greased bowl, turning to grease top. Cover; let rise in a warm place (85°), free from drafts, 45 minutes or until doubled in bulk. Punch dough down; divide in half.

Roll half of dough into a 15- x 7-inch rectangle on a lightly floured surface. Roll up dough, starting at short side. Pinch seams and ends to seal. Place loaf, seam side down, in a greased 8½- x 4½- x 3-inch loafpan. Repeat procedure with remaining dough. Cover; let rise in a warm place, free from drafts, 30 minutes or until doubled in bulk.

Bake at 350° for 35 to 40 minutes or until loaves sound hollow when tapped. Remove loaves from pans, and let cool completely on wire racks. Yield: 2 loaves.   Wally Engelmann

Quad City Cookin'
Queen of Heaven Circle of OLV Ladies Council
Davenport, Iowa

Raisin-Nut Cocoa Bread

2 cups water
1 cup regular oats
1 teaspoon salt, divided
6 cups all-purpose flour, divided
½ cup cocoa
2 packages active dry yeast
½ cup warm water (105° to 115°)
1 cup firmly packed brown sugar
2 tablespoons butter, softened
1 cup chopped walnuts
1 cup raisins
Melted butter

Combine 2 cups water, oats, and ½ teaspoon salt in a medium saucepan. Bring to a boil; reduce heat, and simmer, uncovered, 5 minutes, stirring occasionally. Pour oat mixture into a large mixing bowl, and let cool to lukewarm.

Combine 2 cups flour, cocoa, and remaining ½ teaspoon salt. Combine yeast and warm water in a 1-cup liquid measuring cup; let stand 5 minutes. Add flour mixture, yeast mixture, sugar, and softened butter to oat mixture. Beat at low speed of an electric mixer until moistened. Beat at medium speed 2 minutes. Stir in walnuts and raisins.

Gradually stir in enough remaining flour to make a soft dough. Turn dough out onto a floured surface, and knead until smooth and elastic (6 to 8 minutes). Place dough in a well-greased bowl, turning to grease top. Cover and let rise in a warm place (85°), free from drafts, 45 minutes or until doubled in bulk. Punch dough down, and divide in half.

Roll half of dough into a 15- x 7-inch rectangle on a lightly floured surface. Roll up dough, starting at short side, pressing firmly to eliminate air pockets; pinch seams and ends to seal. Place loaf, seam side down, in a greased 9- x 5- x 3-inch loafpan. Repeat procedure with remaining portion of dough. Cover and let rise in a warm place, free from drafts, 30 minutes or until doubled in bulk.

Bake at 375° for 35 to 40 minutes or until loaves sound hollow when tapped. Remove bread from pans; immediately brush with melted butter. Cool completely on wire racks. Yield: 2 loaves.

Swap Around Recipes
Delmarva Square Dance Federation
Salisbury, Maryland

Light Wheat Rolls

The "light" in the title refers to the delicate color of the crumb of these delectable spiral-shaped rolls–they received our highest rating.

2 packages active dry yeast
½ cup sugar
1 teaspoon salt
1¾ cups warm water (105° to 115°)
¼ cup butter or margarine, melted

1 large egg, lightly beaten
2¼ cups whole wheat flour
2¼ to 2¾ cups all-purpose flour
Melted butter

Combine yeast, sugar, and salt in warm water in a large mixing bowl; let stand 5 minutes. Add ¼ cup melted butter, egg, and whole wheat flour to yeast mixture, beating at medium speed of an electric mixer until well blended. Gradually stir in enough all-purpose flour to make a soft dough.

Turn dough out onto a well-floured surface, and knead until smooth and elastic (about 5 minutes). Place in a well-greased bowl, turning to grease top.

Cover and let rise in a warm place (85°), free from drafts, 45 minutes or until doubled in bulk.

Punch dough down, and divide in half. Roll each portion into a 12- x 7-inch rectangle. Cut each portion into 12 (7- x 1-inch) strips. Roll each strip of dough into a spiral; place in well-greased muffin pans.

Brush with melted butter; let rise, uncovered, in a warm place, free from drafts, 20 to 25 minutes or until doubled in bulk.

Bake at 400° for 12 minutes or until lightly browned. Brush again with melted butter. Yield: 2 dozen.   Cyndi Bradt

Moments, Memories & Manna
Restoration Village
Rogers, Arkansas

Chocolate Cinnamon Rolls

For a chocolaty treat, you can't beat these yummy rolls. Try this tip for glazing them: Simply place glaze in a heavy-duty, zip-top plastic bag, and seal securely. Then snip off one tiny corner of the bag, and pipe glaze over rolls.

1 package active dry yeast
¾ cup warm water (105° to 115°)
¼ cup butter or margarine, softened
1 teaspoon salt
¼ cup sugar
1 large egg
⅓ cup cocoa
2½ cups all-purpose flour, divided

1 tablespoon butter or margarine, softened
1½ teaspoons ground cinnamon
3 tablespoons sugar
½ cup chopped pecans
2 cups sifted powdered sugar
2½ tablespoons milk

Combine yeast and warm water in a 2-cup liquid measuring cup; let stand 5 minutes.

Combine yeast mixture, ¼ cup softened butter, salt, ¼ cup sugar, egg, cocoa, and 1 cup flour in a large mixing bowl; beat at medium speed of an electric mixer until well blended. Gradually stir in enough remaining flour to make a soft dough. Place dough in a well-greased bowl, turning to grease top. Cover and let rise in a warm place (85°), free from drafts, 50 minutes or until doubled in bulk.

Punch dough down; turn out onto a lightly floured surface, and knead until smooth and elastic (about 2 minutes). Roll dough into a 12- x 9-inch rectangle; spread 1 tablespoon softened butter over dough. Combine cinnamon and 3 tablespoons sugar; sprinkle over butter. Sprinkle pecans over cinnamon mixture. Roll up dough, starting at short side, pressing firmly to eliminate air pockets; pinch seams to seal. Slice dough into 9 rolls; place rolls on a greased baking sheet. Cover; let rise in a warm place, free from drafts, 15 minutes or until doubled in bulk. Bake at 425° for 8 minutes or until golden.

Meanwhile, combine powdered sugar and milk, stirring until blended. Drizzle hot rolls with powdered sugar glaze. Yield: 9 large rolls.

Dolores Wilson

Madalene Cooks–50 Years of Good Taste
Church of the Madalene
Tulsa, Oklahoma

Cakes

Triple Chocolate Cake, page 99

Coconut Cake with Pineapple Filling

3 large egg whites
1¾ cups sugar, divided
½ cup butter, softened
2 cups all-purpose flour
2½ teaspoons baking powder
¼ teaspoon salt
1 cup milk
1 teaspoon vanilla extract
1 (15½-ounce) can crushed
  pineapple, well drained
1½ teaspoons cornstarch
2 egg yolks
Seven-Minute Frosting
1½ cups flaked coconut

Beat egg whites in a mixing bowl at high speed of an electric mixer until foamy. Gradually add ¼ cup sugar, 1 tablespoon at a time, beating until stiff peaks form and sugar dissolves (2 to 4 minutes). Set aside.

Beat butter at medium speed until creamy; gradually add 1 cup sugar, beating well. Combine flour, baking powder, and salt; add to butter mixture alternately with milk, beginning and ending with flour mixture. Mix at low speed after each addition until blended.

Fold beaten egg whites and vanilla into batter. Pour batter into three greased and floured 8-inch round cakepans.

Bake at 350° for 20 minutes or until a wooden pick inserted in center comes out clean. Cool in pans on wire racks 10 minutes; remove from pans, and cool completely on wire racks.

Combine remaining ½ cup sugar, pineapple, cornstarch, and egg yolks in top of a double boiler; bring water to a boil. Reduce heat to medium; cook, stirring constantly, until mixture thickens. Cool.

Spread filling between layers. Frost top and sides of cake with frosting. Sprinkle coconut over top and sides of cake. Store in refrigerator. Yield: one 3-layer cake.

Seven-Minute Frosting

1½ cups sugar
¼ cup plus 1 tablespoon cold
  water
2 egg whites
1½ teaspoons light corn syrup
1 teaspoon vanilla extract

Combine first 4 ingredients in top of a large double boiler. Beat at low speed of an electric mixer 30 seconds. Place over boiling water; beat at high speed 7 minutes or until stiff peaks form. Remove from heat. Add vanilla; beat 2 minutes or until thick. Yield: 3½ cups.

Ambrosia
The Junior Auxiliary of Vicksburg, Mississippi

Luscious Orange Sponge Cake

1⅓ cups all-purpose flour,
  divided
1 teaspoon baking powder
¼ teaspoon salt
½ cup finely chopped walnuts
3 large eggs
1¾ cups sugar, divided
⅓ cup orange juice
½ teaspoon orange extract
2 tablespoons powdered sugar
3 egg yolks

¼ teaspoon grated orange rind
½ cup orange juice
1 tablespoon lemon juice
Dash of salt
3 tablespoons orange juice
2 cups whipping cream,
  whipped
1 cup coarsely chopped
  walnuts
Garnishes: orange slices, fresh
  mint leaves

Grease bottom and sides of a 15- x 10- x 1-inch jellyroll pan; line with wax paper. Grease wax paper; set aside.

Combine 1 cup flour, baking powder, and salt; stir in ½ cup finely chopped walnuts. Set aside.

Beat 3 eggs in a medium mixing bowl at high speed of an electric mixer until foamy. Gradually add ¾ cup sugar, beating until thick and pale. Add ⅓ cup orange juice and orange extract; beat until blended. Gradually fold in flour mixture. Spread evenly in prepared pan.

Bake at 375° for 15 minutes or until cake springs back when lightly touched. Sprinkle powdered sugar in a 15- x 10-inch rectangle on a cloth towel. When cake is done, immediately loosen from sides of pan, and turn out onto prepared towel. Peel off wax paper. Let cool completely on towel on a wire rack.

While cake bakes, combine remaining ⅓ cup flour, 1 cup sugar, and 3 egg yolks in top of a double boiler; beat with a wire whisk until blended. Stir in orange rind, ½ cup orange juice, lemon juice, and salt. Bring water to a boil; reduce heat to low, and cook, stirring constantly, 20 minutes or until thickened; cool, stirring often.

Cut cake crosswise into 3 (5- x 10-inch) rectangles. Drizzle 3 tablespoons orange juice over cake rectangles. Fold cooled orange juice mixture into whipped cream. Spread one-third of mixture on 2 of the cake rectangles. Layer cake rectangles with plain cake rectangle on top. Spread remaining mixture on top and sides of cake. Sprinkle with 1 cup coarsely chopped walnuts. Chill. Garnish, if desired. Yield: 8 servings.

Beneath the Palms
The Brownsville Junior Service League
Brownsville, Texas

Butter Sponge Cake

Sponge cakes typically contain egg whites and no butter, so this cake is in a class by itself. You'll agree once you taste its beautiful layers. Prepare Lemon Filling first so it can be chilling as you bake the cake.

2¼ cups sifted cake flour	1 teaspoon vanilla extract
2 teaspoons baking powder	½ cup butter, melted
1 cup milk	Lemon Filling
11 egg yolks	Marshmallow Frosting
2 cups sugar	

Combine cake flour and baking powder, stirring with a wire whisk; set aside.

Place milk in a small saucepan. Cook over medium heat until thoroughly heated (do not boil).

Beat egg yolks in a large mixing bowl at high speed of an electric mixer until thick and pale. Gradually add sugar, beating until light and fluffy. Stir in milk and vanilla. Fold in dry ingredients; add melted butter, and beat gently. Spoon batter into two wax paper-lined 9-inch round cakepans.

Bake at 350° for 25 minutes or until cake springs back when lightly touched. Cool 10 minutes on wire racks. Invert pans, remove pans and wax paper, and cool layers completely on wire racks.

Place 1 cake layer on a cake plate; spread 2 cups Lemon Filling over top layer, leaving a 1-inch border around edges. (Reserve remaining filling for other uses.) Top with remaining cake layer, pressing layer gently until filling flows just to edge of cake. Spread Marshmallow Frosting on top and sides of cake. Store in refrigerator. Yield: one 2-layer cake.

Lemon Filling

1 cup sugar	½ cup fresh lemon juice
3 tablespoons cornstarch	2 tablespoons butter
½ teaspoon salt	4 egg yolks, lightly beaten
1 cup water	

Combine first 3 ingredients in a large heavy saucepan; stir well. Add water, fresh lemon juice, and butter. Bring to a boil over medium heat; cook 1 minute, stirring often. Gradually stir about one-fourth of hot mixture into egg yolks; add to remaining hot mixture, stirring constantly. Cook until thickened, stirring constantly. Cool to room temperature; cover and chill. Yield: 2½ cups.

Marshmallow Frosting

1 cup sugar	13 large marshmallows
⅓ cup water	2 egg whites
1 tablespoon light corn syrup	

Combine first 3 ingredients in a large heavy saucepan; stir well. Bring to a boil; reduce heat, and cook over medium heat, stirring constantly, until mixture reaches soft ball stage or candy thermometer registers 236°. Remove from heat. Add marshmallows, stirring until melted.

Beat egg whites in a large mixing bowl at high speed of an electric mixer until stiff peaks form. Pour hot marshmallow mixture in a heavy stream over beaten egg white while beating at high speed. Beat just until mixture holds its shape (3 to 4 minutes). Immediately spread frosting on cake. Yield: 2 cups.   Margaret Doud

The Flavors of Mackinac
Mackinac Island Medical Center
Mackinac Island, Michigan

Snowflake Cake

½ cup butter, softened
1½ cups sugar
2 large eggs
4 large eggs, separated
2½ cups all-purpose flour
1 tablespoon baking powder
1 cup milk

2 teaspoons vanilla extract,
   divided
½ cup finely chopped pecans
1¾ cups sugar
½ cup water
½ teaspoon cream of tartar
2 cups flaked coconut

Beat butter at medium speed of an electric mixer until creamy; gradually add 1½ cups sugar, beating well. Add 2 eggs and 4 egg yolks, one at a time, beating after each addition.

Combine flour and baking powder; add to butter mixture alternately with milk, beginning and ending with flour mixture. Mix at low speed after each addition until blended. Stir in 1 teaspoon vanilla. Fold in pecans. Pour batter into 3 greased and floured 9-inch round cakepans.

Bake at 350° for 18 to 20 minutes or until a wooden pick inserted in center comes out clean. Cool in pans on wire racks 10 minutes; remove from pans, and cool completely on wire racks.

Combine 1¾ cups sugar and water in a heavy saucepan. Cook over medium heat, stirring until mixture is clear. Cover and cook 2 minutes to wash down sugar crystals from sides of pan. Uncover and cook, without stirring, until syrup reaches firm ball stage or candy thermometer registers 242°.

While syrup cooks, beat reserved 4 egg whites and cream of tartar at high speed of an electric mixer until soft peaks form; continue to beat egg whites, adding the hot syrup mixture in a heavy stream. Add remaining 1 teaspoon vanilla. Beat until stiff peaks form and frosting is thick enough to spread. Spread frosting between layers and on top and sides of cake, sprinkling ¼ cup coconut evenly between each layer. Sprinkle remaining 1½ cups coconut on top and sides of cake. Yield: one 3-layer cake.

Arthur Mae Maloy

Meet Me in the Kitchen
Northside Church of Christ
Waco, Texas

Vermont Maple Nut Cake

1 cup butter or margarine, softened
½ cup firmly packed brown sugar
2 large eggs
1 (8.5-ounce) bottle maple syrup (1 cup)
2½ cups all-purpose flour
2 teaspoons baking powder
½ teaspoon baking soda
½ teaspoon salt
2 teaspoons ground nutmeg
½ cup hot water
½ cup cooking sherry or apple juice
2 cups coarsely chopped walnuts
1 tablespoon all-purpose flour
Frozen whipped topping, thawed (optional)

Beat butter at medium speed of an electric mixer until creamy; gradually add sugar, beating well. Add eggs, one at a time, beating after each addition. Add maple syrup, beating well.

Combine 2½ cups flour and next 4 ingredients; add to butter mixture alternately with hot water and sherry, beginning and ending with flour mixture. Mix at low speed after each addition until blended.

Toss walnuts in 1 tablespoon flour, coating well. Stir walnuts into batter. Pour batter into a greased 9-inch square pan.

Bake at 350° for 45 to 47 minutes or until a wooden pick inserted in center comes out clean. Cool in pan on a wire rack. Cut cake into squares, and top each serving with a dollop of whipped topping, if desired. Yield: 9 servings.   Ella E. Bassett

Vermont Children's Aid Society Cookbook
Vermont Children's Aid Society
Winooski, Vermont

Forbidden Cake

German chocolate cake mix and caramel ice cream topping keep preparation for this rich cake simple.

1 (18.25-ounce) package
  German chocolate cake mix
  (we tested with Duncan
  Hines)
1 (12-ounce) jar caramel ice
  cream topping
1 (14-ounce) can sweetened
  condensed milk

1 (8-ounce) container frozen
  whipped topping, thawed
3 (2.3-ounce) chocolate-covered
  crispy peanut-buttery candy
  bars, crushed
¼ cup chopped pecans

Prepare cake mix according to package directions. Pour batter into a greased 13- x 9- x 2-inch pan.

Bake at 350° for 38 minutes or until a wooden pick inserted in center comes out clean. Prick holes in top of cake at 1-inch intervals with a wooden pick. Gently spread caramel topping over cake. Pour sweetened condensed milk over caramel topping. Spread evenly over cake so mixture will soak into cake. Cool in pan on a wire rack. Cover and chill 2 hours.

Spread whipped topping over cake. Sprinkle with crushed candy and chopped pecans. Yield: 15 servings.   Doris Fromm

Kitchen Keepsakes
United Methodist Church Women
Beloit, Kansas

Holiday Cake

This nutty, prune-filled spice cake is a real treat, whether or not it's holiday time.

3 large eggs
1½ cups sugar
1 cup vegetable oil
2 cups all-purpose flour
1 teaspoon salt
1 teaspoon baking soda
1 teaspoon ground cinnamon
1 teaspoon ground nutmeg

1 teaspoon ground allspice
1 cup buttermilk
1 teaspoon vanilla extract
1 cup chopped pecans
1 cup chopped dried, pitted prunes
Buttermilk Icing

Beat eggs, sugar, and oil at medium speed of an electric mixer until smooth.

Combine flour and next 5 ingredients; add to egg mixture alternately with buttermilk, beginning and ending with flour mixture. Mix at low speed after each addition until blended. Stir in vanilla, pecans, and prunes. Pour batter into a greased 13- x 9- x 2-inch pan.

Bake at 300° for 1 hour or until a wooden pick inserted in center comes out clean. Cool in pan on a wire rack. Pour warm Buttermilk Icing evenly over cooled cake. Yield: 15 servings.

Buttermilk Icing

1 cup sugar
½ cup buttermilk
¼ cup plus 2 tablespoons butter

1 teaspoon baking soda
1 teaspoon vanilla extract
1 teaspoon light corn syrup

Combine all ingredients in a saucepan; bring mixture to a boil over medium heat. Cook 1 minute without stirring. Remove from heat. Yield: 1 cup.

Diana Clark

Renaissance of Recipes
Iao Intermediate School Renaissance Ke 'ala hou
Wailuku, Hawaii

Jam Sheet Cake

¾ cup butter, softened
1 cup sugar
2 large eggs, separated
1 cup seedless blackberry jam
1 cup unsweetened applesauce
½ cup buttermilk
2 cups self-rising flour
1 teaspoon baking soda
1 teaspoon ground cinnamon
1 teaspoon ground nutmeg
1 teaspoon ground allspice
1 teaspoon ground cloves
1 cup chopped pecans
1 cup chopped dates
1 cup raisins
Easy Caramel Icing

Beat butter at medium speed of an electric mixer until creamy; gradually add sugar, beating well. Add egg yolks, jam, applesauce, and buttermilk. Combine flour and next 5 ingredients; add to butter mixture, beating well. Stir in pecans, dates, and raisins. Beat egg whites until stiff peaks form; fold into batter. Pour batter into a greased 13- x 9- x 2-inch pan.

Bake at 350° for 45 minutes or until a wooden pick inserted in center comes out clean. Cool in pan on a wire rack. Spread Easy Caramel Icing over top of cooled cake. Yield: 15 servings.

Easy Caramel Icing

½ cup butter
1 cup firmly packed brown
  sugar
¼ cup milk
2½ cups sifted powdered sugar

Melt butter in a medium saucepan; add brown sugar, and bring to a boil over low heat. Cook 2 minutes. Remove from heat, and add milk; bring to a boil over low heat. Cook 2 more minutes. Remove from heat. When mixture stops boiling, add powdered sugar; beat with a wooden spoon until frosting is spreading consistency. Immediately spread over cake. Yield: 2 cups.

Linen Napkins to Paper Plates
The Junior Auxiliary of Clarksville, Tennessee

Easy and Delicious Pineapple Cream Cake

This moist cake is the perfect choice for a covered-dish dinner because of its preparation and make-ahead ease.

1 (15-ounce) can crushed
   pineapple, undrained
1 (18.25-ounce) package yellow
   cake mix (we tested with
   Duncan Hines)
2 large eggs
1 (11-ounce) can mandarin
   oranges, drained

½ cup mayonnaise
1 (12-ounce) container frozen
   whipped topping, thawed
1 (5.1-ounce) package instant
   vanilla pudding mix

Drain pineapple, reserving juice; set pineapple aside.

Combine pineapple juice, cake mix, eggs, mandarin oranges, and mayonnaise in a large mixing bowl. Beat at medium speed of an electric mixer until blended. Pour batter into a greased 13- x 9- x 2-inch baking dish.

Bake at 350° for 30 minutes or until a wooden pick inserted in center comes out clean. Cool in dish on a wire rack.

Combine pineapple, whipped topping, and pudding mix in a medium mixing bowl; beat at low speed until mixture is blended. Spread pineapple mixture evenly over cake. Cover and store cake in refrigerator. Yield: 15 servings.   Hope Hase

The Great Delights Cookbook
Genoa Serbart United Methodist Churches
Genoa, Colorado

German Apple Cake

4 large eggs
2 cups sugar
3 cups all-purpose flour
1 tablespoon baking powder
1 teaspoon salt
1 cup vegetable oil
½ cup orange juice

2½ teaspoons vanilla extract
4 cups peeled, thinly sliced
  Gala apples
3 tablespoons sugar
2 teaspoons ground cinnamon
Powdered sugar (optional)

Beat eggs and 2 cups sugar in a large mixing bowl at medium speed of an electric mixer until blended. Combine flour, baking powder, and salt. Combine oil and orange juice. Add flour mixture to egg mixture alternately with orange juice mixture, beginning and ending with flour mixture. Mix at low speed after each addition until blended. Stir in vanilla.

Pour half of batter into a greased and floured 10-inch tube pan. Carefully arrange half of apples over batter. Combine 3 tablespoons sugar and cinnamon; sprinkle half of mixture over apples. Repeat layers with remaining batter, apples, and cinnamon-sugar mixture.

Bake at 350° for 1 hour and 15 minutes or until a wooden pick inserted in center of cake comes out clean. Cool cake in pan on a wire rack 15 minutes; remove cake from pan, and let cool completely on wire rack. Sprinkle top of cake with powdered sugar, if desired. Yield: one 10-inch cake.   Hulda Oelkers

Our Favorite Recipes
Lutheran Church of the Good Shepherd
Billings, Montana

Cappuccino Cake with Mocha Sauce

Coffee lovers will indulge in every bite of this espresso-flavored chocolate treat.

½ cup (3 ounces) semisweet
  chocolate morsels
½ cup chopped pecans
1 (18.25-ounce) package yellow
  cake mix (we tested with
  Duncan Hines)
¼ cup instant espresso granules

2 teaspoons ground cinnamon
3 large eggs
1¼ cups water
⅓ cup vegetable oil
Powdered sugar
Mocha Sauce

Sprinkle chocolate morsels and pecans in bottom of a greased and floured 12-cup Bundt pan; set aside.

Combine cake mix, espresso granules, and cinnamon in a large mixing bowl. Add eggs, water, and oil. Beat at medium speed of an electric mixer 2 minutes. Pour batter into prepared pan.

Bake at 325° for 45 minutes or until a wooden pick inserted in center comes out clean. Cool in pan on a wire rack 15 minutes; remove cake from pan, and cool completely on wire rack. Sprinkle with powdered sugar, and serve with Mocha Sauce. Yield: one 10-inch cake.

Mocha Sauce

⅔ cup (4 ounces) semisweet
  chocolate morsels
1 teaspoon instant espresso
  granules

½ cup heavy whipping cream
2 tablespoons light corn syrup
2 tablespoons Kahlúa or other
  coffee-flavored liqueur

Place chocolate morsels and espresso granules in a medium bowl; set aside. Combine whipping cream and corn syrup in a small saucepan; bring to a simmer over low heat, stirring constantly. Pour whipping cream mixture over chocolate morsels and espresso granules. Let stand 30 seconds, and stir until mixture is smooth. Stir in Kahlúa. Yield: about ¾ cup.

Cyndy Kuhlman

The Cookbook Tour
Good Shepherd Lutheran Church
Plainview, Minnesota

Colonial Carrot Pecan Cake

2 cups all-purpose flour
2 teaspoons baking powder
1 teaspoon baking soda
1 teaspoon salt
2 teaspoons ground cinnamon
2 cups sugar

1¼ cups vegetable oil
4 large eggs
3 cups grated carrot (about 6)
1 cup finely chopped pecans
Orange Glaze

Combine first 5 ingredients; set aside.

Combine sugar and vegetable oil in a large mixing bowl; beat at medium speed of an electric mixer until blended. Add dry ingredients to oil mixture alternately with eggs, one at a time, mixing well at low speed after each addition. Add carrot and pecans to oil mixture; beat well. Pour batter into a lightly greased 10-inch tube pan.

Bake at 325° for 1 hour and 10 minutes or until a wooden pick inserted in center comes out clean. Cool in pan on a wire rack 15 minutes; remove cake from pan, and cool completely on wire rack. Spoon Orange Glaze over top of cake, allowing it to drizzle down sides. Yield: one 10-inch cake.

Orange Glaze

1 cup sugar
2 tablespoons cornstarch
1 cup orange juice
1 teaspoon lemon juice

2 tablespoons butter or
  margarine
2 teaspoons grated orange rind
½ teaspoon salt

Combine sugar and cornstarch in a medium saucepan. Gradually add juices, stirring until blended. Add butter, orange rind, and salt.

Cook over medium heat, stirring constantly, until mixture thickens and comes to a boil. Let cool before spooning over cake. Yield: 1 cup.

Moments, Memories & Manna
Restoration Village
Rogers, Arkansas

Triple Chocolate Cake

Chocolate cake mix and pudding mix add to the convenient nature of this rich, moist Bundt cake. The final chocolate in the trio? A full 2 cups of morsels that melt throughout the cake as it bakes.

1 (18.25-ounce) package chocolate cake mix (we tested with Duncan Hines)
1 (3.9-ounce) package chocolate instant pudding mix
2 cups (12 ounces) semisweet chocolate morsels
1 (8-ounce) carton sour cream
4 large eggs
½ cup chopped pecans
½ cup water
½ cup vegetable oil
Powdered sugar

Combine first 8 ingredients in a large bowl; stir with a wire whisk until ingredients are blended. Pour batter into a well-greased 12-cup Bundt pan.

Bake at 350° for 1 hour or until cake begins to pull away from sides of pan. Cool in pan on a wire rack 15 minutes; remove cake from pan, and cool completely on wire rack. Sift a small amount of powdered sugar over top of cake. Yield: one 10-inch cake.   Teresa M. White

Tasty Temptations
Our Lady of the Mountains Church
Sierra Vista, Arizona

Lemon-Amaretto Bundt Cake

1½ cups sliced almonds,
   toasted and divided
1 cup unsalted butter, softened
2 cups sugar
1 tablespoon grated lemon rind
5 large eggs
2 cups all-purpose flour

¼ cup fresh lemon juice,
   divided
1 teaspoon vanilla extract
½ teaspoon lemon extract
¼ cup plus 2 tablespoons sugar
¼ cup amaretto

Sprinkle ½ cup almonds evenly in bottom of a greased and floured 12-cup Bundt pan; set aside.

Beat butter at medium speed of an electric mixer 2 minutes or until creamy. Gradually add 2 cups sugar and lemon rind, beating 5 to 7 minutes. Add eggs, one at a time, beating just until yellow disappears.

Add flour; mix at low speed just until blended. Stir in remaining 1 cup almonds, 1 tablespoon lemon juice, and flavorings. Spoon batter into prepared pan.

Bake at 350° for 1 hour and 5 minutes or until a wooden pick inserted in center comes out clean. Transfer cake in pan to a wire rack.

Immediately combine remaining 3 tablespoons lemon juice, ¼ cup plus 2 tablespoons sugar, and amaretto in a small saucepan. Cook over medium heat, stirring until sugar melts. Prick cake at 1-inch intervals with a long wooden skewer or a cake tester. Brush cake with half of amaretto syrup. Cool in pan 15 minutes. Remove cake from pan; place on wire rack. Brush cake with remaining half of syrup. Cool completely on wire rack. Yield: one 10-inch cake.   Ann Martens

Scent from P.E.O. Sisterhood
Philanthropic Educational Organization, Chapter AG
Newcastle, Wyoming

Marmalade Cake

¾ cup butter, softened
1 cup sugar
3 large eggs
1 cup orange marmalade
1 tablespoon grated orange rind
1 tablespoon vanilla extract
3 cups all-purpose flour

1½ teaspoons baking soda
1 teaspoon salt
½ cup fresh orange juice
½ cup evaporated milk
1 cup chopped pecans
⅓ cup fresh orange juice
⅓ cup sugar

Beat butter at medium speed of an electric mixer until creamy; gradually add 1 cup sugar, beating well. Add eggs, one at a time, beating after each addition. Stir in marmalade, orange rind, and vanilla.

Combine flour, baking soda, and salt. Combine ½ cup orange juice and evaporated milk. Add flour mixture to butter mixture alternately with orange juice mixture, beginning and ending with flour mixture. Mix at low speed after each addition until blended. Stir in pecans. Pour batter into a buttered 12-cup Bundt pan.

Bake at 350° for 45 minutes or until a wooden pick inserted in center comes out clean. Cool in pan on a wire rack 15 minutes; remove cake from pan, and place on wire rack.

Immediately combine ⅓ cup orange juice and ⅓ cup sugar in a small saucepan; cook over medium-low heat until sugar dissolves, stirring often. Prick cake at 1-inch intervals with a long wooden skewer or cake tester. Brush hot juice mixture over top of warm cake; cool completely on wire rack. Yield: one 10-inch cake.

The Cook's Canvas
St. John's Museum of Art
Wilmington, North Carolina

Banana Pound Cake

Banana bread lovers will crave this dense rich pound cake of the same persuasion. It's equally at home for breakfast or dessert.

1½ cups shortening
2 cups sugar
4 large eggs
2 cups mashed ripe banana
¼ cup plus 2 tablespoons
  buttermilk

1 teaspoon vanilla extract
3 cups all-purpose flour
1¼ teaspoons baking soda
¼ teaspoon salt
½ cup chopped pecans

Beat shortening at medium speed of an electric mixer 2 minutes or until creamy. Gradually add sugar, beating 5 to 7 minutes. Add eggs, one at a time, beating just until yellow disappears.

Combine banana, buttermilk, and vanilla. Combine flour, soda, and salt; add to shortening mixture alternately with banana mixture, beginning and ending with flour mixture. Mix at low speed after each addition just until blended. Stir in pecans. Spoon batter into a greased and floured 10-inch tube pan.

Bake at 325° for 1 hour and 30 minutes or until a wooden pick inserted in center comes out clean. Cool in pan on a wire rack 15 minutes; remove cake from pan, and cool completely on wire rack. Yield: one 10-inch cake.

Evelyn Criswell

Bread from the Brook
The Church at Brook Hills
Birmingham, Alabama

Chocolate-Coffee Liqueur Pound Cake

The fudge-like frosting makes more than enough to top this cake. Pour the desired amount carefully over the cake, and enjoy the rest over ice cream or cupcakes.

1 (18.25-ounce) package
  German chocolate cake mix
  with pudding (we tested with
  Betty Crocker)
1½ cups sugar, divided
3 large eggs
¾ cup water
¾ cup strong brewed coffee
½ cup Kahlúa or other coffee-
  flavored liqueur

⅓ cup vegetable oil
¼ cup bourbon
2 teaspoons cocoa
⅛ teaspoon vanilla extract
½ cup butter
⅓ cup evaporated milk
1½ cups (9 ounces) semisweet
  chocolate morsels

Combine cake mix, ½ cup sugar, and next 8 ingredients in a large mixing bowl. Beat at medium speed of an electric mixer 4 minutes. Pour batter into a greased 12-cup Bundt pan.

Bake at 350° for 50 minutes or until a wooden pick inserted in center comes out clean. Cool in pan on a wire rack 15 minutes; remove cake from pan, and cool completely on wire rack.

Butter sides of a heavy saucepan; add remaining 1 cup sugar, butter, and milk. Bring to a boil, stirring gently and constantly, until butter melts and sugar dissolves. Reduce heat to low; add chocolate morsels, and cook, stirring constantly, until chocolate melts. Pour over cake immediately. Yield: one 10-inch cake.

Have You Heard . . . A Tasteful Medley of Memphis
Subsidium, Inc.
Memphis, Tennessee

Sweet Potato Pound Cake

1 cup unsalted butter, softened
1 cup sugar
¼ cup firmly packed brown sugar
2½ cups mashed, cooked sweet potato (about 2½ large) or 1½ (14½-ounce) cans sweet potatoes, mashed
4 large eggs
3 cups all-purpose flour
2 teaspoons baking powder
1 teaspoon baking soda
1 teaspoon salt
1½ teaspoons ground cinnamon
¼ teaspoon ground nutmeg
¼ teaspoon ground mace
1 teaspoon vanilla extract
Whipped cream (optional)

Beat butter at medium speed of an electric mixer 2 minutes or until creamy. Gradually add sugars, beating at medium speed 5 to 7 minutes. Add sweet potato; beat until blended. Add eggs, one at a time, beating just until yellow disappears.

Combine flour and next 6 ingredients; add to butter mixture. Mix at low speed just until blended; stir in vanilla. Pour batter into two greased and floured 8½- x 4½- x 3-inch loafpans.

Bake at 350° for 1 hour and 10 minutes or until a wooden pick inserted in center comes out clean. Cool in pans on wire racks 10 minutes. Remove cakes from pans; cool completely on wire racks. Serve with whipped cream, if desired. Yield: 2 loaves.   Evelyn Brown

Star-Spangled Recipes
American Legion Auxiliary, Department of West Virginia
Belmont, Ohio

Golden Fruitcake

6 large eggs, separated
½ teaspoon cream of tartar
1½ cups butter, softened
2 cups sugar
1 cup milk
1 teaspoon vanilla extract
1 teaspoon brandy extract
3½ cups all-purpose flour
½ teaspoon salt
2 cups golden raisins
1 (6-ounce) package dried apricots, chopped
1 cup coarsely chopped walnuts
½ cup chopped candied orange peel

Beat egg whites and cream of tartar at high speed of an electric mixer until stiff peaks form; set aside.

Beat butter at medium speed 2 minutes or until creamy. Gradually add sugar, beating 5 to 7 minutes. Add egg yolks, one at a time, beating just until yellow disappears.

Combine milk and flavorings. Combine flour and salt; add flour mixture to butter mixture alternately with milk mixture, beginning and ending with flour mixture. Mix at low speed after each addition just until blended. Fold in raisins and remaining 3 ingredients. Fold in egg whites. Spoon batter into a greased and floured 10-inch tube pan with a removable bottom.

Bake at 275° for 2 hours and 30 minutes or until a wooden pick inserted in center comes out clean. Cool in pan on a wire rack 15 minutes; remove cake from pan, and cool completely on wire rack. Yield: one 10-inch cake.

Lillian Bancale

Meet Me in the Kitchen
Northside Church of Christ
Waco, Texas

Chocolate Apricot Walnut Cake

Serve this soft, gooey cake with unsweetened whipped cream and a demitasse of espresso for a perfect ending to a special evening.

3 tablespoons cocoa	2 cups sugar
1 cup walnuts, finely chopped	6 large eggs, separated
1 cup bourbon	1 cup all-purpose flour
2 cups (12 ounces) semisweet chocolate morsels	¼ teaspoon cream of tartar
1 cup butter or margarine, softened	1 (6-ounce) package dried apricots, coarsely chopped
	Sifted powdered sugar

Grease a 10-inch springform pan; sprinkle cocoa in pan, and shake to coat. Set aside.

Combine walnuts and bourbon; let stand 30 minutes. Drain walnuts, reserving bourbon; set walnuts aside.

Combine bourbon and chocolate morsels in top of a double boiler; bring water to a boil. Reduce heat to low; cook until chocolate melts, stirring often. Remove chocolate mixture from heat; set aside, and let cool to room temperature.

Beat butter at medium speed of an electric mixer until creamy; gradually add 2 cups sugar, beating well. Add egg yolks, one at a time, beating after each addition. Add flour; mix well, and set aside.

Beat egg whites and cream of tartar at high speed until stiff peaks form. Gently fold one-fourth of beaten egg whites into chocolate mixture; fold chocolate mixture into remaining beaten egg whites.

Gently fold butter mixture into chocolate mixture. Gently stir in reserved walnuts and apricots. Pour batter into prepared pan.

Bake at 325° for 1 hour and 15 minutes. Cool in pan on a wire rack.

Carefully remove sides of pan, and place cake on a serving plate. Place a doily over cake; sift a small amount of powdered sugar over doily. Carefully lift the doily off to reveal a decorative design. Yield: one 10-inch cake.

Lavinia Seide

Savoring Cape Cod
Massachusetts Audubon Society's Wellfleet Bay Wildlife Sanctuary
South Wellfleet, Massachusetts

Flourless Chocolate Cake

This decadent chocolate cake is similar to a soufflé, so expect it to fall slightly and to crack on top shortly after removing it from the oven.

2 (8-ounce) packages semisweet baking chocolate squares, chopped (we tested with Baker's)
1 cup unsalted butter
2 tablespoons Frangelico or other hazelnut-flavored liqueur
8 large eggs, separated
1½ cups sugar
Chocolate Sauce
Garnish: fresh raspberries

Combine chocolate and butter in a heavy saucepan. Cook over low heat until chocolate melts, stirring occasionally. Remove from heat, and stir in liqueur; let cool slightly.

Beat egg yolks and sugar in a large mixing bowl at medium speed of an electric mixer until thick and pale. Beat egg whites in a large mixing bowl at high speed just until stiff peaks form.

Fold one-third of chocolate mixture into egg yolk mixture. Gently fold in one-third of egg whites. Fold in remaining chocolate mixture and egg whites. Pour batter into a greased and floured 10-inch springform pan.

Bake at 350° for 30 minutes or until edges are set (center will not be set). Cool to room temperature in pan on a wire rack; cover and chill 8 hours. Remove sides of springform pan just before serving. Serve with warm Chocolate Sauce. Garnish, if desired. Yield: one 10-inch cake.

Chocolate Sauce

1 (6-ounce) package bittersweet baking chocolate squares, chopped (we tested with Baker's)
¾ cup heavy whipping cream

Place chocolate in a small bowl. Pour cream into a small saucepan; place over low heat. Cook just until thoroughly heated; pour over chocolate. Let stand 5 minutes; stir until smooth. Yield: 1⅓ cups.

Sterling Service
The Dothan Service League
Dothan, Alabama

Pumpkin Cupcakes

Here's a perfect treat for fall! For the freshest taste, use one small cooking pumpkin (about 2½ to 3 pounds), if available. We also suggest using fresh orange juice in the icing.

½ cup butter or margarine, softened
1⅓ cups sugar
2 large eggs
1 cup mashed, cooked pumpkin (1 small)
2¼ cups all-purpose flour
1 tablespoon baking powder

½ teaspoon baking soda
½ teaspoon salt
¾ teaspoon ground ginger
½ teaspoon ground nutmeg
½ teaspoon ground cinnamon
¾ cup milk
¾ cup chopped walnuts

Beat butter at medium speed of an electric mixer until creamy. Gradually add sugar, beating well. Add eggs, and beat until frothy. Add pumpkin; beat well.

Combine flour and next 6 ingredients; add to sugar mixture alternately with milk, beginning and ending with flour mixture. Stir in walnuts. Spoon batter by rounded tablespoonfuls into paper-lined muffin pans.

Bake at 375° for 25 minutes. Remove from pans immediately, and cool completely on wire racks. Frost lightly with Orange Icing. Yield: 22 cupcakes.

Orange Icing

1 tablespoon butter or margarine, softened
2 tablespoons fresh orange juice

1 tablespoon grated orange rind
1 to 1½ cups sifted powdered sugar

Combine first 3 ingredients, beating with a wire whisk until blended. Gradually whisk in powdered sugar until spreading consistency. Yield: ½ cup.

Joyce Marshall

A Cookery & Memories from Old Bourne
The Bourne Society for Historic Preservation
Bourne, Massachusetts

Raspberry-Lemon Cheesecake

2 cups graham cracker crumbs
¼ cup sugar
¼ cup unsalted butter, melted
1 egg white, lightly beaten
2 cups fresh raspberries
½ cup sugar
1 teaspoon lemon juice

3 (8-ounce) packages cream
   cheese, softened
1 cup sugar
1 tablespoon grated lemon rind
¼ cup lemon juice
1 cup heavy whipping cream
4 large eggs

Combine first 4 ingredients in a medium bowl. Stir until blended. Press crumb mixture in bottom and 1 inch up sides of a 9-inch spring-form pan. Place on a baking sheet, and bake at 350° for 10 to 12 minutes or until lightly browned. Remove pan from oven, and place on a wire rack. Reduce oven temperature to 300°.

Combine raspberries, ½ cup sugar, and 1 teaspoon lemon juice in a medium saucepan; bring to a boil, stirring until sugar dissolves. Pour mixture through a wire-mesh strainer lined with cheesecloth into a bowl, discarding seeds. Cool.

Combine cream cheese, 1 cup sugar, lemon rind, and ¼ cup lemon juice in a large mixing bowl; beat at medium speed of an electric mixer until smooth. Gradually add cream, beating at low speed. Add eggs, one at a time, beating after each addition (do not overbeat after eggs are added). Pour into prepared crust. Gently spoon ¼ cup reserved raspberry mixture over filling; swirl with a wooden pick to form a lacy pattern.

Place a shallow pan of water on bottom rack of oven. Place cheesecake on rack directly above pan of water.

Bake at 300° for 2 hours or until cheesecake is almost set (center will be soft but will firm up when chilled). Cool completely in pan on a wire rack. Cover and chill 8 hours. Remove sides of springform pan just before serving. Yield: 12 servings.

Bully's Best Bites
The Junior Auxiliary of Starkville, Mississippi

The Best Cheesecake

This New York-style cheesecake rated high in our test kitchens. We especially liked the sweet graham cracker crust.

2½ cups graham cracker crumbs
½ cup sugar
½ cup butter or margarine, melted
5 (8-ounce) packages cream cheese, softened
1¾ cups sugar

3 tablespoons all-purpose flour
1 teaspoon lemon juice
¼ teaspoon vanilla extract
5 large eggs
2 egg yolks
¼ cup whipping cream
1½ cups sour cream

Combine cracker crumbs and ½ cup sugar in a medium bowl; add melted butter, stirring well. Press crumb mixture in bottom and 2½ inches up sides of a 10-inch springform pan. Chill thoroughly.

Beat cream cheese at medium speed of an electric mixer until creamy; gradually add 1¾ cups sugar, beating well. Add flour, lemon juice, and vanilla; beat well. Add eggs and egg yolks, one at a time, beating after each addition. Stir in whipping cream. Pour batter into prepared pan.

Bake at 500° for 10 minutes. Reduce oven temperature to 250°, and bake 1 hour and 10 minutes. (Cheesecake will brown on top.)

Carefully remove from oven, and place on a wire rack. Immediately spread sour cream over top of cheesecake. Cool completely in pan on wire rack. Cover and chill at least 8 hours. Remove sides of pan just before serving. Yield: 16 servings.

Landmark Entertaining
The Junior League of Abilene, Texas

Cookies & Candies

Almond-Toffee Triangles, page 119

Apricot Jewel Cookies

1¼ cups all-purpose flour
1½ teaspoons baking powder
¼ teaspoon salt
¼ cup sugar
½ cup butter or margarine, softened

1 (3-ounce) package cream cheese, softened
½ cup flaked coconut
½ cup chopped pecans
½ cup apricot preserves
Frosting

Combine first 4 ingredients in a large bowl. Cut in butter and cream cheese with a pastry blender until mixture is crumbly. Add coconut, pecans, and preserves; stir well.

Drop dough by heaping teaspoonfuls onto greased cookie sheets. Bake at 350° for 8 to 10 minutes or until lightly browned. Remove to wire racks to cool slightly. Spread with frosting while cookies are still warm. Yield: 4 dozen.

Frosting

1 cup sifted powdered sugar
¼ cup apricot preserves

1 teaspoon butter or margarine, melted

Combine all ingredients; stir well. Yield: 1 cup.   Gloria Arndt

Cook Bookery
The University of Illinois College of Medicine at Peoria
Peoria, Illinois

Chocolate-Chocolate Chip Cookies

These double chocolate cookies are similar in texture to a brownie. For jumbo cookies, drop dough by ¼-cup measures and bake slightly longer.

½ cup butter
4 (1-ounce) squares
   unsweetened chocolate,
   chopped
3 cups (18 ounces) semisweet
   chocolate morsels, divided
1½ cups all-purpose flour

½ teaspoon baking powder
½ teaspoon salt
4 large eggs
1½ cups sugar
2 teaspoons vanilla extract
2 cups chopped pecans,
   toasted

Combine butter, unsweetened chocolate, and 1½ cups chocolate morsels in a large heavy saucepan. Cook over low heat, stirring constantly, until butter and chocolate melt; cool.

Combine flour, baking powder, and salt in a small bowl; set aside.

Beat eggs, sugar, and vanilla in a medium mixing bowl at medium speed of an electric mixer. Gradually add flour mixture to egg mixture, beating well. Add chocolate mixture; beat well. Stir in remaining 1½ cups chocolate morsels and pecans.

Drop dough by 2 tablespoonfuls 1 inch apart onto parchment paper- or wax paper-lined cookie sheets. Bake at 350° for 10 minutes. Cool slightly on cookie sheets; remove to wire racks to cool completely. Yield: about 2½ dozen.

Janeyce Michel-Cupito

The Kansas City Barbeque Society Cookbook
Kansas City Barbeque Society
Kansas City, Missouri

Marvelous Macaroons

2⅔ cups shredded coconut
⅔ cup sugar
¼ cup all-purpose flour
¼ teaspoon salt

4 egg whites
1 teaspoon almond extract
1 cup slivered almonds

Combine first 4 ingredients in a medium bowl; stir well. Add egg whites and almond extract; stir well. Stir in almonds.

Drop dough by teaspoonfuls onto greased cookie sheets. Bake at 325° for 22 minutes or until golden. Remove immediately to wire racks to cool completely. Yield: 2 dozen.   Rosetta Cowell

Let's Get Cooking
Monvale Health Resources Auxiliary
Monongahela, Pennsylvania

Oatmeal Scotch Chippers

1¼ cups butter-flavored
  shortening
1¼ cups extra-crunchy peanut
  butter
1½ cups firmly packed brown
  sugar
1 cup sugar
3 large eggs

4½ cups regular oats,
  uncooked
2 teaspoons baking soda
1 cup (6 ounces) semisweet
  chocolate morsels
1 cup butterscotch morsels
1 cup chopped pecans

Beat shortening and peanut butter at medium speed of an electric mixer until creamy; gradually add sugars, beating well. Add eggs, one at a time, beating well after each addition.

Combine oats and baking soda; add to shortening mixture, beating well. Stir in chocolate morsels, butterscotch morsels, and pecans.

Drop dough by rounded teaspoonfuls onto ungreased cookie sheets. Bake at 350° for 9 to 11 minutes or until lightly browned. Cool 2 minutes on cookie sheets; remove to wire racks to cool completely. Yield: 6 dozen.   Melanie Knight

Best and Blessed
Sweet Spirit Singers
Liberty, Mississippi

Chocolate Mint Cookies

Mint and chocolate make a winning combination in these cookies that won a blue ribbon at a county fair.

2 cups (12 ounces) semisweet chocolate morsels
¾ cup butter or margarine
1½ cups firmly packed brown sugar
2 tablespoons water
2 large eggs

2½ cups all-purpose flour
1¼ teaspoons baking soda
½ teaspoon salt
2 (4.67-ounce) packages chocolate-covered mint wafer candies, cut into halves (we tested with Andes)

Combine chocolate morsels and butter in a medium saucepan; cook over medium-low heat until chocolate and butter melt, stirring occasionally. Combine chocolate mixture, brown sugar, and water in a large bowl; beat at low speed of an electric mixer until blended. Cool slightly. Add eggs, beating well.

Combine flour, baking soda, and salt; gradually add to chocolate mixture, beating well at low speed. Cover and chill 1 hour.

Shape dough into 1-inch balls. Place 2 inches apart on greased cookie sheets. Bake at 350° for 10 minutes. Place half of a mint on top of each warm cookie. Remove cookies to wire racks, and cool 1 minute. Gently spread melted mint over top of each cookie. Cool completely. Yield: 8 dozen.

Jennifer Meyer

Iowa: A Taste of Home
Iowa 4-H Foundation
Ames, Iowa

Honey-Nut-Filled Cookies

This tender bite-size cookie has a ground pecan filling similar to baklava.

1 cup butter or margarine, softened	2 cups all-purpose flour
	Pinch of salt
3 (3-ounce) packages cream cheese, softened	Pecan Filling
	Powdered sugar

Beat butter and cream cheese at medium speed of an electric mixer until creamy. Combine flour and salt; add to butter mixture, beating well. Shape dough into 1-inch balls; place 1 inch apart on ungreased cookie sheets.

Flatten balls slightly. Place about 1 teaspoon Pecan Filling in center of each flattened ball. Bring edges of dough up to center, and pinch together to seal. Bake at 350° for 20 minutes or until lightly browned. (Cookies will open during baking to expose filling.) Cool slightly on cookie sheets; remove to wire racks to cool completely. Sprinkle with powdered sugar. Yield: 4 dozen.

Pecan Filling

⅓ pound pecan pieces, ground (about 1½ cups pieces)	2 teaspoons butter or margarine, melted
⅓ cup sugar	½ teaspoon ground cinnamon
⅓ cup honey	

Combine all ingredients in a small bowl; stir well. Yield: 1¼ cups.

Ambrosia
The Junior Auxiliary of Vicksburg, Mississippi

Lemon Whippers

1 (18.25-ounce) package lemon cake mix (we tested with Betty Crocker)	1 large egg, lightly beaten
	Powdered sugar
2 cups frozen whipped topping, thawed	

Combine first 3 ingredients in a large bowl, stirring well.

Shape dough into balls, using 1 teaspoon of dough for each; roll in powdered sugar. Place on greased cookie sheets.

Bake at 350° for 8 to 10 minutes or until edges are golden. Cool 1 minute on cookie sheets; remove to wire racks to cool completely. Yield: 5 dozen.

Jean M. Linville

Quad City Cookin'
Queen of Heaven Circle of OLV Ladies Council
Davenport, Iowa

New Year's Seed Cookies

Anise-flavored caraway seeds and only a hint of sweetness flavor these tender cookies more for adults than for children. They're a grand afternoon snack with a cup of tea. Legend has it that sprinkling them with sesame seeds brings good luck for the New Year.

1½ **cups all-purpose flour**	½ **cup firmly packed brown**
1½ **teaspoons baking powder**	**sugar**
½ **teaspoon salt**	½ **cup heavy whipping cream**
½ **teaspoon ground nutmeg**	2 **teaspoons caraway seeds**
1 **large egg**	**Sesame seeds (optional)**

Combine first 4 ingredients in a medium bowl.

Beat egg in a large mixing bowl at medium speed of an electric mixer. Gradually add sugar and cream, beating well. Stir in flour mixture and caraway seeds. Cover and chill overnight.

Divide dough in half. Work with 1 portion of dough at a time, storing remaining dough in refrigerator. Roll each portion of dough to ⅛-inch thickness on a heavily floured surface. Cut with a 3-inch cookie cutter, and place cookies on lightly greased cookie sheets. Sprinkle with sesame seeds, if desired.

Bake at 350° for 10 minutes or until lightly browned. Cool slightly on cookie sheets; remove to wire racks to cool completely. Yield: 2 dozen.

A Cookery & Memories from Old Bourne
The Bourne Society for Historic Preservation
Bourne, Massachusetts

Sarah's Prizewinning Shortbread

1 cup butter, softened
½ cup sugar
⅛ teaspoon vanilla extract

2¼ cups all-purpose flour
⅛ teaspoon salt
Sugar

Beat butter at medium speed of an electric mixer until creamy; gradually add ½ cup sugar, beating well. Stir in vanilla.

Combine flour and salt; gradually add to butter mixture, beating at low speed after each addition.

Roll dough to ½-inch thickness on a lightly floured surface. Cut with a 3-inch heart-shaped cookie cutter, and place 2 inches apart on ungreased cookie sheets. Sprinkle with additional sugar.

Bake at 275° for 45 minutes or until edges begin to brown. Remove to wire racks to cool completely. Yield: 1 dozen.   Sarah Henderson

From ANNA's Kitchen
Adams-Normandie Neighborhood Association (ANNA)
Los Angeles, California

English Madeleines

Brew a fresh cup of tea to sip and to daintily dip these scalloped delights. Their texture is like a sponge cake.

2 tablespoons butter, melted
½ cup butter, softened
½ cup sugar
2 large eggs

1 tablespoon milk
¾ teaspoon vanilla extract
1 cup sifted cake flour
¾ teaspoon baking powder

Brush madeleine pans with 1 tablespoon melted butter. Place madeleine pans in freezer 5 minutes. Repeat procedure with remaining 1 tablespoon melted butter.

Beat softened butter, sugar, eggs, milk, and vanilla at high speed of an electric mixer until thick and pale. Combine flour and baking powder; fold into sugar mixture, 2 tablespoons at a time. Spoon batter into prepared madeleine pans, filling half full.

Bake at 375° for 12 to 14 minutes or until lightly browned. Let cool in pans 1 minute. Remove from pans, and cool completely on wire racks. Yield: 1½ dozen.   LaJunta Jewell

Note: If desired, brush ½ cup melted currant jelly over tops of cooled madeleines. Sprinkle 1 cup flaked coconut over jelly.

Party Pleasers
GFWC Philomathic Club
Duncan, Oklahoma

Almond-Toffee Triangles

2 cups all-purpose flour
⅔ cup butter or margarine, softened
½ cup firmly packed brown sugar

½ cup light corn syrup
1 large egg, lightly beaten
1 teaspoon vanilla extract
¼ teaspoon salt
Topping

Combine all ingredients except topping in a bowl; stir well. Spread dough in a greased 15- x 10- x 1-inch jellyroll pan. Bake at 350° for 18 minutes or until golden. Cool completely in pan on a wire rack.

Spread topping evenly over cooled layer. Bake at 350° for 18 minutes or until lightly browned. Cool completely in pan on wire rack. Cut into 24 (2½-inch) squares. Cut each square diagonally into triangles. Yield: 4 dozen.

Topping

⅓ cup firmly packed brown sugar
⅓ cup light corn syrup
¼ cup butter or margarine

¼ cup whipping cream
1 cup sliced almonds
1 teaspoon vanilla extract

Combine brown sugar and corn syrup in a small saucepan; cook over low heat until sugar dissolves, stirring often. Stir in butter and cream. Bring just to a boil. Remove from heat, and stir in almonds and vanilla. Yield: 1¼ cups.

Joan Meyer

Food for the Soul
Matt Talbot Kitchen
Lincoln, Nebraska

S'Mores Cookies

Enjoy this cookie version of the favorite campfire treat in the comforts of your own home. Our rendition has a chunky peanut butter crust that's layered with marshmallow cream, chocolate, and peanuts.

½ cup butter or margarine, softened
½ cup sugar
½ cup firmly packed brown sugar
½ cup chunky peanut butter
1 large egg
½ teaspoon vanilla extract

1½ cups all-purpose flour
2 teaspoons baking powder
½ teaspoon salt
1 (7-ounce) jar marshmallow cream
1 cup (6 ounces) semisweet chocolate morsels
¾ cup salted roasted peanuts

Beat butter at medium speed of an electric mixer until creamy; add sugars, beating well. Add peanut butter, egg, and vanilla; beat well.

Combine flour, baking powder, and salt; add to butter mixture, beating well.

Press dough into a greased 13- x 9- x 2-inch pan. Spread marshmallow cream over dough. Sprinkle chocolate morsels and peanuts over marshmallow cream. Bake at 375° for 16 to 18 minutes or until marshmallow cream is lightly browned. Cool completely in pan on a wire rack; cut into bars. Yield: 2 dozen.   Ione Lebo

United Church of Tekoa Cookbook
United Church of Tekoa
Tekoa, Washington

Brownies Kahlúa

½ cup butter or margarine
4 (1-ounce) squares
　unsweetened chocolate
4 large eggs
2 cups sugar
1 cup all-purpose flour
1 cup miniature marshmallows

1 cup chopped walnuts,
　divided
1 cup (6 ounces) semisweet
　chocolate morsels, divided
1 tablespoon Kahlúa
1 teaspoon vanilla extract

Combine butter and unsweetened chocolate in a heavy saucepan; cook over low heat until butter and chocolate melt, stirring often. Cool mixture.

Beat eggs at medium speed of an electric mixer until thick and pale. Gradually add sugar, beating until thickened. Stir in chocolate mixture. Add flour, marshmallows, ½ cup walnuts, ½ cup chocolate morsels, Kahlúa, and vanilla; mix well.

Spread batter in a greased 9-inch square pan. Sprinkle with remaining ½ cup walnuts and ½ cup chocolate morsels. Bake at 325° for 50 minutes. Cool completely in pan on a wire rack; cut into squares. Yield: 20 brownies.

Mary Lutesinger

St. Andrew's Foods for the Multitudes and Smaller Groups
St. Andrew's Episcopal Church
Cripple Creek, Colorado

Mint Chocolate Chip Brownies

Top these brownies with a scoop of vanilla ice cream for a satisfying dessert. For easier cleanup, line your pan with aluminum foil before pouring the batter.

1 cup sugar
½ cup all-purpose flour
½ teaspoon baking powder
¼ teaspoon salt
¼ cup plus 3 tablespoons cocoa
2 large eggs, lightly beaten

½ cup butter or margarine, melted
1 teaspoon vanilla extract
1 cup (6 ounces) mint chocolate morsels
1 cup chopped walnuts (optional)

Combine first 5 ingredients in a large bowl; set aside. Combine eggs, butter, and vanilla; stir into flour mixture. Stir in chocolate morsels and, if desired, walnuts.

Pour batter into a greased 8-inch square pan. Bake at 350° for 30 minutes. Cool completely in pan on a wire rack; cut into squares. Yield: 1 dozen.

Marilyn Roberts

Recipes from Our Home to Yours
Hospice of North Central Florida
Gainesville, Florida

Can't Fail Divinity

Marshmallow cream gives this candy a denser texture than regular divinity, and it's oh so tasty!

2 cups sugar
½ cup water
⅛ teaspoon salt
2 (7-ounce) jars marshmallow cream

1 teaspoon vanilla extract
½ cup chopped pecans

Combine first 3 ingredients in a large heavy saucepan; cook over low heat, stirring constantly, until sugar dissolves. Cover and cook over medium heat 2 to 3 minutes to wash down sugar crystals from sides of pan. Uncover and cook, without stirring, to hard ball stage or until candy thermometer registers 260°. Remove from heat.

Place marshmallow cream in a large mixing bowl. Pour hot sugar mixture in a heavy stream over marshmallow cream, beating at high speed of an electric mixer. Add vanilla, beating just until mixture holds its shape (3 to 4 minutes). Stir in pecans.

Working quickly, drop divinity by rounded teaspoonfuls onto wax paper; cool. Yield: 28 pieces (1¾ pounds).   Nancy Hendricks

Fire Gals' Hot Pans Cookbook
Garrison Emergency Services Auxiliary
Garrison, Iowa

Peanut Butter Cups

⅔ **cup creamy peanut butter**
½ **cup sifted powdered sugar**
2 **teaspoons vanilla extract**

1 **pound chocolate-flavored candy coating**
48 **(1½-inch) paper candy cups**

Combine first 3 ingredients in a small bowl; stir well.

Cover and chill 1 hour or until firm. Shape mixture by teaspoonfuls into balls, and flatten slightly.

Melt candy coating in a microwave-safe bowl according to package directions. Spoon ½ teaspoon melted candy coating into 48 paper-lined miniature (1¾-inch) muffin pans. Place 1 peanut butter ball in each cup; spoon remaining melted candy coating over peanut butter balls to cover completely. Cover and chill until firm. Store in an airtight container in refrigerator. Yield: 4 dozen.   Kyle Danielle Sexton

Iowa: A Taste of Home
Iowa 4-H Foundation
Ames, Iowa

Chocolate-Raspberry Truffles

These chocolate delights make a wonderful gift for any occasion.

1⅓ cups (8 ounces) semisweet
    chocolate morsels
2 tablespoons whipping cream
1 tablespoon butter
2 tablespoons seedless
    raspberry jam

6 ounces white chocolate or
    milk chocolate (we tested
    with Ghirardelli)
2 teaspoons shortening

Combine chocolate morsels, cream, and butter in a heavy saucepan. Cook over low heat, stirring constantly, until chocolate morsels melt; stir in jam. Remove from heat; cover and freeze mixture 30 minutes or until firm.

Shape mixture into ¾-inch balls. Place on wax paper-lined baking sheets; chill 5 minutes. If necessary, reroll to smooth balls. Freeze 8 hours.

Place white chocolate and shortening in top of a double boiler; bring water to a boil. Reduce heat to low; cook, stirring constantly, until chocolate and shortening melt.

Place each ball on a candy dipper or fork, and hold over double boiler. Quickly spoon melted chocolate mixture over each ball, allowing excess to drip back into double boiler. Return each ball to lined baking sheets; chill until firm. Store in an airtight container in refrigerator. Yield: 2½ dozen.

Secrets of Amelia
McArthur Family Branch YMCA
Fernandina Beach, Florida

Desserts

Coffee Charlotte, page 134

Balsamic Berries over Ice Cream

The crunchy nut topping that crowns this strawberry sundae resembles peanut brittle.

¼ cup pine nuts
1 pint fresh strawberries, sliced
¼ cup plus 2 tablespoons sugar, divided

2 tablespoons balsamic vinegar
⅛ teaspoon ground cloves
Vanilla ice cream

Toast pine nuts in a small skillet over medium heat until lightly browned. Set aside.

Combine strawberries, 2 tablespoons sugar, and balsamic vinegar in a small bowl, stirring gently.

Combine remaining ¼ cup sugar and cloves in a small heavy skillet. Cook over medium-low heat until sugar dissolves; add toasted pine nuts, and cook until sugar and nuts are golden. Spoon nut mixture onto wax paper, and let cool completely. Break nut mixture into small pieces.

To serve, spoon strawberries over ice cream, and sprinkle with nut mixture. Yield: 4 servings.

Special Selections of Ocala
Ocala Royal Dames for Cancer Research, Inc.
Ocala, Florida

Peach Perfect

Fresh peaches make a dramatic presentation in this flaming dessert sauce spooned over ice cream.

½ cup plus 2 tablespoons butter
½ cup firmly packed brown sugar
2 tablespoons flaked coconut
¼ teaspoon ground cinnamon

5 fresh peaches, sliced
2 teaspoons peach liqueur or 1 teaspoon vanilla extract
¼ cup rum
Vanilla ice cream

Melt butter in a large skillet over medium heat. Add brown sugar, coconut, and cinnamon to skillet. Cook, stirring constantly, until sugar dissolves. Stir in peach slices; cook 2 minutes. Add peach liqueur; cook, stirring constantly, 1 minute. Remove from heat, and add rum. Ignite mixture, using a long match. Let flames die down; serve warm sauce over ice cream. Yield: 4 servings.

Gracious Gator Cooks
The Junior League of Gainesville, Florida

Spiced Pears

1 (15¼-ounce) can pear halves in heavy syrup, undrained	2 whole cloves
⅓ cup fresh orange juice	½ cup red currant jelly
1 tablespoon lemon juice	3 drops of red food coloring
⅛ teaspoon ground ginger	⅔ cup plain yogurt
½ (3-inch) stick cinnamon	2 teaspoons sugar
	½ teaspoon vanilla extract

Drain pears, reserving juice; set pears aside. Combine reserved pear juice, orange juice, and next 4 ingredients in a small saucepan; bring to a boil. Reduce heat, and simmer 10 minutes; discard cinnamon stick and cloves.

Place jelly in a small bowl. Add 1 tablespoon heated juice mixture and food coloring, stirring well with a wire whisk. Set aside.

Place reserved pears in a small deep bowl. Pour remaining juice mixture over pears; cover and chill.

Combine yogurt, sugar, and vanilla.

Using a slotted spoon, place pear halves evenly in four dessert dishes; discard juice mixture. Top each with jelly mixture and yogurt mixture. Serve immediately. Yield: 4 servings.

Notable Feasts
Friends of the Cape Cod Symphony Orchestra
Yarmouth Port, Massachusetts

Strawberry Cream Crêpes

Extra crêpes freeze well to make a quick dessert with ice cream and chocolate syrup or strawberries and powdered sugar.

2 pints fresh strawberries,
   sliced
¼ cup sugar
1 (3-ounce) package cream
   cheese, softened

1 cup whipping cream
2 tablespoons sugar
24 Crêpes
⅓ cup brandy

Toss strawberries with ¼ cup sugar; set aside. Beat cream cheese at medium speed of an electric mixer until smooth. Gradually add cream and 2 tablespoons sugar, beating until thick and smooth. Fill each crêpe with 1 tablespoon whipped cream mixture; roll up. Chill.

Cook brandy in a small saucepan over medium heat until hot but not boiling. Pour brandy over berries, and ignite, using a long match; let flames die down. Spoon mixture over crêpes. Yield: 12 servings.

Crêpes

1½ cups all-purpose flour
⅓ cup sugar
⅛ teaspoon salt
5 large eggs
2 cups milk

½ teaspoon vanilla extract
½ teaspoon grated orange rind
¼ teaspoon grated lemon rind
2 tablespoons Cointreau
Melted butter

Combine flour, sugar, and salt in a large bowl. Beat eggs and milk in a medium bowl, using a wire whisk. Add to flour mixture; stirring until smooth. Add vanilla and next 3 ingredients; stir well. Cover and chill at least 30 minutes.

Brush bottom of a 6-inch crêpe pan or heavy skillet with melted butter; place over medium heat until hot. Pour 3 tablespoons batter into pan; quickly tilt pan in all directions so batter covers bottom of pan. Cook 1 minute or until crêpe can be shaken loose from pan. Turn crêpe; cook about 30 seconds. Place crêpe on a cloth towel or wire rack to cool. Repeat procedure with additional melted butter and batter. Stack crêpes between sheets of wax paper to prevent sticking. Yield: 25 crêpes.

Seaboard to Sideboard
The Junior League of Wilmington, North Carolina

Lemon Bavarian Cream

It's worth squeezing fresh lemons to make this tangy-sweet temptation. You'll need 4 or 5 lemons for this dessert.

1 tablespoon unflavored
   gelatin
¼ cup cold water
1 cup boiling water
1 cup sugar
¼ teaspoon grated lemon rind
¾ cup fresh lemon juice

1 cup whipping cream
6 stale macaroon cookies,
   crumbled (we tested with
   Archway)
10 maraschino cherries with
   stems

Sprinkle gelatin over cold water; stir and let stand 1 minute.

Add boiling water and sugar to gelatin mixture, stirring until sugar and gelatin dissolve. Add lemon rind and lemon juice; stir well. Chill until consistency of unbeaten egg white (about 1 hour).

Beat gelatin mixture at medium speed of an electric mixer until foamy; set aside.

Beat whipping cream at high speed until stiff peaks form. Fold whipped cream and crumbled macaroons into gelatin mixture. Spoon mixture into a lightly greased 5-cup mold. Cover and chill at least 4 hours or until firm.

To serve, unmold dessert onto a serving plate. Top with cherries. Yield: 10 servings.

Priscilla Flint

Expressions
National League of American Pen Women, Chester County
Coatesville, Pennsylvania

Crème Framboise

The chilling time for this easy raspberry dessert allows you time to prepare and serve dinner, and then present your guests with this fabulous finale.

1 (14-ounce) package frozen raspberries, thawed
1 envelope unflavored gelatin
¾ cup sugar
2 cups whipping cream
1 tablespoon vanilla extract
1 (16-ounce) carton sour cream
1 tablespoon brandy

Process raspberries in container of an electric blender until smooth. Pour pureed raspberries through a wire-mesh strainer into a bowl, discarding seeds. Set puree aside.

Combine gelatin, sugar, and whipping cream in a saucepan; let stand 5 minutes. Cook over low heat, stirring constantly, 2 minutes or until gelatin dissolves; let cool to room temperature. Add vanilla and sour cream; stir well with a wire whisk.

Stir brandy into raspberry puree. Place 1 teaspoon raspberry sauce in bottom of each of six clear stemmed wine goblets. Fill goblets with cream mixture; cover and chill at least 2 hours. Serve with remaining raspberry sauce. Yield: 6 servings.

The Cook's Canvas
St. John's Museum of Art
Wilmington, North Carolina

White Chocolate Mousse

2 cups whipping cream
¼ cup Grand Marnier or other
    orange-flavored liqueur
½ pound finely chopped
    premium white chocolate
    baking squares (we tested
    with Baker's)

¾ cup sugar
¼ cup plus 2 tablespoons water
⅛ teaspoon cream of tartar
4 egg whites
Raspberry Sauce

Combine whipping cream and Grand Marnier in a chilled bowl. Beat at high speed of an electric mixer until stiff peaks form; chill.

Place white chocolate in a double boiler; bring water to a boil. Reduce heat to low, and cook until chocolate melts; keep warm over hot water.

Combine sugar, ¼ cup plus 2 tablespoons water, and cream of tartar in a heavy saucepan; cook over medium heat, stirring constantly, until clear. Cook, without stirring, to soft ball stage (240°).

While syrup cooks, beat egg whites at high speed until soft peaks form; continue to beat, adding hot syrup in a heavy stream. Continue beating just until stiff peaks form.

Immediately fold melted white chocolate into egg white mixture; fold whipped cream mixture into egg white mixture. Pour into individual parfait glasses, and freeze 1 hour. Serve with Raspberry Sauce. Yield: 10 servings.

Raspberry Sauce

1 (14-ounce) package frozen
    raspberries

2 tablespoons water
2 teaspoons cornstarch

Place raspberries in a saucepan, and bring to a boil; cook 5 minutes or until berries are crushed, stirring often. Remove from heat. Pour raspberries through a wire mesh strainer; press with back of a spoon against sides of strainer to squeeze out juice, discarding solids. Return juice to pan; bring to a boil.

Whisk together water and cornstarch; stir into raspberry juice. Cook, stirring constantly, 1 minute or until thickened. Yield: ¾ cup.

Sterling Service
The Dothan Service League
Dothan, Alabama

Chocolate Croissant Pudding with Jack Daniel's Custard Sauce

After baking, this dessert should be crusty on the edges with a soft pudding in the middle. Look for large croissants in the bakery of your supermarket.

⅔ cup sugar
4 large eggs
2 egg yolks
¾ cup heavy whipping cream
1 (4-ounce) bar bittersweet
   chocolate, melted and cooled

6 large croissants, torn into
   bite-size pieces (about 7
   cups)
Jack Daniel's Custard Sauce

Combine first 3 ingredients in a large bowl; beat at medium speed of an electric mixer 3 minutes or until thick and pale. Set aside.

Beat whipping cream at high speed until soft peaks form. Gently fold melted chocolate into whipped cream. Fold whipped cream mixture into egg mixture. Add croissants, folding gently. Spoon mixture into a buttered 11- x 7- x 1½-inch baking dish. Place in a large shallow pan. Add hot water to pan to depth of 1 inch.

Bake at 350° for 45 minutes. Let stand 5 minutes before serving. Spoon croissant pudding into individual dessert dishes; top evenly with Jack Daniel's Custard Sauce. Yield: 6 servings.

Jack Daniel's Custard Sauce

2 cups milk
⅔ cup sugar

6 egg yolks
¼ cup Jack Daniel's bourbon

Place milk in a medium saucepan over medium heat, and bring to a simmer. Beat sugar and egg yolks at high speed of an electric mixer until thick and pale. Gradually add hot milk to egg yolk mixture, stirring with a wire whisk until blended; return to saucepan. Cook over low heat, stirring constantly, until slightly thickened. Remove from heat; pour through a wire-mesh strainer into a bowl. Stir in bourbon. Yield: 3 cups.

Mary Hayward

Newport Cooks & Collects
Preservation Society of Newport County
Newport, Rhode Island

Apple Pudding with Caramel Sauce

1 cup sugar
¼ cup shortening
1 large egg
2 cups peeled, diced Granny
   Smith apple
1 cup all-purpose flour
1 teaspoon baking soda

½ teaspoon ground cinnamon
¼ teaspoon salt
¼ teaspoon ground nutmeg
½ cup chopped walnuts or
   pecans
Caramel Sauce

Combine first 3 ingredients, stirring well with a wire whisk. Stir in apple; set aside.

Combine flour and next 5 ingredients. Add to apple mixture, stirring well. Spread in a greased 8-inch square pan. Bake at 350° for 35 to 40 minutes.

Spoon warm Caramel Sauce over warm pudding. Yield: 6 servings.

Caramel Sauce

1 cup firmly packed brown
   sugar
1 cup boiling water
½ cup sugar

2 tablespoons cornstarch
2 tablespoons butter or
   margarine
1 teaspoon vanilla extract

Combine first 4 ingredients in a heavy saucepan. Bring to a boil over medium heat, and cook, stirring constantly, until thickened. Remove from heat. Stir in butter and vanilla. Yield: 1½ cups.   Ellen Bails

Morrisonville's 125th Anniversary Cookbook
Morrisonville Historical Society & Museum
Morrisonville, Illinois

Coffee Charlotte

Prepare this dessert the night before to get a head start on dinner.

⅔ cup sugar
2 tablespoons instant coffee
  granules
¼ teaspoon salt
2 envelopes unflavored gelatin
3 cups milk

¼ cup cognac
24 ladyfingers, split
2 cups whipping cream,
  whipped
Garnish: chocolate curls

Combine first 4 ingredients in a large saucepan. Add milk, and cook over medium heat just until sugar and gelatin dissolve. Remove from heat; stir in cognac. Chill 1 hour or until mixture is consistency of unbeaten egg white.

Line bottom and sides of a 9-inch springform pan with ladyfingers, cut side in.

Fold whipped cream into gelatin mixture. Pour into prepared pan. Cover and chill 8 hours or until firm. Remove sides of pan just before serving. Garnish, if desired. Yield: 10 servings.

Carolina Sunshine, Then & Now
The Charity League of Charlotte, North Carolina

Creamy Mocha Frozen Dessert

2 teaspoons instant coffee
  granules
1 tablespoon hot water
1½ cups crushed cream-filled
  chocolate sandwich cookies
  (we tested with Oreos)
¾ cup finely chopped pecans,
  divided

½ cup butter, melted
2 (8-ounce) packages cream
  cheese, softened
1 (14-ounce) can sweetened
  condensed milk
½ cup chocolate syrup
1 (8-ounce) container frozen
  whipped topping, thawed

Dissolve coffee granules in hot water; set aside.

Combine cookie crumbs, ½ cup pecans, and melted butter; press in bottom of a 13- x 9- x 2-inch pan.

Beat cream cheese at medium speed of an electric mixer until light and fluffy. Add coffee mixture, condensed milk, and chocolate syrup, beating until blended. Fold in whipped topping.

Spoon mixture into prepared pan; sprinkle with remaining ¼ cup pecans. Cover and freeze until firm. Cut into squares to serve. Yield: 20 servings. Amy Smith

Somethin's Cookin' with Married Young Adults
Houston's First Baptist Church
Houston, Texas

Pumpkin Crunch

Substitute two teaspoons of pumpkin pie spice for the four spices listed, if desired.

3 large eggs
½ cup sugar
½ cup firmly packed dark
   brown sugar
1 (12-ounce) can evaporated
   milk
1½ teaspoons ground
   cinnamon
1 teaspoon ground ginger
½ teaspoon ground cloves
½ teaspoon grated whole
   nutmeg
½ teaspoon salt

1 teaspoon vanilla extract
1 tablespoon brandy (optional)
1 (29-ounce) can pumpkin
1 (18.25-ounce) package yellow
   cake mix without pudding
   (we tested with Duncan
   Hines)
2 cups walnut pieces
¾ cup butter or margarine,
   melted

Beat eggs at medium speed of an electric mixer; add sugars, and beat 5 more minutes. Add evaporated milk; beat well. Stir in cinnamon, next 5 ingredients, and, if desired, brandy. Gradually add pumpkin, and blend well. Pour batter into a lightly greased 13- x 9- x 2-inch baking dish. Sprinkle dry cake mix on top of pumpkin mixture; top evenly with walnut pieces. Drizzle melted butter over top.

Bake at 325° for 1½ hours or until a wooden pick inserted in center comes out clean. (Cover dessert with aluminum foil during last 15 minutes of baking to prevent excessive browning of walnuts, if necessary.) Yield: 15 servings. Helen Bowman

Renaissance of Recipes
Iao Intermediate School Renaissance Ke 'ala hou
Wailuku, Hawaii

Kokomo Trifle

Make preparation easy by buying a store-bought pound cake. You'll need about 2 pounds to equal 10 cups of cubed pound cake. You can also buy pre-cut tropical fruit in the produce department of your supermarket.

Orange Sauce
½ cup dark rum, divided
1 (12-ounce) jar guava jelly (we tested with Cross and Blackwell)
¾ cup pineapple juice
¾ cup cream of coconut
10 cups pound cake cubes

4 cups chopped mixed tropical fruit (such as guava, pineapple, mango, and papaya)
1½ cups sliced strawberries
Garnishes: sliced kiwifruit, starfruit, and strawberries; toasted coconut

Prepare Orange Sauce, and set aside.

Combine ¼ cup rum and jelly in a small saucepan; cook over low heat until jelly melts, stirring often. Set aside.

Combine remaining ¼ cup rum, pineapple juice, and cream of coconut in a medium bowl; stir well. Set aside.

Layer one-fourth each of pound cake cubes, jelly mixture, cream of coconut mixture, chopped mixed fruit, sliced strawberries, and Orange Sauce in a 3-quart trifle bowl or large glass serving bowl (bowl will be very full). Repeat layers 3 times, ending with Orange Sauce. Cover and chill 8 hours. Garnish, if desired. Yield: 14 servings.

Orange Sauce

¾ cup orange juice
½ cup sugar
¼ cup curaçao

8 egg yolks, lightly beaten
1 cup whipping cream

Combine first 4 ingredients in top of a double boiler; bring water to a boil. Reduce heat to medium; cook, stirring constantly, 10 minutes or until mixture thickens. Remove from heat; cool completely.

Beat whipping cream at high speed of an electric mixer until soft peaks form. Gently fold into orange juice mixture. Cover and chill thoroughly. Yield: 3½ cups.

Made in the Shade
The Junior League of Greater Fort Lauderdale, Florida

Raspberry Cheese Delight

2 cups flaked coconut
2 tablespoons sugar
1 tablespoon all-purpose flour
2 tablespoons butter or
  margarine, melted
¾ cup raspberry preserves
1 (8-ounce) package cream
  cheese, softened

¾ cup sifted powdered sugar,
  divided
½ cup chopped pecans
1 teaspoon milk
1 teaspoon vanilla extract
1 cup heavy whipping cream

Combine first 4 ingredients in a medium bowl; mix well. Press evenly into an 8-inch square pan. Bake at 350° for 10 minutes. Chill 10 minutes or until firm.

Spread raspberry preserves gently over crust. Chill 30 minutes or until set.

Combine cream cheese, ½ cup powdered sugar, pecans, milk, and vanilla in a large mixing bowl; beat at medium speed of an electric mixer until well blended. Spread evenly over raspberry layer.

Combine cream and remaining ¼ cup powdered sugar. Beat at medium speed until stiff peaks form. Spread sweetened whipping cream evenly over cream cheese layer. Freeze 1 hour or until firm. Cut into squares to serve. Yield: 9 servings.

Hearthside: A Country Community Cookbook
Christ Community Church
Weare, New Hampshire

Scrumptious Dessert

2 cups peeled and sliced fresh peaches
2 cups sliced fresh strawberries
2 cups fresh blueberries
2 cups fresh raspberries
Sauce

1 (10.5-ounce) angel food cake, cut into thin slices
1 cup whipping cream
2 tablespoons sifted powdered sugar

Combine first 4 ingredients in a large bowl; pour sauce over fruit, stirring to blend. Cover and chill.

Line bottom and sides of a 3-quart dish or trifle bowl with cake slices; cover with fruit mixture.

Beat whipping cream at medium speed of an electric mixer until foamy; gradually add powdered sugar, beating until soft peaks form. Dollop or pipe whipped cream over fruit mixture. Yield: 12 servings.

Sauce

½ cup sugar
½ cup water, divided
½ cup white grape juice

½ teaspoon ground cinnamon
1 teaspoon cornstarch

Combine sugar, ¼ cup water, juice, and cinnamon in a small saucepan; bring to a boil. Combine cornstarch and remaining ¼ cup water; add to juice mixture, and cook over medium-high heat, stirring constantly, 1 minute or until sauce is thickened. Cool slightly. Yield: 1 cup.   Carolyn Driggs

A Bite of the Best
Relief Society Church of Jesus Christ of Latter Day Saints
Provo, Utah

Dacquoise

Dazzle guests with this spectacular dessert of two meringue layers filled with luscious chocolate cream and topped with whipped cream. Serve it right away, and the meringue layers stay crisp and nicely contrast with the texture of the rich fillings. Cover and chill the dessert several hours, and the meringues soften a little and meld more with the fillings. Either way, the dessert will bring rave reviews.

¾ cup plus 2 tablespoons
  sugar, divided
¾ teaspoon cream of tartar
1 cup finely chopped pecans
2 tablespoons plus 1 teaspoon
  cornstarch
1 cup plus 2 tablespoons sifted
  powdered sugar

6 egg whites
2 cups heavy whipping cream,
  divided
¾ cup (4½ ounces) semisweet
  chocolate morsels
Garnish: chocolate curls or
  shaved chocolate

Line two baking sheets with parchment paper. Trace an 8-inch circle on each. Turn paper over, and place on baking sheets.

Combine ¼ cup plus 3 tablespoons sugar and cream of tartar in a small bowl; set aside.

Combine remaining ¼ cup plus 3 tablespoons sugar, pecans, cornstarch, and powdered sugar in a medium bowl; set aside.

Beat egg whites at medium speed of an electric mixer until foamy. Gradually add cream of tartar mixture, beating constantly until stiff peaks form. Fold in powdered sugar mixture. Spread over circles on parchment paper. Bake at 250° for 2 hours; let cool. Gently peel paper off meringues.

Pour ½ cup whipping cream into a saucepan; bring almost to a boil. Pour over morsels; stir until chocolate melts. Cool.

Beat ½ cup whipping cream at medium speed until stiff peaks form. Fold ¼ cup whipped cream into chocolate mixture; gently fold in remaining whipped cream. Spread chocolate mixture over 1 meringue; top with second meringue.

Beat remaining 1 cup whipping cream until stiff peaks form. Spread over top layer. Garnish, if desired. Cut into wedges to serve. Yield: 8 to 10 servings.

Becky Conroy

Southern Settings
Decatur General Foundation, Inc.
Decatur, Alabama

Raspberry Torte

1¼ cups all-purpose flour
1¼ cups sugar, divided
¼ teaspoon salt
1 cup butter or margarine,
   softened
3 tablespoons cornstarch

5 cups frozen unsweetened
   raspberries (about 20 ounces)
45 large marshmallows
1 cup milk
1 cup whipping cream,
   whipped

Combine flour, ¼ cup sugar, and salt in a large bowl; cut in butter with a pastry blender until mixture is crumbly. Press mixture into a 13- x 9- x 2-inch pan. Bake at 350° for 15 minutes or until lightly browned. Cool completely in pan on a wire rack.

Combine remaining 1 cup sugar and cornstarch in a large saucepan. Add raspberries. Cook over medium heat, stirring constantly, until mixture thickens and boils; cool slightly. Spoon raspberry mixture over baked layer; cover and chill.

Combine marshmallows and milk in a large saucepan. Cook over medium-low heat, stirring constantly, until marshmallows melt. Chill 30 minutes or until marshmallow mixture is cool. Fold in whipped cream. Spread over raspberry mixture. Cover and chill until ready to serve. Yield: 12 to 15 servings.

Great Lake Effects
The Junior League of Buffalo, New York

Lynne's Chilled Chocolate Tortoni

Chocoholics will enjoy the chunks of chocolate wafers in every bite of this frozen Italian dessert. Lynne freezes hers in pretty stemware; just make sure whatever you use is freezerproof.

⅔ cup light corn syrup
1 (8-ounce) package semisweet
   chocolate
2 cups heavy whipping cream,
   divided

24 chocolate wafer cookies,
   coarsely crumbled (we tested
   with Nabisco)
1 cup chopped walnuts

Combine corn syrup and chocolate in a heavy saucepan; cook over medium-low heat, stirring constantly, until chocolate melts. Stir in ½ cup cream. Cover and chill 15 minutes.

Beat remaining 1½ cups cream in a large bowl at medium speed of an electric mixer until soft peaks form. Gently fold into chocolate mixture. Stir in cookies and walnuts. Spoon dessert evenly into 6-ounce custard cups or paper-lined muffin pans. Freeze 2 hours or until firm. Let stand at room temperature 5 minutes before serving. Yield: 12 servings.   Lynne Mouw

St. Ansgar Heritage Cookbook
St. Ansgar Heritage Association
St. Ansgar, Iowa

Buster Bars

Reminiscent of a hot fudge sundae, this ice cream treat sports similar toppings but is frozen and cut into bars.

½ cup butter or margarine, melted

1 (16-ounce) package cream-filled chocolate sandwich cookies, crushed (we tested with Oreos)

½ gallon vanilla ice cream, softened

1 (12-ounce) jar hot fudge sauce

1 (12-ounce) jar salted peanuts

1 (8-ounce) container frozen whipped topping, thawed

Combine butter and crushed cookies, reserving 1 cup. Press mixture firmly into a 13- x 9- x 2-inch pan. Spread ice cream evenly over crust. Freeze 1 hour or until firm.

Heat hot fudge sauce according to directions on jar. Pour evenly over ice cream. Sprinkle peanuts over hot fudge sauce. Spread whipped topping evenly over peanuts. Sprinkle reserved crushed cookie mixture over whipped topping. Freeze 8 hours or until firm. Remove from freezer 15 minutes before serving. Cut into bars to serve. Yield: 15 servings.   Danelle Krapfl

Quad City Cookin'
Queen of Heaven Circle of OLV Ladies Council
Davenport, Iowa

Butter Pecan Ice Cream

2 cups chopped pecans
3 tablespoons butter or
  margarine, melted
2 quarts milk
2½ cups sugar

1 teaspoon vanilla extract
3 (12-ounce) cans evaporated
  milk
2 (3.4-ounce) packages vanilla
  instant pudding mix

Sauté pecans in butter in a large skillet 3 to 5 minutes or until toasted. Set aside to cool.

Combine milk and remaining 4 ingredients, stirring well with a wire whisk. Pour mixture into freezer container of a 1½- to 2-gallon hand-turned or electric freezer. Freeze 10 minutes or until ice cream begins to thicken. Remove dasher, and add pecans to ice cream mixture. Return dasher; freeze according to manufacturer's instructions. Pack freezer with additional ice and rock salt, and let stand 1 hour before serving. Yield: about 1 gallon. Elise Finch

Shared Treasures
First Baptist Church
Monroe, Louisiana

Strawberry Ice Cream

A hint of banana flavor surprises the palate in this creamy treat.

1 quart half-and-half
2 cups whipping cream
3 tablespoons fresh lemon juice
3 tablespoons frozen orange
  juice concentrate
3 cups sugar

2 ripe bananas, mashed
2 (16-ounce) packages frozen
  unsweetened whole
  strawberries, thawed and
  mashed

Combine all ingredients. Pour into freezer container of a 1-gallon hand-turned or electric freezer. Freeze according to manufacturer's instructions. Pack freezer with additional ice and rock salt, and let stand 1 hour before serving. Yield: 1 gallon. Jill Tietjen

Cookin' in the Canyon
Jarbidge Community Hall
Jarbidge, Nevada

Eggs & Cheese

Creole Deviled Eggs, page 146

Eggs-ceptional over Artichokes

8 large eggs
4 egg yolks
2 tablespoons lemon juice
1½ tablespoons cold water
½ teaspoon salt
½ teaspoon sweet red pepper
  flakes
⅛ teaspoon pepper
2 to 3 dashes of hot sauce
1 cup butter, cut into thirds
8 canned artichoke bottoms
1 (12-ounce) package bacon,
  cooked and crumbled

Lightly grease a large skillet; add water to depth of 2 inches. Bring to a boil; reduce heat, and maintain a light simmer. Working in batches to poach 4 eggs at a time, break eggs, one at a time, into a cup; slip egg into water, holding cup close to water. Simmer 5 minutes or until done. Remove eggs with a slotted spoon; trim edges of eggs, if desired. Set aside.

Combine 4 eggs yolks and next 6 ingredients in top of a double boiler, stirring well with a wire whisk. Add one-third of butter to egg yolk mixture; cook over hot, not boiling, water, stirring constantly with a wire whisk until butter melts. Add another third of butter, stirring constantly. As sauce thickens, stir in remaining butter. Cook, stirring constantly, until temperature reaches 160°. Remove sauce from double boiler.

On individual serving plates, place one poached egg on each artichoke bottom. Spoon sauce evenly over eggs. Sprinkle with bacon. Yield: 4 to 8 servings.

Back to the Table
Episcopal Church Women—Christ Church
Raleigh, North Carolina

Easy Eggs Benedict

8 large eggs
¾ cup mayonnaise
¼ teaspoon salt
¼ cup whipping cream,
  whipped
1 teaspoon grated lemon rind
1 tablespoon fresh lemon juice
4 English muffins, split and
  toasted
Butter or margarine
8 slices Canadian bacon or
  thinly sliced ham

Lightly grease a large skillet; add water to depth of 2 inches. Bring to a boil; reduce heat, and maintain a light simmer. Working in batches to poach 4 eggs at a time, break eggs, one at a time, into a cup; slip egg into water, holding cup close to water. Simmer 5 minutes or until done. Remove eggs with a slotted spoon; trim edges of eggs, if desired. Set aside.

Combine mayonnaise and salt in a small saucepan. Cook over low heat, stirring constantly, 3 minutes. Stir in whipped cream, lemon rind, and lemon juice; remove from heat, and keep warm.

Spread split sides of muffin halves with butter. Arrange bacon on muffin halves; top each bacon slice with a poached egg. Spoon reserved sauce over eggs. Yield: 4 to 8 servings. Rita Boyd

Our Family's Favorite Recipes
University Family Fellowship
Sparks, Nevada

Eggs Florcntine

Pecorino is an Italian cheese made from goat's milk; it has a sharp, pungent flavor. If pecorino is not available in your area, substitute Romano or Parmesan.

3 tablespoons olive oil
1 (10-ounce) package fresh
 spinach
⅛ teaspoon salt

¼ teaspoon pepper
4 large eggs
¼ cup freshly grated pecorino
 cheese

Heat oil in a large skillet over medium heat; add spinach. Cover and cook 8 minutes or until tender, stirring occasionally. Sprinkle with salt and pepper; toss well.

Arrange spinach evenly in four 4-ounce ramekins. Break one egg over spinach in each ramekin; sprinkle 1 tablespoon cheese over each egg. Bake at 350° for 15 minutes or until eggs reach desired doneness. Yield: 4 servings. Marcelle L. Crisona

Food for Thought
Friends of Centerville Public Library
Centerville, Massachusetts

Creole Deviled Eggs

Hot sauce and red pepper deliver a powerful punch to these stuffed eggs.

16 large hard-cooked eggs
½ cup mayonnaise
1 tablespoon lemon juice
5 drops of hot sauce
¼ teaspoon salt
½ teaspoon ground red
   pepper
2 tablespoons finely chopped
   fresh chives

2 tablespoons finely chopped
   fresh parsley
2 tablespoons finely chopped
   sweet red pepper
Garnishes: sweet red pepper
   strips, chopped chives,
   parsley sprigs
Ground red pepper

Slice eggs in half lengthwise, and carefully remove yolks. Process yolks, mayonnaise, and next 4 ingredients in a food processor until smooth, stopping once to scrape down sides. Add chives, parsley, and chopped sweet red pepper; pulse just until blended.

Spoon yolk mixture into egg whites. Garnish, if desired; sprinkle with additional ground red pepper. Chill thoroughly before serving. Yield: 16 servings.

Jan Lester

Somethin's Cookin' with Married Young Adults
Houston's First Baptist Church
Houston, Texas

Rise and Shine Casserole

The ease of this recipe makes it a perfect addition for a weekend brunch. For the ultimate eye-opening entrée, use hot salsa instead of mild or medium.

¾ cup salsa
Vegetable cooking spray
2 cups (8 ounces) shredded
   Monterey Jack and Colby
   cheese blend

1 cup canned chopped
   artichokes
¼ cup grated Parmesan cheese
6 large eggs, lightly beaten
1 (8-ounce) carton sour cream

Spread salsa in a 2-quart baking dish coated with cooking spray. Layer shredded cheese, artichokes, and Parmesan cheese over salsa. Combine eggs and sour cream, stirring with a wire whisk. Pour over cheese mixture. Bake, uncovered, at 350° for 35 to 40 minutes or until set. Cut into squares to serve. Yield: 6 servings.

Linen Napkins to Paper Plates
The Junior Auxiliary of Clarksville, Tennessee

Pipérade with Ham

Tomatoes and sweet peppers cooked in olive oil are the mainstay of this French dish. Adding prosciutto and eggs makes this a hearty main dish. You can easily halve this recipe, if desired.

2 large onions, sliced
6 cloves garlic, minced
3 tablespoons olive oil
2 (15-ounce) jars roasted sweet red peppers, drained
3 medium tomatoes, peeled, seeded, and chopped
¼ teaspoon ground red pepper
½ teaspoon salt
½ teaspoon freshly ground black pepper
¼ cup plus 3 tablespoons butter or margarine
10 large eggs, lightly beaten
⅓ cup thinly sliced fresh basil
¼ pound prosciutto, cut into very thin strips
8 (1-inch-thick) slices French bread, toasted, or 8 English muffins, split and toasted

Cook onion and garlic in hot oil in a large skillet over medium-high heat 8 minutes or until tender, stirring often. Add peppers, tomato, and ground red pepper; cover, reduce heat, and cook 20 minutes, stirring occasionally. Uncover and cook 20 minutes or until mixture is slightly thickened. Stir in salt and black pepper.

Melt butter in a large skillet over medium-low heat; add eggs and basil. Cook, without stirring, until egg mixture begins to set on bottom. Draw a spatula across bottom of skillet to form large curds. Continue cooking until eggs are firm but still moist (do not stir constantly).

Combine tomato mixture, prosciutto, and egg mixture, stirring gently. Serve pipérade with French bread or English muffins. Yield: 8 servings.

Victorian Thymes and Pleasures
The Junior League of Williamsport, Pennsylvania

Holiday Strata

10 slices white bread
2 cups finely chopped ham
1½ cups (6 ounces) shredded
   sharp Cheddar cheese
1½ cups diced sweet red
   pepper
1 cup sliced fresh
   mushrooms

1 cup chopped green onions
9 large eggs, lightly beaten
4 cups milk
1½ teaspoons dry mustard
½ teaspoon pepper
½ teaspoon paprika

Cut bread slices into fourths. Layer bread in a greased 13- x 9- x 2-inch baking dish; cover with ham and next 4 ingredients.

Combine eggs and remaining 4 ingredients; stir well. Pour over ingredients in baking dish. Cover and chill at least 8 hours. Remove from refrigerator; let stand 30 minutes. Bake, uncovered, at 350° for 1 hour or until a knife inserted in center comes out clean. Let stand 10 minutes before serving. Yield: 10 to 12 servings.   Ginny Cole

'Pon Top Edisto
Trinity Episcopal Church
Edisto Island, South Carolina

Pizza Quiche

Here's a clever recipe to introduce kids to quiche—who could resist this pepperoni pizza rendition? It was a prizewinner at the Iowa State Fair.

3 cups (12 ounces) shredded
   mozzarella cheese
2 cups (8 ounces) shredded
   Cheddar cheese
1 unbaked 9-inch pastry shell
1 (4-ounce) can sliced
   mushrooms, drained
½ (3.5-ounce) package sliced
   pepperoni, finely chopped

¾ cup milk
2 large eggs, beaten
1 teaspoon dried Italian
   seasoning
1 (14-ounce) jar spaghetti
   sauce, heated

Place cheeses in pastry shell; top with mushrooms and pepperoni. Combine milk, eggs, and Italian seasoning in a bowl, stirring well. Pour mixture into prepared pastry shell.

Bake at 400° for 45 minutes or until quiche is set (cover with aluminum foil after 25 minutes to prevent excessive browning). Let stand 10 minutes. Serve quiche with warm spaghetti sauce. Yield: one 9-inch quiche.

Erin Summy

Iowa: A Taste of Home
Iowa 4-H Foundation
Ames, Iowa

Spinach Quiche

This crustless quiche is abundant in fresh vegetables mixed with savory ricotta and feta cheese.

1 (10-ounce) package frozen chopped spinach, thawed
1½ cups sliced fresh mushrooms
1½ cups sliced zucchini
1 medium-size green pepper, chopped
1 medium onion, chopped
1½ teaspoons minced garlic
3 tablespoons vegetable oil
5 large eggs, lightly beaten

1 (15-ounce) carton ricotta cheese
7 ounces crumbled feta cheese (about 1½ cups)
1 tablespoon chopped fresh parsley
1½ teaspoons chopped fresh thyme
¾ teaspoon salt
¼ teaspoon freshly ground pepper

Drain spinach, and press between layers of paper towels to remove excess moisture. Set aside.

Cook mushrooms, zucchini, green pepper, onion, and garlic in hot oil in a large skillet over medium-high heat, stirring constantly, 8 minutes or until tender; drain. Combine eggs and ricotta cheese, stirring until blended. Stir in sautéed vegetables, spinach, feta cheese, and remaining 4 ingredients. Pour into a lightly greased 10-inch springform pan. Bake at 350° for 1 hour or until set. Let stand 10 minutes. Carefully remove sides of springform pan, and cut quiche into wedges. Yield: 8 servings.

Seaboard to Sideboard
The Junior League of Wilmington, North Carolina

Mock Cheese Soufflé

These flavors resemble a classic Cheddar soufflé, but the method and texture resemble a strata. Serve squares of this meatless entrée for brunch or lunch.

Butter
6 slices white bread, crusts removed
2 cups (8 ounces) shredded sharp Cheddar cheese
4 large eggs, lightly beaten

2½ cups milk
1 teaspoon seasoned salt
1 teaspoon dry mustard
⅛ teaspoon garlic powder
⅛ teaspoon Worcestershire sauce

Butter 1 side of each bread slice. Line a lightly greased 11- x 7- x 1½-inch baking dish with bread slices, buttered side up, overlapping if necessary. Sprinkle cheese over bread.

Combine eggs and remaining 5 ingredients in a medium bowl; stir well. Pour over cheese; cover and chill 8 hours or overnight. Remove from refrigerator; let stand 30 minutes. Bake, uncovered, at 350° for 50 minutes or until a knife inserted in center comes out clean. Yield: 6 servings.

Marilyn Conklin

Recipes and Remembrances
Otsego County Historical Society
Gaylord, Michigan

Stuffed Italian Pancakes

These pancakes are really crêpes–in this case, a triple cheese-vegetarian version drenched with marinara sauce. Two crêpes per serving make a hearty lunch or supper with a salad and crusty loaf bread on the side.

3 large eggs
¾ cup milk
½ cup beer
1 cup all-purpose flour
¼ cup butter or margarine, divided
1 (15-ounce) carton ricotta cheese
1 large egg

1 clove garlic, minced
½ teaspoon salt
½ teaspoon pepper
½ cup (2 ounces) shredded mozzarella, Cheddar, or Swiss cheese
1 (16-ounce) jar marinara sauce
2 tablespoons freshly grated Parmesan or Romano cheese

Process first 4 ingredients in container of an electric blender until smooth, stopping once to scrape down sides. Chill batter 1 hour.

For each crêpe, melt 1 teaspoon butter in a 10-inch nonstick crêpe pan or skillet over medium heat. Pour ¼ cup batter into pan; quickly tilt pan in all directions so batter covers bottom of pan. Cook 1 minute or until crêpe can be shaken loose from pan. Turn crêpe over, and cook 1 minute or until done. Place crêpe on a cloth towel to cool.

Combine ricotta and next 5 ingredients in a large bowl; stir well. Spoon cheese mixture evenly down center of each crêpe; fold sides over. Place crêpes, seam side down, in a lightly greased 13- x 9- x 2-inch baking dish. Spoon marinara sauce evenly over crêpes; sprinkle evenly with Parmesan cheese. Bake at 400° for 10 to 15 minutes or until thoroughly heated. Yield: 6 servings.   Sayre Uhler

Classic Italian Cooking
Italian American Society of San Marco Island
Marco Island, Florida

Eggnog Custard French Toast

Traditional flavors of the holiday feast find their way to the breakfast table in this French toast dipped in a mixture of eggnog and nutmeg and topped with a simple homemade cranberry sauce.

2 large eggs
1 egg white
2 cups refrigerated eggnog
1 tablespoon rum extract
½ teaspoon ground nutmeg, divided

16 (1-inch-thick) slices French bread
Vegetable cooking spray
2 tablespoons powdered sugar
Berry Sauce

Combine eggs and egg white in a medium bowl; beat well. Add eggnog, rum extract, and ¼ teaspoon nutmeg; stir well. Dip bread slices in eggnog mixture, coating both sides. Place in a single layer in two 13- x 9- x 2-inch baking dishes. Pour remaining eggnog mixture evenly over bread slices. Cover and chill 8 hours.

Place bread slices on a baking sheet coated with cooking spray. Bake at 425° for 16 minutes or until golden, turning once. Sprinkle each slice evenly with powdered sugar and remaining ¼ teaspoon nutmeg. Spoon Berry Sauce over each serving. Yield: 8 servings.

Berry Sauce

1 cup frozen cranberry-raspberry juice concentrate, thawed (we tested with Welch's)

1 cup jellied cranberry sauce
3 tablespoons sugar

Combine juice concentrate, cranberry sauce, and sugar in a medium saucepan; cook over low heat until sugar melts, stirring often. Yield: 2 cups.

Gracious Goodness Christmas in Charleston
Bishop England High School Endowment Fund
Charleston, South Carolina

Sour Cream Brunch Bake

This soufflélike dish tastes like a cheese blintz but without the crêpes, so it's easy to make and serve. Just cut it into squares, and top each serving with sour cream and preserves.

1 (15-ounce) carton ricotta cheese
⅔ cup sifted powdered sugar, divided
1 large egg, separated

9 large eggs
1½ cups sour cream
¼ teaspoon salt
Sour cream
Raspberry preserves

Combine ricotta cheese, ⅓ cup powdered sugar, and egg yolk in a medium bowl; stir well. Spread cheese mixture evenly in bottom of a greased and floured 11- x 7- x 1½-inch baking dish.

Combine remaining ⅓ cup powdered sugar, egg white, 9 eggs, 1½ cups sour cream, and salt in a mixing bowl. Beat at medium speed of an electric mixer 2 minutes. Pour egg mixture over cheese mixture.

Bake at 350° for 45 to 50 minutes or until almost set and edges are lightly browned. Let stand 10 minutes before serving. Cut into squares, and serve with sour cream and raspberry preserves. Yield: 9 servings.

Food Fabulous Food
Women's Board to Cooper Hospital/University Medical Center
Camden, New Jersey

Spiced Yogurt Cheese

Spice up your morning by serving homemade yogurt cheese, seasoned with fragrant spices, with your bagel. The yogurt cheese also makes a great low-fat snack served with fruit.

1 (32-ounce) carton plain
  low-fat yogurt
2 tablespoons sugar

¼ teaspoon ground cinnamon
⅛ teaspoon ground cloves
⅛ teaspoon ground nutmeg

Place a colander in a medium bowl. Line colander with four layers of cheesecloth, allowing cheesecloth to extend over edges of bowl. Spoon yogurt into colander, and cover loosely with plastic wrap; let stand in refrigerator at least 8 hours.

Discard liquid; spoon yogurt into bowl. Stir sugar, cinnamon, cloves, and nutmeg into yogurt. Serve with gingersnaps or sliced apples or pears. Yield: about 2 cups.   Margie Caley

Canton McKinley Bulldogs Pup's Pantry
McKinley Booster Club
Canton, Ohio

Tomato Cheeserole

This rustic casserole simmers cheese dumplings atop a chunky tomato sauce on the cooktop. Spoon the duo into serving bowls to savor all the juices.

2 tablespoons chopped onion
1 tablespoon chopped green
  pepper
2 tablespoons shortening,
  melted
1 tablespoon all-purpose flour
1 (28-ounce) can whole
  tomatoes, undrained and
  coarsely chopped

1 (14½-ounce) can whole
  tomatoes, undrained and
  coarsely chopped
1 tablespoon chopped celery
  leaves
1 teaspoon sugar
½ teaspoon salt
⅛ teaspoon pepper
Cheese Dumplings

Cook chopped onion and green pepper in shortening in a Dutch oven or a deep 12-inch skillet, stirring constantly, 5 minutes. Stir in flour. Gradually add chopped tomatoes, stirring constantly. Add celery leaves, sugar, salt, and pepper; bring to a boil. Reduce heat, and simmer 5 minutes.

Drop dumpling batter by tablespoonfuls over tomato mixture. Cover and simmer 20 minutes or until dumplings are done. Serve immediately. Yield: 6 servings.

Cheese Dumplings

1 cup all-purpose flour
2 teaspoons baking powder
½ teaspoon salt
2 tablespoons shortening
½ cup (2 ounces) shredded
   Cheddar or American cheese

1 tablespoon chopped fresh
   parsley
½ cup milk

Combine flour, baking powder, and salt. Cut in shortening with a pastry blender until crumbly. Add cheese and parsley; stir well. Add milk, stirring just until dry ingredients are moistened. Yield: batter for 18 dumplings.

Nancy Curtis

Crossroads Cookbook
New Albany-Plain Township Historical Society
New Albany, Ohio

Sausage Coffee Cake

Sausage and a pair of cheeses lend a savory twist to these hearty breakfast squares. Serve them with fresh fruit for a simple yet satisfying morning meal.

1 **pound ground pork sausage**
½ **cup chopped onion**
½ **cup (2 ounces) shredded Swiss cheese**
¼ **cup grated Parmesan cheese**
1 **large egg, lightly beaten**
2 **tablespoons minced fresh parsley**

½ **teaspoon salt**
¼ **teaspoon hot sauce**
2 **cups biscuit mix**
¾ **cup milk**
¼ **cup mayonnaise**
1 **egg yolk**
1 **tablespoon water**

Brown sausage and onion in a large skillet, stirring until meat crumbles; drain. Add Swiss cheese and next 5 ingredients; set aside.

Combine biscuit mix, milk, and mayonnaise. Spread half of batter in a greased 9-inch square pan. Spread sausage mixture over batter. Spread remaining batter over sausage mixture.

Combine egg yolk and water; stir with a wire whisk. Brush egg mixture over top of batter. Bake at 400° for 20 to 25 minutes or until golden; remove from oven, and let stand 5 minutes. Cut into squares. Yield: 6 servings.

Bettye Hutt

Blessings
First Presbyterian Church
Pine Bluff, Arkansas

Toulouse Tarts

"Toulouse" refers to a French sausage spiced with wine, garlic, and seasonings. These tarts call for regular sausage; caraway seeds, leeks, two types of mustard, and two kinds of cheese make up the French connection.

3 cups all-purpose flour
1 tablespoon caraway seeds
1 tablespoon dry mustard
1 cup butter or margarine, cut into 1-inch pieces
¼ cup plus 3 tablespoons ice water
¾ pound ground pork sausage
2 tablespoons freshly grated Parmesan cheese
2 tablespoons fine, dry breadcrumbs (store-bought)
2 leeks, thinly sliced (about 2 cups)

2 tablespoons butter or margarine, melted
3 large eggs, beaten
2 cups milk
⅓ cup butter or margarine, melted
½ cup (2 ounces) shredded Swiss cheese
¼ cup freshly grated Parmesan cheese
1½ teaspoons Dijon mustard
1 teaspoon salt

Process flour, caraway seeds, and dry mustard in a food processor until blended. Add 1 cup butter, processing until mixture is crumbly.

With processor running, slowly add ice water, 1 tablespoon at a time; process just until pastry begins to form a ball and leaves sides of bowl. Shape dough into 24 balls; press into muffin pans to form crusts. Set aside.

Brown sausage in a large skillet, stirring until it crumbles; drain. Combine 2 tablespoons Parmesan cheese and breadcrumbs; sprinkle over dough in muffin pans. Crumble sausage evenly over breadcrumb mixture.

Cook leeks in 2 tablespoons melted butter in a large skillet over medium-high heat, stirring constantly, until tender. Remove from heat. Add beaten eggs, milk, and remaining 5 ingredients, stirring well. Spoon egg mixture evenly into each muffin pan (about 2 tablespoons each). Bake at 350° for 45 to 50 minutes or until lightly browned. Yield: 2 dozen.

Lois Clark

Quad City Cookin'
Queen of Heaven Circle of OLV Ladies Council
Davenport, Iowa

Herbed Cheese Tarts

A simple sprinkling of breadcrumbs forms the crust for these three-cheese tarts. Heavily coat the mini-muffin pans with cooking spray to help the crumbs adhere.

⅓ cup fine, dry breadcrumbs (store-bought)
Vegetable cooking spray
1 (8-ounce) package cream cheese, softened
¾ cup cottage cheese
½ cup (2 ounces) shredded Swiss cheese

1 tablespoon all-purpose flour
¼ teaspoon dried basil
⅛ teaspoon garlic powder
2 large eggs
Sour cream
Sliced olives
Snipped fresh chives
Ground red pepper

Sprinkle breadcrumbs on bottom and up sides of miniature (1¾-inch) muffin pans heavily coated with cooking spray; shake pans to remove any excess crumbs. Set aside.

Combine cream cheese and next 5 ingredients in a large bowl; beat at medium speed of an electric mixer until fluffy. Add eggs; beat at low speed just until blended. Spoon mixture evenly into prepared muffin pans, filling each cup about two-thirds full.

Bake at 375° for 15 minutes or until edges are golden. Cool 10 minutes in pans; remove from pans, and cool on wire racks. Chill until ready to serve. Top with sour cream, olives, chives, or red pepper. Yield: 2½ dozen.

A Capital Affair
The Junior League of Harrisburg, Pennsylvania

Fish & Shellfish

Florida Clambake, page 171

Waquoit Bluefish with Mustard Sauce

2 pounds bluefish or mackerel fillets
1 teaspoon salt
½ teaspoon pepper
⅓ cup butter or margarine, melted

3 tablespoons fresh lemon juice
1½ teaspoons chopped fresh thyme or ½ teaspoon dried thyme
Mustard Sauce

Cut fish into serving-size pieces. Sprinkle with salt and pepper; place in a greased 13- x 9- x 2-inch baking dish. Combine butter, lemon juice, and thyme; pour over fish.

Bake, uncovered, at 350° for 15 to 20 minutes or until fish flakes easily when tested with a fork. Serve immediately with Mustard Sauce. Yield: 6 servings.

Mustard Sauce

2 tablespoons butter or margarine
1½ tablespoons all-purpose flour
2 teaspoons dry mustard

¼ teaspoon salt
⅛ teaspoon hot sauce
1 cup half-and-half
1 egg yolk, beaten

Melt butter in a small saucepan over medium heat; stir in flour and next 3 ingredients, using a wire whisk. Gradually stir in half-and-half. Cook, stirring constantly, 2 minutes or until thickened and bubbly. Reduce heat to low; stir in egg yolk. Cook, stirring constantly, until thickened. Yield: about 1 cup.   Toni David

Flavors of Falmouth
Falmouth Historical Society
Falmouth, Massachusetts

Baked Pecan Catfish

Pecans highlight the batter and topping of this easy catfish entrée.

1 cup buttermilk	⅛ teaspoon pepper
1 large egg, lightly beaten	¼ cup butter, melted
1 cup ground pecans	4 (8-ounce) catfish fillets
½ cup all-purpose flour	¼ cup pecan halves
¼ cup sesame seeds	Garnish: fresh parsley sprigs
1 tablespoon paprika	Lemon wedges
2 teaspoons salt	

Combine buttermilk and egg; stir well. Combine ground pecans and next 5 ingredients. Add to buttermilk mixture; stir until blended.

Pour melted butter into a 13- x 9- x 2-inch baking dish. Dip catfish fillets in batter, allowing excess to drain off. Arrange fillets in dish. Place pecan halves on top. Bake, uncovered, at 400° for 35 minutes or until fish flakes easily when tested with a fork. Garnish, if desired. Serve with lemon wedges. Yield: 4 servings.

Pick of the Crop, Two
North Sunflower Academy PTA
Drew, Mississippi

Parmesan Catfish

½ cup grated Parmesan cheese	8 catfish fillets (about 3
2 tablespoons yellow cornmeal	pounds)
1 teaspoon paprika	Vegetable cooking spray
¼ teaspoon ground red pepper	

Combine first 4 ingredients, stirring well. Rinse fish in cold water, and drain.

Dredge fish in cheese mixture. Place coated fish on a rack in a broiler pan coated with cooking spray. Broil 5½ inches from heat (with electric oven door partially opened) 10 minutes or until fish flakes easily when tested with a fork. Yield: 8 servings. Kathleen Powell

From ANNA's Kitchen
Adams-Normandie Neighborhood Association (ANNA)
Los Angeles, California

Crab-Stuffed Flounder

These succulent flounder fillets sport a double dose of a fresh crabmeat and Parmesan mixture—they're stuffed as well as topped with the savory blend.

1 stalk celery, chopped
3 green onions, chopped
2 cloves garlic, minced
¼ cup olive oil
½ pound fresh lump crabmeat, drained
1 cup soft breadcrumbs (homemade)
½ cup grated Parmesan cheese
1 plum tomato, chopped
1 large egg, lightly beaten
2 tablespoons fresh lemon juice
1 tablespoon chopped fresh parsley
¼ teaspoon salt
¼ teaspoon pepper
6 (4-ounce) flounder fillets
½ cup butter or margarine, melted
Garnish: lemon wedges

Cook celery, green onions, and garlic in hot oil in a large skillet over medium-high heat, stirring constantly, until tender. Remove from heat; add crabmeat and next 8 ingredients, stirring well.

Brush fillets evenly with melted butter. Spoon 1 heaping tablespoon crabmeat mixture on top of each fillet. Roll up fillets, and secure each with a wooden pick. Place fillets in a lightly greased 13 - x 9- x 2-inch baking dish. Spoon remaining crabmeat mixture over each stuffed fillet, and drizzle with any remaining butter.

Cover and bake at 375° for 20 minutes. Uncover and bake 10 more minutes or until fish flakes easily when tested with a fork. Garnish, if desired. Yield: 6 servings.

Texas Ties
The Junior League of North Harris County
Spring, Texas

Monkfish with Herbs and Cognac

Mild-flavored monkfish nicely showcases the bold herb and cognac sauce that bathes the fillets. If you're unable to find monkfish in your area, substitute snapper or grouper.

⅓ cup all-purpose flour
¾ teaspoon salt, divided
¾ teaspoon pepper, divided
2 (7-ounce) monkfish fillets
¼ cup olive oil
¼ cup plus 2 tablespoons cognac or brandy, divided
1 cup white wine
2 tablespoons tomato paste

1½ tablespoons chopped fresh thyme
Dash of ground nutmeg
2 whole cloves
½ cup fish stock
1 small onion, diced (about 1 cup)
1 clove garlic, finely chopped
2 teaspoons grated lemon rind

Combine flour, ½ teaspoon salt, and ½ teaspoon pepper in a shallow dish. Dredge fish in flour mixture.

Heat oil in a large skillet over medium-high heat; add fish. Sauté 2 minutes on each side. Pour ¼ cup cognac into skillet; remove from heat. Ignite with a long match; shake skillet until flames die down. Remove fish from skillet; keep warm.

Add remaining 2 tablespoons cognac, wine, and remaining 8 ingredients to cognac mixture in skillet. Stir in remaining ¼ teaspoon salt and ¼ teaspoon pepper; bring to a boil. Reduce heat to medium-high, and simmer, uncovered, 15 minutes or until reduced to about 1 cup. Remove and discard whole cloves. Return fish to Dutch oven; cover and simmer 12 minutes or until fish flakes easily when tested with a fork. To serve, spoon sauce over fish. Yield: 2 servings.

Note: For fish stock, you can use a fish bouillon cube dissolved in water according to package directions. We tested with Knorr.

International Home Cooking
The United Nations International School Parents' Association
New York, New York

400 Capitol Street Fish

4 (6-ounce) orange roughy
  fillets
¾ teaspoon salt, divided
¼ cup all-purpose flour
⅓ cup plus 1 tablespoon dry
  white wine, divided
⅔ cup chicken broth
½ teaspoon instant minced
  onion

2 teaspoons cornstarch
2 tablespoons chopped ripe
  olives
2 tablespoons olive oil
1 large tomato, chopped
2 tablespoons chopped fresh
  parsley

Sprinkle fillets with ¼ teaspoon salt. Dredge fillets in flour, and set aside.

Combine ⅓ cup wine, broth, and onion in a saucepan. Combine cornstarch and remaining 1 tablespoon wine; add to pan, and cook over medium heat, stirring constantly, 1 minute or until thickened. Add olives; set aside.

Fry fish fillets in hot oil in a large skillet 4 minutes on each side or until fish flakes easily when tested with a fork. Pour reserved sauce over fish. Sprinkle with remaining ½ teaspoon salt, tomato, and parsley. Cook 1 more minute or until thoroughly heated. Serve immediately. Yield: 4 servings.

Bully's Best Bites
The Junior Auxiliary of Starkville, Mississippi

Roast Salmon with Mushroom Rice

Roast salmon is accentuated with a rub of tarragon and rosemary and served over a bed of rice combined with shiitake and button mushrooms. A tangy dill and mustard sauce tops off this dish.

1 teaspoon olive oil
3 green onions, thinly sliced
1 clove garlic, minced
2 cups thinly sliced fresh
   mushrooms
2 cups thinly sliced shiitake
   mushrooms
1½ cups water, divided
⅔ cup uncooked long-grain
   rice
¾ teaspoon salt, divided

¾ teaspoon dried tarragon,
   divided
¾ teaspoon dried rosemary,
   divided
1 (1¾-pound) center-cut
   salmon fillet with skin
¼ cup fresh lemon juice
3 tablespoons water, divided
1 teaspoon cornstarch
¼ cup chopped fresh dill
½ teaspoon Dijon mustard

Heat oil in a large saucepan over medium heat; add green onions and garlic. Cook until tender, stirring often. Add mushrooms; stir well. Stir in ¼ cup water; cook, uncovered, 7 minutes. Stir in rice, remaining 1¼ cups water, ½ teaspoon each salt, tarragon, and rosemary; bring to a boil. Cover, reduce heat, and simmer 20 minutes or until rice is tender. Fluff rice with a fork, and spoon evenly down center of a 13- x 9- x 2-inch pan.

Rub remaining ¼ teaspoon salt, ¼ teaspoon tarragon, and ¼ teaspoon rosemary into flesh side of salmon. Lay salmon, skin side up, over rice; score salmon skin with a sharp knife. Bake, uncovered, at 425° for 20 to 25 minutes or until salmon flakes easily when tested with a fork.

Meanwhile, combine lemon juice and 2 tablespoons water in a small saucepan; bring to a boil. Combine cornstarch and remaining 1 tablespoon water; add to lemon juice mixture, stirring with a wire whisk. Cook, stirring constantly, 1 minute or until slightly thickened. Remove from heat; stir in dill and mustard.

Remove and discard skin from salmon. Cut salmon into 4 pieces; serve over rice, and top with sauce. Yield: 4 servings.   Carmen Perry

25 Years of Food, Fun & Friendship
Clifton Community Woman's Club
Clifton, Virginia

Red Snapper with Leeks and Chives

1 (750-milliliter) bottle dry red wine
6 shallots, minced
1 tablespoon red wine vinegar
¼ cup plus 2 tablespoons unsalted butter
¼ teaspoon salt, divided

¼ teaspoon freshly ground pepper, divided
2 (8-ounce) red snapper fillets
3 leeks, cut into very thin strips
2 tablespoons minced fresh chives

Combine wine, shallot, and vinegar in a large saucepan. Bring to a boil over medium heat; cook until reduced to ⅓ cup. Remove from heat, and add butter (shake pan to melt butter). Add ⅛ teaspoon salt and ⅛ teaspoon pepper; keep warm.

Sprinkle fillets with remaining ⅛ teaspoon salt and ⅛ teaspoon pepper. Arrange fillets in a steamer basket over boiling water. Place leek strips over fillets. Cover and steam 10 to 12 minutes or until fish flakes easily when tested with a fork. Carefully transfer fish fillets to two serving plates. Spoon wine sauce around fillets. Spoon leeks on top of fillets. Sprinkle with chives. Yield: 2 servings.

A Capital Affair
The Junior League of Harrisburg, Pennsylvania

Swordfish with Parmesan Crust

Round out this cheese-crusted fish with a serving of rice pilaf or orzo.

1 cup all-purpose flour
¼ teaspoon salt
¼ teaspoon pepper
2½ cups freshly grated Parmesan cheese
2 tablespoons all-purpose flour

3 large eggs, beaten
¼ cup milk
1½ to 2 pounds swordfish steaks (about 1 inch thick)
½ cup butter, divided
Garnish: lemon wedges

Combine 1 cup flour, salt, and pepper in a shallow dish. Combine Parmesan cheese and 2 tablespoons flour in a separate dish. Combine eggs and milk in a small bowl. Dredge swordfish in flour mixture; dip in egg mixture. Dredge in cheese mixture, patting on extra cheese mixture, if necessary, to coat thoroughly.

Melt ¼ cup butter in a large nonstick skillet over medium-high heat; add half of swordfish. Sauté 2 minutes on each side or until golden. (Fish may stick to skillet; turn carefully with a spatula.) Transfer fish to a baking sheet; repeat procedure with remaining butter and fish.

Bake at 350° for 8 to 12 minutes or until fish flakes easily when tested with a fork. Garnish, if desired. Yield: 4 servings.

Capital Celebrations
The Junior League of Washington, DC

Swordfish Rum Rickey

A rum-inspired marinade gives salmon a refreshing taste of the tropics. A rickey is a drink made with lime or lemon juice, soda water, and liquor.

¼ **cup dark rum**	1 **tablespoon molasses**
3 **tablespoons Dijon mustard**	1 **clove garlic, pressed**
3 **tablespoons fresh lime juice**	2½ **pounds swordfish steaks**
2 **tablespoons vegetable oil**	**(about 1 inch thick)**
2 **tablespoons soy sauce**	**Vegetable cooking spray**

Combine first 7 ingredients in a small bowl; stir well with a wire whisk. Set aside ½ cup marinade. Arrange swordfish steaks in a single layer in a shallow dish; pour remaining marinade over fish, turning fish to coat. Marinate at room temperature 30 minutes.

Coat grill rack with cooking spray; place on grill over medium-hot coals (350° to 400°). Place fish on rack; grill, covered, 5 to 7 minutes on each side or until fish flakes easily when tested with a fork. Serve with reserved marinade. Yield: 6 servings.

Perennial Palette
Southborough Gardeners
Southborough, Massachusetts

Panfried Mountain Trout

8 medium whole trout, dressed
1½ teaspoons salt, divided
1½ teaspoons pepper, divided
16 fresh basil sprigs
16 fresh oregano sprigs
16 flat-leaf parsley sprigs

8 (¼-inch-thick) lemon slices
Fresh chives (optional)
2 cups all-purpose flour
1 cup butter or margarine
½ cup olive oil
Fresh lemon juice

Sprinkle inside of fish evenly with ½ teaspoon salt and ½ teaspoon pepper. Stuff each fish with 2 basil sprigs, 2 oregano sprigs, 2 parsley sprigs, and 1 lemon slice. Tie fish around the middle with chives, if desired, or string. Combine flour, remaining 1 teaspoon salt, and 1 teaspoon pepper. Dredge trout in flour mixture.

Heat butter and olive oil in a large deep skillet over medium-high heat. Add trout; cook 5 minutes on each side, adjusting heat as necessary to avoid burning crust. Drain on paper towels. Drizzle with lemon juice, and serve immediately. Yield: 8 servings.

Southern . . . On Occasion
The Junior League of Cobb-Marietta
Marietta, Georgia

Tuna Patties

1 (6-ounce) can tuna in water,
   drained and flaked
½ cup soft French
   breadcrumbs (homemade)
½ cup finely chopped celery
2 tablespoons minced onion
¼ cup mayonnaise

2 tablespoons chili sauce
1 teaspoon lemon juice
1 egg white, beaten
1 tablespoon vegetable oil
4 hamburger buns, toasted
Green leaf lettuce leaves
Tomato slices

Combine first 8 ingredients, stirring well. Shape into 4 patties.

Fry patties in hot oil in a large skillet 5 minutes on each side or until browned. Serve patties on buns with lettuce leaves and tomato slices. Yield: 4 servings.
Laura Pawlowski

Our Saviour's Lutheran Church 75th Anniversary Cookbook
Our Saviour's Lutheran Church
Casper, Wyoming

Seared Sesame Tuna with Cucumber Sambal

A sambal is a multipurpose condiment. Here it is made with a medley of cucumber, carrot, purple onion, and fresh herbs that accompany these sesame-crusted tuna steaks.

4 (8-ounce) yellowfin tuna
   steaks (1½ inches thick)
⅛ teaspoon salt

¾ cup black sesame seeds
1 tablespoon vegetable oil
Cucumber Sambal

Season tuna with salt. Coat tuna evenly with sesame seeds on all sides. Heat oil in a large skillet over high heat. Cook steaks in hot oil 4 minutes on each side or until fish flakes easily when tested with a fork (cook steaks 2 at a time, if necessary, so as not to crowd skillet).

Mound Cucumber Sambal in center of each of 4 serving plates. Slice tuna; arrange in a fan pattern around sambal. Yield: 4 servings.

Cucumber Sambal

2 large cucumbers
½ cup scraped and shredded
   carrot
¾ cup finely chopped purple
   onion
½ to 1 tablespoon dried
   crushed red pepper
½ cup white vinegar
2 tablespoons sugar

1 tablespoon minced fresh
   cilantro
1 tablespoon minced fresh
   mint
1 tablespoon minced fresh
   basil
⅛ teaspoon salt
⅛ teaspoon ground black
   pepper

Cut cucumbers in half lengthwise, and slice thinly.

Combine cucumber, carrot, and remaining ingredients in a medium bowl; mix well. Yield: 5 cups.

Secrets of Amelia
McArthur Family Branch YMCA
Fernandina Beach, Florida

Tuna Niçoise with Mustard Anchovy Vinaigrette

This versatile vinaigrette is so good that it is used as a marinade for all three accompanying vegetables as well as a topping to these tuna steaks.

1½ pounds small round red
    potatoes
Mustard Anchovy Vinaigrette
2 medium tomatoes, cut into
    ½-inch cubes
1 pound fresh green beans,
    trimmed and cut into ½-inch
    pieces

2 tablespoons olive oil, divided
4 (5-ounce) tuna steaks (1 inch
    thick)
½ teaspoon salt
1 teaspoon freshly ground
    pepper
¼ cup Niçoise olives

Cook potatoes in boiling salted water to cover 15 minutes or until tender; drain well. Place in a medium bowl; add 3 tablespoons Mustard Anchovy Vinaigrette, stirring gently. Keep warm.

Combine tomato and 1 tablespoon vinaigrette in a medium bowl, stirring well; set in a warm place.

Cook green beans in 1 tablespoon oil in a large skillet over medium-high heat, stirring constantly, 4 minutes or until crisp-tender. Place in a bowl; add 1 tablespoon vinaigrette, stirring well. Keep warm.

Sprinkle tuna with salt and pepper. Heat remaining 1 tablespoon olive oil in skillet; add tuna. Cook 2 to 3 minutes on each side or until fish flakes easily when tested with a fork. Place tuna steaks on individual serving plates. Arrange vegetables around tuna. Drizzle remaining vinaigrette as desired over tuna and vegetables. Reserve any remaining vinaigrette as a salad dressing. Top tuna and vegetables with olives. Yield: 4 servings.

Mustard Anchovy Vinaigrette

2 tablespoons anchovy paste
2 cloves garlic, minced
1 tablespoon plus 1 teaspoon
    stone-ground mustard
¼ cup plus 2 tablespoons
    balsamic vinegar

½ cup olive oil
1 tablespoon plus 1 teaspoon
    capers, rinsed
½ teaspoon salt
½ teaspoon freshly ground
    pepper

Combine all ingredients in a jar; cover tightly, and shake vigorously. Yield: 1 cup.

Jill and Mike Wallock

Fishing for Compliments
Shedd Aquarium Society
Chicago, Illinois

Florida Clambake

Here's a perfect recipe for the beach or backyard! Be sure to select small potatoes and ears of corn so they will cook in the same amount of time as the seafood.

4 large lettuce leaves	1 cup unsalted butter, melted
4 small ears fresh corn	1 (1-ounce) envelope onion
4 (8- to 10-ounce) rock or	soup mix
Florida lobster tails, split	2 cloves garlic, pressed
12 littleneck clams, scrubbed	2 teaspoons dried oregano
8 new potatoes, halved	

Cut 4 large sheets of aluminum foil. Place 1 lettuce leaf in the center of each sheet. Pull back husks from corn, leaving husks attached at base of cob; remove silks. Rinse corn, and pat dry. Pull husks up over corn. Arrange 1 lobster tail, 3 clams, 1 ear of corn, and 4 potato halves over lettuce.

Combine butter and remaining 3 ingredients; brush over seafood mixture. Fold aluminum foil loosely around seafood mixture, sealing edges. Grill, covered, over medium-hot coals (350° to 400°) 20 to 30 minutes or until clams open. Yield: 4 servings.

Made in the Shade
The Junior League of Greater Fort Lauderdale, Florida

Carolina Crab Cakes with Basil Tartar Sauce

This easy-to-prepare dish makes an exceptional appetizer or light dinner.

1 large egg, lightly beaten
1 egg yolk, lightly beaten
2 tablespoons chopped green onions
2 tablespoons chopped fresh parsley
1½ tablespoons half-and-half
1 teaspoon lemon juice
½ teaspoon ground red pepper
½ teaspoon dry mustard
¼ teaspoon ground black pepper
¼ teaspoon Worcestershire sauce
1 pound fresh lump crabmeat, drained
½ cup plus 2 tablespoons round buttery cracker crumbs, divided
Vegetable cooking spray
2 tablespoons butter, melted
Basil Tartar Sauce

Combine first 10 ingredients; stir in crabmeat and 2 tablespoons cracker crumbs. Chill 30 minutes.

Shape crab mixture into 8 patties; dredge in remaining ½ cup cracker crumbs. Place patties on a baking sheet coated with cooking spray. Drizzle with melted butter. Bake at 475° for 10 minutes or until lightly browned. Serve with Basil Tartar Sauce. Yield: 4 servings.

Basil Tartar Sauce

½ cup firmly packed fresh basil leaves
½ cup mayonnaise
1 tablespoon sour cream
1 teaspoon lemon juice
½ teaspoon minced garlic
⅛ teaspoon salt
⅛ teaspoon ground red pepper
⅛ teaspoon hot sauce

Process all ingredients in a food processor until smooth, stopping once to scrape down sides; chill. Yield: ½ cup.

Back to the Table
Episcopal Church Women—Christ Church
Raleigh, North Carolina

Crawfish Jambalaya

Crawfish and jambalaya are hallmarks of Louisiana cooking. Enjoy this dish that teams the two regional classics in one fantastic entrée.

1 medium onion, chopped
4 cloves garlic, minced
½ cup chopped green pepper
½ cup chopped celery
½ cup butter, melted
1 (14.5-ounce) can stewed
   tomatoes, undrained

1 pound frozen crawfish tails,
   thawed
1 cup chopped green onions
3 cups cooked long-grain rice
¼ teaspoon salt
⅛ teaspoon pepper

Sauté first 4 ingredients in butter in a large skillet over medium-high heat until tender. Add tomatoes; reduce heat, and simmer, uncovered, 40 minutes. Add crawfish; cook 10 minutes. Stir in green onions, rice, salt, and pepper. Yield: 4 to 6 servings.   Charlotte Champagne

Nun Better: Tastes and Tales from Around a Cajun Table
St. Cecilia School
Broussard, Louisiana

Baked Mussels with Feta and Tomatoes

2 pounds raw mussels in shells
1 medium onion, finely
   chopped
¼ cup olive oil
3 medium or 4 large Roma
   tomatoes, chopped
1 cup dry white wine
1 teaspoon dried oregano
⅛ teaspoon dried crushed red
   pepper

1 teaspoon red wine vinegar
1 (4-ounce) package crumbled
   feta cheese
⅛ teaspoon salt
⅛ teaspoon freshly ground
   black pepper
1 tablespoon minced fresh
   parsley

Scrub mussels with a brush; remove beards. Discard cracked or heavy mussels (they're filled with sand) or opened mussels that won't close when tapped.

Sauté onion in oil in a large skillet over medium-high heat 5 minutes or until tender. Add tomato and next 4 ingredients. Bring to a boil; reduce heat, and simmer, uncovered, 20 minutes. Add mussels. Cover and cook over medium heat 4 minutes or until mussels open.

Remove mussels from skillet. Discard any unopened mussels. Gently remove mussels from shells; discard shells. Spoon mussels into a 1-quart baking dish. Add tomato mixture, feta cheese, salt, and pepper. Bake at 400° for 15 minutes or until bubbly. Sprinkle with parsley. Serve with pasta, rice, or crusty French bread, if desired. Yield: 3 to 4 servings.   Kim Farino

The Monarch's Feast
Mary Munford PTA
Richmond, Virginia

Oyster Fritters

Complement these tasty fritters with a rémoulade or cocktail sauce.

1 cup all-purpose flour
1 teaspoon salt
⅛ teaspoon ground red pepper
⅔ cup water
2 tablespoons butter or
   margarine, melted

1 large egg, separated
Vegetable oil
3 (8-ounce) containers Select
   oysters, drained

Combine flour, salt, and pepper in a medium bowl. Combine water, butter, and egg yolk in a small bowl, beating well with a fork. Gradually add egg mixture to dry ingredients, stirring until blended. Beat egg white until soft peaks form; fold into batter.

Pour oil to depth of 2 to 3 inches into a Dutch oven; heat to 375°. Dip oysters in batter; fry in batches in hot oil 2 to 3 minutes or until golden, turning once. Drain on paper towels. Serve immediately. Yield: 4 servings.   Melissa Sthrom

In the Breaking of Bread
Catholic Committee on Scouting and Camp Fire
Lake Charles, Louisiana

Grilled Oysters

Corn relish and crumbled bacon top these grilled oysters on the half shell. Serve them by the dozen for dinner or by the half dozen for an appetizer.

¼ cup olive oil
2 tablespoons balsamic vinegar
2 tablespoons dry red wine
2 cups fresh whole kernel corn, or frozen whole kernel corn, thawed
2 tablespoons chopped fresh basil

⅓ cup minced shallot
¾ teaspoon freshly ground pepper
½ teaspoon salt
4 slices bacon
3 dozen oysters in shell, scrubbed

Combine first 3 ingredients in a bowl; stir well with a wire whisk. Stir in corn and next 4 ingredients. Cover and let stand 1 hour.

Grill bacon, uncovered, over medium-hot coals (350° to 400°) 4 minutes or until crisp, turning occasionally. Remove from grill; crumble.

Grill oysters, covered, 10 to 15 minutes or until opened slightly (remove oysters from grill as they open). To open oyster, insert an oyster knife between top and bottom shells next to hinge; twist knife to pry shells apart. Scrape knife between oyster and bottom shell to free meat. Spoon corn mixture evenly over meat in each oyster shell. Sprinkle with crumbled bacon. Yield: 3 servings.   Beth Philion

The Kansas City Barbeque Society Cookbook
Kansas City Barbeque Society
Kansas City, Missouri

Oven-Roasted Prawns with Garlic and Feta

Yes this dish calls for two heads of garlic, and it's simply delightful. The garlic mellows and sweetens as it cooks. Serve this entrée immediately to appreciate the full flavor this Mediterranean-inspired dish offers. Sourdough or pumperknickel bread is a good accompaniment.

1 pound unpeeled jumbo fresh prawns
2 large heads garlic, separated and peeled
½ cup olive oil, divided
Dash of hot sauce
½ cup dry white wine
1 (10-ounce) package fresh spinach leaves
½ cup chopped fresh parsley
2 tablespoons chopped fresh cilantro
2 teaspoons chopped fresh oregano
2 teaspoons chopped fresh rosemary
1 tablespoon fresh lemon juice
½ teaspoon salt
½ teaspoon pepper
Dash of nutmeg
4 ounces feta cheese, crumbled
Lemon wedges (optional)

Peel prawns, leaving tails intact; devein, if desired.

Sauté garlic in ¼ cup olive oil and hot sauce in a Dutch oven over medium heat 5 minutes. Add wine; cook 3 minutes. Add spinach leaves; cook just until wilted. Place spinach mixture evenly in a 13- x 9- x 2-inch baking dish. Add prawns in a single layer. Sprinkle with parsley and next 7 ingredients. Drizzle with remaining ¼ cup olive oil.

Bake at 425° for 10 minutes or until prawns turn pink. Remove from oven, and sprinkle with feta cheese. Serve with lemon wedges, if desired. Yield: 4 servings.

Symphony of Flavors
The Associates of the Redlands Bowl
Redlands, California

Scallops and Shrimp with Orzo and Spinach

Spinach and orzo team with shrimp and scallops, making this a hearty one-dish meal for four.

¾ pound unpeeled medium-size fresh shrimp
2 quarts water
8 ounces bay scallops
1½ cups uncooked orzo
1 teaspoon salt (optional)
3 tablespoons olive oil
6 cloves garlic, minced
⅓ cup minced dried tomato in oil

2 (10-ounce) packages frozen chopped spinach, thawed and drained
¾ cup grated Parmesan cheese
¼ cup plus 2 tablespoons pine nuts, toasted
¼ cup dry white wine
½ teaspoon salt
¼ teaspoon pepper

Peel shrimp, and devein, if desired.

Bring water to a boil in a large saucepan. Add shrimp and scallops. Cover and remove from heat. Let stand 8 minutes or until shrimp turn pink and scallops are opaque. Remove seafood with a slotted spoon; cover seafood to keep warm. Bring water to a boil again; add orzo and, if desired, 1 teaspoon salt. Cook 8 minutes or until tender, and drain.

Heat oil in a large skillet over medium-high heat until hot. Add garlic and dried tomato; cook 1 minute. Add spinach and cooked orzo; cook, stirring constantly, until thoroughly heated. Stir in seafood, cheese, and remaining ingredients. Cook until thoroughly heated. Yield: 4 servings.

Out of the Ordinary
The Hingham Historical Society
Hingham, Massachusetts

Grilled Shrimp and Scallops

For a smoky flavor, partially cook bacon in the microwave; then wrap a half piece of bacon around each shrimp before grilling.

1½ pounds unpeeled large or
    jumbo fresh shrimp
1 bunch green onions,
    chopped
½ cup firmly packed brown
    sugar

½ cup Dijon mustard
½ cup bourbon
½ cup soy sauce
2 tablespoons Worcestershire
    sauce
1 pound sea scallops

Peel shrimp, and devein, if desired. Set aside.

Combine green onions and next 5 ingredients in a large bowl. Add shrimp and scallops, stirring well. Cover and marinate in refrigerator 1 hour.

Remove shrimp and scallops from marinade, discarding marinade. Thread shrimp and scallops evenly onto six 12-inch metal skewers. Grill, covered, over medium-hot coals (350° to 400°) 2 to 3 minutes on each side or until shrimp turn pink. Yield: 6 servings.

Beneath the Palms
The Brownsville Junior Service League
Brownsville, Texas

Shrimp Élégante

1½ pounds unpeeled large
    fresh shrimp
2 tablespoons butter or
    margarine
2 tablespoons minced shallot
1¼ cups sliced fresh
    mushrooms
1⅓ cups water

3 tablespoons chili sauce
1 teaspoon salt
⅛ teaspoon pepper
1⅓ cups uncooked instant rice
1 (8-ounce) carton sour cream
1 tablespoon all-purpose flour
1 tablespoon chopped fresh
    chives

Peel shrimp, and devein, if desired. Set aside.

Melt butter in a large skillet over medium-high heat; add shallot, and cook, stirring constantly, 3 minutes or until tender. Add shrimp and mushrooms; cook 1 minute, stirring constantly.

Combine water and next 3 ingredients; add to shrimp mixture, and bring to a boil. Add rice; cover, reduce heat, and simmer 5 minutes.

Combine sour cream and flour, stirring to blend. Add to rice mixture, and cook until thoroughly heated. Sprinkle with chopped chives. Yield: 4 servings.   Margaret Wilson

75 Years and Still Cooking
Lakeside Presbyterian Church
Richmond, Virginia

Shrimp Sauté Piquant

For extra zip, add the whole teaspoon of hot sauce to this saucy dish.

1½ pounds unpeeled large fresh shrimp	⅓ cup chopped celery
⅓ cup vegetable oil	3 cups water
⅓ cup all-purpose flour	1 (14.5-ounce) can diced tomatoes
1 medium onion, chopped	½ to 1 teaspoon hot sauce
3 cloves garlic, minced	2 teaspoons salt
½ cup chopped green pepper	Hot cooked rice

Peel shrimp, and devein, if desired. Set aside.

Combine oil and flour in a large Dutch oven; cook over medium heat, stirring constantly, until roux is caramel-colored (about 15 minutes). Add onion and next 3 ingredients. Cook until vegetables are tender, stirring often. Add water and next 3 ingredients. Bring to a boil; reduce heat, and simmer, uncovered, 1 hour.

Add shrimp, and simmer 10 minutes or until shrimp turn pink. Serve over rice. Yield: 4 servings.   Jeanie Adkins

7 Alarm Cuisine
East Mountain Volunteer Fire Department
Gladewater, Texas

Super Easy Thai Shrimp and Noodles

A peanut butter sauce with chili oil, fresh ginger, and garlic gives this easy shrimp dish its Oriental flavor.

1 pound unpeeled medium-size fresh shrimp
4 quarts water
12 ounces uncooked thin spaghetti, broken
1½ pounds fresh broccoli flowerets
⅓ cup creamy peanut butter
¼ cup soy sauce

3 tablespoons rice vinegar
2 tablespoons sesame oil
1 tablespoon chili oil
1 tablespoon grated fresh ginger
3 cloves garlic, minced
4 green onions, chopped
⅓ cup almonds

Peel shrimp, and devein, if desired. Set aside.

Bring water to a boil in a Dutch oven. Add pasta, and cook 4 minutes. Add broccoli and shrimp, and cook 3 minutes or until shrimp turn pink.

Combine peanut butter and next 6 ingredients in a small bowl; stir well with a wire whisk.

Drain spaghetti mixture, and return to Dutch oven. Add peanut butter mixture, green onions, and almonds; toss to coat well. Yield: 4 servings.

Kathy Thames

Recipes & Remembrances
Frank P. Tillman Elementary PTO
Kirkwood, Missouri

Meats

Peach-Glazed Virginia Ham, page 204

Chili Spiced Brisket

The pan juices from this brisket provide a flavorful topping for mashed potatoes.

1 (4-pound) beef brisket
1 tablespoon vegetable oil
¼ teaspoon salt
¼ teaspoon pepper
4 black peppercorns, crushed
1 bay leaf
1 cup chili sauce

1½ cups chopped onion
1 (10.5-ounce) can beef broth
1½ tablespoons brown sugar
1 tablespoon Worcestershire
  sauce
⅛ teaspoon garlic salt

Trim excess fat from brisket. Brown brisket in hot oil in a large Dutch oven on all sides. Add salt and next 5 ingredients to Dutch oven. Combine beef broth and remaining 3 ingredients; stir well. Pour over brisket. Cover and bake at 350° for 4 hours or until tender. Remove meat to a serving platter; keep warm.

Pour pan juices through a wire-mesh strainer into a bowl, discarding solids. Slice meat across grain into thin slices, and serve with pan juices. Yield: 8 to 10 servings.

Beyond Chicken Soup
Jewish Home of Rochester Auxiliary
Rochester, New York

Garofaloto (Italian Pot Roast)

10 whole cloves
1 (4-pound) beef chuck roast
3 tablespoons olive oil, divided
3 cloves garlic, crushed
¼ teaspoon pepper

1 cup dry red wine
1 (14.5-ounce) can diced
  tomatoes, undrained
1½ teaspoons salt
1 teaspoon sugar

Press cloves into 1 side of roast. Poke holes in opposite side of roast, using a metal skewer. Pour 1 tablespoon oil into holes in roast. Let roast stand 30 minutes in refrigerator.

Brown roast on all sides in remaining 2 tablespoons hot oil in a large Dutch oven. Add garlic and next 3 ingredients. Bring to a boil; cover, reduce heat, and simmer 3 to 3½ hours or until tender.

Remove roast to a serving platter; discard cloves. Pour pan juices through a fine wire-mesh strainer, and return to Dutch oven, discarding solids; skim off fat. Add salt and sugar to pan juices. Bring to a boil over high heat; cook, uncovered, until reduced by half. Serve sauce over roast. Yield: 10 to 12 servings.

Judith Merrill

Expressions
National League of American Pen Women, Chester County
Coatesville, Pennsylvania

South-of-the-Border Stir-Fry

Turn up the heat by using hot salsa to this southwestern dish.

1 cup chunky salsa, divided
  (we tested with Old El Paso)
¼ cup water
2 tablespoons minced fresh
  parsley
2 teaspoons white vinegar
¾ teaspoon cornstarch
½ teaspoon sugar
½ teaspoon ground cumin
¼ teaspoon salt
¼ teaspoon pepper
⅛ teaspoon ground cinnamon
1 tablespoon vegetable oil

1 clove garlic, minced
1 small onion, chopped
1 (1-pound) beef top round
  steak, sliced diagonally
  across grain into wafer-thin
  slices
1 (11-ounce) can Mexican-style
  corn, drained
1 (9-ounce) package tortilla
  chips
1 cup shredded lettuce
½ cup (2 ounces) shredded
  Monterey Jack cheese

Combine ½ cup salsa, water, and next 8 ingredients in a small bowl. Set salsa mixture aside.

Pour oil around top of a preheated wok, coating sides, and heat at medium-high (375°) for 2 minutes. Add garlic and onion; stir-fry 1 minute. Push onion and garlic to side of wok. Add beef; stir-fry 2 minutes or until browned. Push beef to side of wok; add salsa mixture, and cook until thickened and bubbly. Cook 2 more minutes, stirring to coat meat and vegetables with sauce. Cover and cook 1 minute; add corn, and cook until corn is thoroughly heated.

Divide tortilla chips evenly among four serving plates. Top evenly with meat mixture, remaining ½ cup salsa, shredded lettuce, and cheese. Yield: 4 servings.   Mary Jean Dzurisin

Cook Bookery
The University of Illinois College of Medicine at Peoria
Peoria, Illinois

Beef Tenderloin

Simple ingredients from your pantry parlay phenomenal flavor in this tenderloin.

½ cup dry red wine
⅓ cup tarragon vinegar
¼ cup olive oil
¼ cup soy sauce
1½ teaspoons seasoned salt

1 teaspoon dried parsley flakes
1 teaspoon paprika
1 (4- to 6-pound) beef
    tenderloin, trimmed

Combine first 7 ingredients; stir well. Place meat in a 13- x 9- x 2-inch baking dish. Pour marinade over meat, and cover tightly. Marinate in refrigerator 2 hours, turning meat after 1 hour.

Uncover meat, and broil 8 inches from heat (with electric oven door partially opened) 15 to 20 minutes on each side. Cover and bake at 350° for 30 more minutes or until a meat thermometer inserted in thickest part of tenderloin registers 145° (medium-rare) or 160° (medium). Remove to a serving platter. Let stand 10 minutes before slicing. Yield: 12 to 15 servings.

Joan White

75 Years and Still Cooking
Lakeside Presbyterian Church
Richmond, Virginia

Beef Tenderloin au Poivre

1 (4-pound) beef tenderloin,
  trimmed
⅓ cup Dijon mustard
1½ tablespoons black
  peppercorns, crushed

1½ tablespoons white
  peppercorns, crushed

Evenly shape tenderloin by tucking small end underneath; tie with string. Rub tenderloin with mustard.

Combine crushed peppercorns, and press evenly over surface of tenderloin. Place on a rack in a shallow roasting pan; bake, uncovered, at 425° for 45 minutes or until a meat thermometer inserted in thickest part of tenderloin registers 145° (medium-rare) or 160° (medium). Let stand 10 minutes before slicing. Yield: 12 servings.

Women Who Can Dish It Out
The Junior League of Springfield, Missouri

Grilled Filet Mignon

No need to light the grill for this steak. Grilled, in this recipe, refers to quick cooking in a skillet.

1 tablespoon cracked pepper
4 (4-ounce) beef tenderloin
  steaks (1 inch thick)
1 tablespoon butter
1 tablespoon olive oil

¼ cup dry sherry
¼ cup heavy whipping cream
2 tablespoons Dijon mustard
Garnish: minced fresh parsley

Press pepper into both sides of each steak. Cover; chill 30 minutes.

Heat butter and olive oil in a heavy skillet over medium-high heat. Cook steaks 10 minutes or to desired degree of doneness, turning once. Remove steaks from skillet, reserving drippings in skillet; keep steaks warm.

Add sherry, cream, and mustard to skillet; bring to a boil, stirring constantly. Pour over steaks. Garnish, if desired. Yield: 4 servings.

Symphony of Flavors
The Associates of the Redlands Bowl
Redlands, California

Grilled Sirloin Steak with Stilton Sauce

Stilton cheese stars in this delectable sauce that provides the perfect topping on grilled steak.

½ cup butter or margarine, melted
⅓ cup Worcestershire sauce
8 ounces Stilton cheese, crumbled

1 clove garlic, crushed
½ teaspoon salt
¼ teaspoon pepper
2 pounds lean boneless top sirloin steak (3 inches thick)

Combine first 4 ingredients in a medium saucepan. Cook over low heat until cheese melts, stirring constantly. Set aside ⅔ cup sauce; keep remaining sauce warm.

Sprinkle salt and pepper over steak. Grill, covered, over medium-hot coals (350° to 400°) 18 minutes on each side or to desired degree of doneness, basting often with ⅔ cup sauce. To serve, cut steak diagonally across grain. Serve with remaining sauce. Yield: 6 servings.

Savour St. Louis
Barnes-Jewish Hospital Auxiliary Plaza Chapter
St. Louis, Missouri

Hot Tamales

Find dry corn husks in the produce section of most supermarkets.

½ (8-ounce) package corn husks or about 9 whole dried corn husks (we tested with Don Enrique)
¾ cup yellow cornmeal
½ cup plus 1 tablespoon chili powder
3 tablespoons onion powder
1 tablespoon plus 1 teaspoon salt
1 tablespoon garlic powder
2 tablespoons ground cumin
1 tablespoon ground red pepper
1 teaspoon black pepper
3 pounds ground beef
1 (8-ounce) can tomato sauce
¾ cup water
1 large egg
Tamale Sauce

Place whole corn husks in a large bowl (each husk should contain several layers); cover with hot water. Let stand 1 to 2 hours or until softened. Remove any silks; wash husks well. Drain well; pat dry.

Combine cornmeal and next 11 ingredients; stir well. Roll meat mixture into 24 (4-inch-long) logs. Separate layers of corn husks. Place 1 log in center of 1 layer of corn husk; wrap husk tightly around meat. Twist ends of husks; tie securely with narrow strips of softened corn husk or pieces of string. Cut off long ends of husks, if necessary. (You may not need all of the corn husk layers.)

Layer tamales in a large Dutch oven. Pour Tamale Sauce over tamales; bring to a boil. Reduce heat; simmer, uncovered, 1½ hours, rearranging tamales every 30 minutes. Yield: 8 to 12 servings.

Tamale Sauce

1 (6-ounce) can tomato paste
¼ cup chili powder
2 tablespoons onion powder
1 tablespoon salt
1 tablespoon ground cumin
2 teaspoons garlic powder
9 cups water

Combine all ingredients in a large bowl, stirring until smooth. Yield: 9¼ cups.

Daniel Rigamer

Cooking from the Heart
Girl Scout Troop 669
Metairie, Louisiana

Stuffed Cabbage

1 medium cabbage (2½ pounds)
1 pound ground chuck
½ pound ground pork sausage
1 cup uncooked long-grain rice
1 medium onion, chopped
1 large egg, lightly beaten
1 clove garlic, minced
1 teaspoon salt
1 teaspoon dried oregano
1 teaspoon paprika
2 (8-ounce) cans tomato sauce

Remove 12 large outer leaves of cabbage; cook leaves in boiling water 5 to 8 minutes or until just tender; drain and set aside. Shred remaining cabbage, and set aside.

Combine ground chuck and next 8 ingredients in a large bowl. Spoon about ⅓ cup mixture in center of each cabbage leaf. Fold left and right sides of large leaf over; roll up, beginning at bottom. Repeat procedure with remaining cabbage leaves.

Arrange half of shredded cabbage in bottom of a Dutch oven. Top with cabbage rolls, seam side down. Place remaining shredded cabbage over rolls. Pour tomato sauce over top. Cover, reduce heat, and simmer 1½ hours. Yield: 6 servings.

Foods from the Homelands
Kingsburg Friends of the Library
Kingsburg, California

Veal Cutlet Provençale

Garlic, tomatoes, and olive oil ensure goodness as well as the authenticity of this dish prepared in the style of Provence, a region of southeastern France.

1½ teaspoons salt, divided
1 teaspoon pepper
2 pounds veal cutlets
1 cup all-purpose flour
½ cup olive oil
2 cloves garlic, minced

2 tomatoes, peeled, seeded, and chopped
½ cup dry red wine
2 tablespoons chopped fresh parsley
12 ripe olives, chopped

Sprinkle 1 teaspoon each salt and pepper over veal cutlets; dredge in flour. In 3 batches, sauté veal over medium-high heat 2 minutes on each side or until browned, using about one-third of olive oil for each batch; remove from pan, and keep warm.

Add garlic to pan; sauté 1 minute. Add tomato and wine, scraping bottom of pan to loosen browned bits. Return veal to pan, coating with sauce. Cover, reduce heat, and simmer over low heat 40 minutes or until veal is tender, stirring sauce and turning veal occasionally.

Transfer veal to a serving platter; keep warm. Stir parsley, olives, and remaining ½ teaspoon salt into sauce in pan. Spoon sauce over veal. Yield: 4 servings.

Ellen Vander Noot

Expressions
National League of American Pen Women, Chester County
Coatesville, Pennsylvania

Veal with Prosciutto and Sage

1 pound veal cutlets
⅓ cup all-purpose flour
½ teaspoon ground sage
2 tablespoons butter
2 tablespoons olive oil
1 cup water
¼ cup dry sherry

¾ teaspoon chicken-flavored
  bouillon granules
¼ pound sliced prosciutto, cut
  into ½-inch strips
⅛ teaspoon cracked pepper
2 teaspoons minced fresh
  parsley

Place veal between two sheets of heavy-duty plastic wrap, and flatten to ⅛-inch thickness, using a meat mallet or rolling pin. Cut veal into serving-size pieces. Pat veal dry. Combine flour and sage; dredge veal in flour mixture.

Heat butter and oil in a large skillet over medium-high heat. Add veal, in two batches, and cook 1 to 2 minutes on each side. Remove veal to a warm platter; cover and keep warm. Add water, sherry, and bouillon granules to drippings in skillet; bring to a boil. Return veal to skillet, and add prosciutto; cook until thoroughly heated. To serve, spoon sauce over veal and prosciutto; sprinkle evenly with pepper and parsley. Yield: 4 servings.

Carol La Nasa

Tasty Temptations
Our Lady of the Mountains Church
Sierra Vista, Arizona

Veal Chops with Caramelized Onions

This caramelized onion topping also complements pork chops.

¾ cup water
¼ cup fresh lemon juice
2 tablespoons minced garlic
½ teaspoon salt
½ teaspoon ground cumin
½ teaspoon paprika
¼ teaspoon black pepper
4 (1-inch-thick) veal chops, trimmed
3 cups sliced purple onion (about 1½ large onions)

¼ cup water
¼ cup firmly packed brown sugar
½ cup dry white wine
¼ cup white vinegar
1 teaspoon olive oil
¼ teaspoon salt
¼ teaspoon black pepper
⅛ teaspoon ground red pepper
Vegetable cooking spray

Combine first 7 ingredients in a large heavy-duty, zip-top plastic bag. Add veal chops; seal bag, turning to coat chops. Marinate in refrigerator 8 hours, turning occasionally.

Combine onion and water in a small Dutch oven; bring to a boil. Cover, reduce heat, and cook over medium heat 5 minutes. Add brown sugar and next 6 ingredients to Dutch oven. Cover and cook over medium-low heat 50 minutes, stirring occasionally. Uncover and cook over medium-high heat 10 minutes or until liquid thickens.

Remove chops from marinade, discarding marinade.

Place a large skillet over medium-high heat until very hot. Coat chops with cooking spray; add to pan. Cook 12 to 15 minutes, turning occasionally, until a meat thermometer inserted in thickest part of chops registers 160°. Spoon caramelized onion over chops. Yield: 4 servings.

Shalom on the Range
Shalom Park
Aurora, Colorado

Spinach Stuffed Leg of Lamb

2 (10-ounce) packages fresh
   spinach, chopped
1 tablespoon salt
½ cup olive oil, divided
1 cup thinly sliced green onions
¼ cup chopped fresh parsley
¼ cup fine, dry breadcrumbs
   (store-bought)
1 large egg, lightly beaten
2 tablespoons dried dillweed
2¼ teaspoons dried oregano,
   divided
⅛ teaspoon freshly ground
   pepper

1 (7-pound) boneless leg of
   lamb, trimmed
3 tablespoons fresh lemon
   juice
2 cloves garlic, minced
2 teaspoons salt
½ teaspoon freshly ground
   pepper
1 cup crumbled feta cheese
1 cup hot water
3 to 4 large red potatoes, cut
   into eighths

Place spinach in a colander; sprinkle with 1 tablespoon salt, tossing well. Let spinach stand 1 hour.

Heat ¼ cup oil in a large skillet; add green onions. Cook over medium heat, 8 minutes, stirring occasionally. Add spinach; cook over high heat 6 minutes or until liquid evaporates, stirring often. Remove from heat; stir in parsley. Cool 5 minutes; stir in breadcrumbs, egg, dillweed, ¼ teaspoon oregano, and ⅛ teaspoon pepper.

Place lamb, skin side down, on work surface; flatten slightly, using a meat mallet. Combine remaining ¼ cup oil, lemon juice, garlic, 2 teaspoons salt, remaining 2 teaspoons oregano, and ½ teaspoon pepper; rub half of mixture over cut side of lamb. Spread spinach mixture over cut side of lamb; sprinkle feta cheese over spinach mixture. Roll up lamb; tie securely. Transfer meat to a rack in a roasting pan. Rub remaining lemon juice mixture over outside of lamb. Add hot water to pan.

Bake lamb, uncovered, at 400° for 30 minutes. Reduce heat to 350°, and bake 30 more minutes. Arrange potato around rack in pan. Bake 1 to 1½ hours or until a meat thermometer inserted in thickest part of lamb registers 150° (medium-rare) or 160° (medium), basting lamb and potato occasionally. Transfer lamb and potato to a serving platter; skim fat from pan. Serve pan juices with lamb and potato. Yield: 10 to 12 servings.

Winnie Fitzpatrick

Flavors of Falmouth
Falmouth Historical Society
Falmouth, Massachusetts

Lamb with Feta Crust

Ask your butcher to french the rack of lamb. This term means to remove the meat from the end of a rib or chop to expose the bone. Frenching adds to the presentation of a rack of lamb.

¼ cup Italian-seasoned breadcrumbs (store-bought)
3 tablespoons crumbled feta cheese
2 cloves garlic, minced
½ teaspoon kosher salt
¼ teaspoon freshly ground pepper
2 teaspoons Dijon mustard
1 (8-rib) lamb rib roast (2¾ to 3 pounds), trimmed

Combine first 5 ingredients in a bowl. Spread mustard over lamb. Pat cheese mixture on lamb. Place lamb, fat side up, on a rack in a roasting pan. Shield exposed bones with strips of aluminum foil to prevent excessive browning.

Bake, uncovered, at 350° for 40 minutes or until a meat thermometer inserted in thickest part of roast registers 145°. Remove lamb from oven; cover loosely with aluminum foil, and let stand 5 minutes or until thermometer registers 150° (medium-rare). Yield: 4 servings.

Apron Strings: Ties to the Southern Tradition of Cooking
The Junior League of Little Rock, Arkansas

Braised Lamb Shanks

1 teaspoon salt
¼ teaspoon black pepper
6 (2-inch) slices cross-cut
   lamb shanks (about 3
   pounds)
2 tablespoons vegetable oil
1 small onion, thinly sliced
½ cup water
½ cup ketchup
¼ cup white vinegar

¼ cup butter or margarine
1 thick lemon slice
2 tablespoons sugar
2 tablespoons Worcestershire
   sauce
1 tablespoon prepared mustard
1½ teaspoons salt
½ teaspoon black pepper
¼ teaspoon ground red pepper

Sprinkle 1 teaspoon salt and ¼ teaspoon black pepper over lamb shanks. Cook in hot oil in a Dutch oven over medium-high heat until shanks brown, turning occasionally.

Combine onion and remaining 11 ingredients in a small saucepan; bring to a boil. Reduce heat, and simmer, uncovered, 10 minutes. Pour mixture over lamb. Cover and simmer 2 hours or until lamb shanks are tender, basting occasionally. Skim off fat; discard lemon. Yield: 4 to 6 servings.   Mrs. Philip D. Block III

Fishing for Compliments
Shedd Aquarium Society
Chicago, Illinois

Grilled Lamb Chops with Gorgonzola Butter

This tasty recipe can be halved easily to serve 4. As an option, shape the butter mixture into an 8-inch log and chill 8 hours or until firm; cut into ½-inch slices to serve.

16 lamb loin chops (1½ inches thick)
1 cup olive oil
8 shallots, minced
¼ cup minced garlic
1 tablespoon plus 1 teaspoon dried rosemary
Gorgonzola Butter

Trim excess fat from lamb chops; place chops in a heavy-duty, zip-top plastic bag or shallow dish.

Combine oil and next 3 ingredients; stir well. Pour over chops. Seal or cover, and marinate in refrigerator 8 hours.

Remove chops from marinade, discarding marinade. Drain excess marinade from chops to prevent flare-ups.

Grill chops, covered, over medium coals (300° to 350°) 8 to 10 minutes on each side or to desired degree of doneness. Top each chop with Gorgonzola Butter. Yield: 8 servings.

Gorgonzola Butter

1 cup butter, softened
6 ounces Gorgonzola cheese, softened
2 tablespoons olive oil
2 tablespoons fresh lemon juice
1 tablespoon plus 1 teaspoon minced shallots
2 teaspoons minced garlic
½ teaspoon kosher salt
½ teaspoon freshly ground pepper

Combine all ingredients in a large mixing bowl; beat at medium speed of an electric mixer until smooth. Shape mixture into 16 (1-inch) patties. Cover and freeze 3 hours or until firm. Yield: 1¾ cups.

Great Lake Effects
The Junior League of Buffalo, New York

Oriental Lamb Chops

You probably have all the ingredients on hand to stir up the tangy-sweet marinade for these lamb chops. The marinade pairs equally well with pork.

6 (1-inch-thick) lamb sirloin chops
⅓ cup soy sauce
¼ cup sugar
1 teaspoon powdered sugar
1 teaspoon minced garlic
¼ teaspoon salt

Trim excess fat from lamb chops; place chops in a heavy-duty, zip-top plastic bag or shallow dish.

Combine soy sauce and remaining 4 ingredients; stir well. Pour over chops. Seal or cover, and marinate in refrigerator 4 hours, turning occasionally.

Remove chops from marinade, reserving marinade. Bring marinade to a boil in a small saucepan; set aside.

Grill chops, covered, over medium coals (300° to 350°) 8 to 10 minutes on each side or to desired degree of doneness, basting often with marinade. Yield: 6 servings.

Kevin Converse

Iowa: A Taste of Home
Iowa 4-H Foundation
Ames, Iowa

Rio Grande Pork Loin

Hickory flavor permeates this pork loin that's slowly smoked and basted with a tangy sauce of chili powder and apple jelly. The results are a mouthwatering entrée that you can't wait to sink your teeth into.

Hickory or mesquite chunks
1 teaspoon chili powder, divided
½ cup apple jelly
½ cup ketchup
1 tablespoon white vinegar
½ teaspoon salt
½ teaspoon garlic salt
1 (4-pound) rolled boneless pork loin roast
Vegetable cooking spray

Soak hickory or mesquite chunks in water 30 minutes. Prepare charcoal fire in smoker, and let burn 10 to 15 minutes. Drain chunks, and place on hot coals. Place water pan in smoker, and fill with water.

Combine ½ teaspoon chili powder and next 3 ingredients in a small saucepan. Bring to a boil; reduce heat to medium, and cook, stirring constantly, 2 minutes. Reserve ¼ cup sauce for basting and ¾ cup sauce to serve with pork loin.

Combine remaining ½ teaspoon chili powder, salt, and garlic salt; mix well. Rub roast with seasoning mix; brush roast with reserved basting sauce. Coat food rack with cooking spray, and place over coals. Place roast on rack; cover with smoker lid, and cook 5 hours or until a meat thermometer inserted in thickest part of roast registers 160° (medium), refilling water pan and adding charcoal as needed. Baste twice while cooking.

Remove roast from food rack. Let stand 10 minutes before slicing. Serve with reserved ¾ cup sauce. Yield: 10 to 12 servings.

Beneath the Palms
The Brownsville Junior Service League
Brownsville, Texas

Apricot-Pecan Stuffed Pork Tenderloins

1½ cups dried apricots
½ cup pecan pieces
1 clove garlic
½ teaspoon salt
¼ teaspoon pepper
2 tablespoons dried thyme, divided

2 tablespoons vegetable oil, divided
1 tablespoon molasses
2 (1-pound) pork tenderloins
1 cup chicken broth

Process first 5 ingredients in a food processor until finely chopped. Add 1 tablespoon thyme, 1 tablespoon oil, and molasses; process until thyme is finely chopped.

Slice each tenderloin lengthwise down center, cutting to, but not through, bottom. Place each tenderloin between two sheets of heavy-duty plastic wrap; pound to ½-inch thickness, using a meat mallet or rolling pin. Spoon half of stuffing onto 1 tenderloin; roll up tenderloin, jellyroll fashion, starting at short side. Tie with heavy string at 1½-inch intervals. Repeat procedure with remaining tenderloin and stuffing.

Place tenderloins, seam side down, in a shallow roasting pan. Brush lightly with remaining 1 tablespoon oil; sprinkle with remaining 1 tablespoon thyme. Pour chicken broth over tenderloins. Bake at 350° for 1 hour and 10 minutes or until a meat thermometer inserted in thickest part of tenderloin registers 160° (medium). Yield: 6 to 8 servings.

Landmark Entertaining
The Junior League of Abilene, Texas

Pork Tenderloin with Maple Mustard Sauce

⅓ cup maple syrup
2 tablespoons Dijon mustard
½ teaspoon nutmeg
½ teaspoon dried thyme, crushed
¼ teaspoon dried basil, crushed
¼ teaspoon ground red pepper
¼ teaspoon ground cloves
¼ teaspoon ground cinnamon
¼ teaspoon black pepper
⅛ teaspoon ground allspice
1 (12- to 16-ounce) pork tenderloin
3 bay leaves
Olive oil-flavored cooking spray

Combine maple syrup and mustard in a small bowl; stir with a wire whisk until blended. Set Maple Mustard Sauce aside.

Combine nutmeg and next 7 ingredients in a bowl; stir well. Rub mixture over tenderloin. Place tenderloin on a large sheet of heavy-duty plastic wrap. Place bay leaves along bottom of tenderloin. Wrap tenderloin in plastic wrap; marinate in refrigerator at least 2 hours.

Remove tenderloin from plastic wrap, and place tenderloin on a rack in a shallow roasting pan. Coat tenderloin with cooking spray. Bake at 425° for 25 to 35 minutes or until a meat thermometer inserted in thickest part of tenderloin registers 160°. Discard bay leaves. Place tenderloin on a serving platter; slice diagonally across grain. Serve with reserved Maple Mustard Sauce. Yield: 3 to 4 servings.

A Taste of the Good Life from the Heart of Tennessee
Saint Thomas Heart Institute
Nashville, Tennessee

Adams' Ribs

We loved the spicy bite these ribs have. For the milder palette, simply reduce the amount of seasonings.

1 tablespoon garlic powder
1 tablespoon Creole seasoning
2 tablespoons pepper
1 tablespoon Worcestershire sauce
2 (3- to 4-pound) slabs pork spareribs
Vegetable cooking spray
Basting Sauce
Serving Sauce

Combine first 4 ingredients; rub on all sides of ribs.

Using a gas grill, light one burner, placing drip pan on opposite side. Coat food rack over drip pan with cooking spray, and place rack on grill.

Arrange ribs on rack over drip pan. Grill, covered, over medium-low coals (275° to 325°) 2 to 3 hours, turning and basting with Basting Sauce every hour. (The longer ribs cook, the more tender they will be.)

Grill, covered, over medium-hot coals (350° to 400°) 1 more hour, basting every 10 minutes. Serve with Serving Sauce. Yield: 8 to 10 servings.

Basting Sauce

3 cups red wine vinegar
1 cup dry white wine
1 cup water
¾ cup ketchup
¼ cup Worcestershire sauce
¼ cup firmly packed brown
   sugar

¼ cup prepared mustard
2 tablespoons black pepper
1 to 2 tablespoons ground red
   pepper or dried crushed red
   pepper

Combine all ingredients in a saucepan; bring to a boil. Reduce heat to medium, and simmer, uncovered, 1 hour. Yield: about 4½ cups.

Serving Sauce

1 medium onion, finely
   chopped
1½ teaspoons minced garlic
   (about 4 cloves)
1 tablespoon butter or
   margarine, melted
1 cup ketchup

½ cup white vinegar
¼ cup lemon juice
¼ cup steak seasoning (we
   tested with Dale's)
2 tablespoons brown sugar
1 tablespoon Cajun seasoning
2 tablespoons liquid smoke

Cook onion and garlic in melted butter in a large skillet over medium heat, stirring constantly, 5 minutes or until tender. Add ketchup and remaining ingredients; bring to a boil. Reduce heat, and simmer, uncovered, 15 minutes. Yield: 2 cups.   Oscar W. Adams

Southern Settings
Decatur General Foundation, Inc.
Decatur, Alabama

Ono Spareribs

Finger-licking good is the way we describe the tasty sauce that cloaks these ribs. Serve the sauce over pork tenderloin for variety, if desired.

5 pounds country-style pork ribs
1 (2-inch) piece fresh ginger, peeled and grated
1 cup ketchup
¾ cup sugar
¾ cup soy sauce
⅓ cup oyster sauce
¼ cup dry red wine

Place ribs and ginger in a large Dutch oven; add water to cover ribs. Bring to a boil; cover, reduce heat, and simmer 45 minutes or until tender. Drain and return ribs to Dutch oven.

Combine ketchup and remaining 4 ingredients; pour over ribs. Cover and simmer over low heat 1 hour and 15 minutes or until ribs are very tender. Yield: 6 servings.

The Tastes and Tales of Moiliili
Moiliili Community Center
Honolulu, Hawaii

Pork Kabobs with Peanut Sauce

¼ cup vegetable oil
¼ cup dry sherry
¼ cup soy sauce
2 tablespoons brown sugar
3 tablespoons fresh lemon
  juice
2 tablespoons honey
1 tablespoon sesame oil

1 tablespoon minced fresh
  ginger
2 cloves garlic, minced
3 pounds lean boneless pork,
  cut into 2-inch cubes
Vegetable cooking spray
Peanut Sauce

Combine first 9 ingredients; stir well. Place pork in a heavy-duty, zip-top plastic bag or shallow dish. Pour marinade over pork. Seal or cover, and marinate in refrigerator 3 hours, turning occasionally.

Remove pork from marinade, reserving ⅓ cup marinade for Peanut Sauce.

Thread pork onto six metal skewers. Coat food rack with cooking spray; place kabobs on grill. Grill, covered, over medium-hot coals (350° to 400°) 20 minutes or until done, turning occasionally. Serve with Peanut Sauce. Yield: 6 servings.

Peanut Sauce

⅓ cup reserved marinade
⅓ cup creamy peanut butter
½ cup heavy whipping cream
2 tablespoons soy sauce

2 tablespoons sesame oil
½ teaspoon chili oil
½ teaspoon fresh lemon juice

Bring reserved ⅓ cup marinade to a boil in a small saucepan over medium heat. Add peanut butter and remaining ingredients, stirring with a wire whisk until smooth. Cook until sauce is thoroughly heated. Yield: 1¼ cups.

Project Open Hand Cookbook
Project Open Hand Atlanta
Atlanta, Georgia

Peach-Glazed Virginia Ham

1 (8-pound) Virginia smoked
   fully cooked ham half
   (shank end)
½ cup peach preserves
1 tablespoon stone-ground
   mustard

¾ teaspoon hot sauce
⅛ teaspoon ground cloves
Peach-Corn Piccalilli
2 large ripe peaches, pitted and
   halved

Score fat on ham in a diamond design. Place ham, fat side up, on a rack in a roasting pan. Insert a meat thermometer, making sure it does not touch fat or bone. Bake, uncovered, at 325° for 1 hour and 45 minutes or until meat thermometer registers 135°.

Combine peach preserves and next 3 ingredients. Remove ham from oven, and brush with glaze. Bake 20 more minutes or until thermometer registers 140°.

Place ham on a serving platter. Spoon Peach-Corn Piccalilli into peach halves. Arrange peach halves on platter around ham. Yield: 16 servings.

Peach-Corn Piccalilli

1 tablespoon vegetable oil
1 sweet red pepper, chopped
2 green onions, sliced
1 (15¼-ounce) can whole
   kernel corn, drained
2 tablespoons brown sugar

2 tablespoons cider vinegar
1 teaspoon hot sauce
¼ teaspoon salt
1 large ripe peach, peeled and
   chopped

Heat oil in a medium saucepan over medium heat until hot. Add pepper and green onions; cook 3 minutes, stirring often. Add corn and next 4 ingredients; bring to a boil. Stir in chopped peach. Cover, reduce heat, and simmer 5 minutes or just until peach is heated. Yield: 2¾ cups.

Shirley Downing

Our Favorite Recipes
Claremont Society for the Prevention of Cruelty to Animals
Serving Sullivan County
Claremont, New Hampshire

Venison Grillades and Grits

2 tablespoons vegetable oil
2 tablespoons all-purpose flour
2 pounds bone-in venison roast
1 (14½-ounce) can diced
  tomatoes, undrained
1 cup chopped onion
½ cup chopped green pepper
3 cloves garlic, pressed

1 tablespoon chopped fresh
  parsley
1½ teaspoons salt
½ teaspoon dried oregano
¼ teaspoon ground red pepper
¼ teaspoon black pepper
Hot cooked grits

Heat oil in a small skillet over medium heat; stir in flour, using a wire whisk. Cook, stirring constantly, until mixture thickens and turns golden; place in a 5-quart electric slow cooker.

Add venison and next 9 ingredients. Cover and cook on HIGH setting 4 to 5 hours. (For longer cooking time, cover and cook on HIGH setting 1 hour; reduce to LOW setting for 7 to 8 hours.) Remove meat from bone; return meat to slow cooker, stirring to blend. Spoon over grits. Yield: 4 to 6 servings.

Randy Wiest

Bartlett Memorial Hospital's 25th Anniversary Cookbook
Bartlett Memorial Hospital
Juneau, Alaska

Venison Steak with Green Peppercorn Sauce

3 cloves garlic, minced
2 tablespoons olive oil
4 (8-ounce) venison steaks
  (1 inch thick)

¼ teaspoon salt
¼ teaspoon pepper
Green Peppercorn Sauce

Rub garlic and olive oil over venison. Place in a large heavy-duty, zip-top plastic bag or shallow dish. Seal or cover, and marinate in refrigerator 4 hours. Remove venison, and sprinkle both sides with salt and pepper.

Grill, covered, over medium-hot coals (350° to 400°) 6 minutes on each side or to desired degree of doneness. Serve with Green Peppercorn Sauce. Yield: 4 servings.

Green Peppercorn Sauce

2 tablespoons whole green
  peppercorns
¼ teaspoon salt

¼ teaspoon pepper
1 tablespoon cognac
¼ cup unsalted butter

Combine first 4 ingredients in a small saucepan. Bring to a boil; reduce heat, and simmer 1 minute, stirring constantly. Add butter, stirring until melted. Yield: ¼ cup.

David Gallup

'Pon Top Edisto
Trinity Episcopal Church
Edisto Island, South Carolina

Pasta, Rice & Grains

Pasta with Tomatoes, Brie, and Basil, page 215

Shrimp and Tasso Pasta

Tasso is a smoked and highly seasoned pork commonly used to impart traditional Cajun flavor. Find it at the meat counter of most large supermarkets.

1 cup chopped onion
½ cup chopped green pepper
¼ cup chopped celery
3 cloves garlic, minced
¼ cup plus 2 tablespoons butter
½ cup chopped tasso
1 teaspoon Cajun seasoning (we tested with Tony Chachere's)
¼ teaspoon salt
¼ teaspoon pepper
1 cup milk or half-and-half, divided
1 tablespoon all-purpose flour

2 (5-ounce) cans evaporated milk
1 pound unpeeled medium-size fresh shrimp, peeled and deveined
8 ounces dried angel hair pasta, uncooked
2 tablespoons freshly grated Parmesan cheese
1 tablespoon chopped fresh basil
1 tablespoon chopped fresh oregano
1 tablespoon chopped fresh thyme

Sauté first 4 ingredients in butter in a large skillet over medium-high heat 5 minutes. Add tasso and next 3 ingredients, stirring well.

Combine 1 tablespoon milk and 1 tablespoon flour, stirring until smooth. Add milk mixture, remaining milk, and evaporated milk to vegetable mixture in skillet; cook, stirring constantly, 3 minutes or until slightly thickened. Add shrimp, and cook 8 minutes or until shrimp turn pink.

Meanwhile, cook pasta according to package directions; drain well. Serve shrimp mixture over hot cooked pasta. Sprinkle with cheese and herbs. Yield: 4 servings.   Ellen Blanchard

Nun Better: Tastes and Tales from Around a Cajun Table
St. Cecilia School
Broussard, Louisiana

Sun-Dried Tomato Pasta

Colorful strips of sweet peppers and chiffonades (thin shreds) of fresh spinach and basil highlight this dried tomato pasta.

¼ cup pine nuts
3 tablespoons plus ½ teaspoon olive oil, divided
1 cup sliced shallot (5 shallots)
1 large sweet red pepper, cut into thin strips
1 large sweet yellow pepper, cut into thin strips
2 cups tightly packed fresh spinach, cut into thin shreds
½ cup shredded fresh basil
½ cup drained oil-packed dried tomatoes
2 (14½-ounce) cans chicken broth
3 cups water
1 (8-ounce) package dried angel hair pasta
¾ cup freshly grated Parmesan cheese

Sauté pine nuts in ½ teaspoon olive oil in a large skillet until golden; set aside. Add remaining 3 tablespoons olive oil, and heat over medium heat; add shallot and peppers, and cook 3 minutes. Add spinach and basil; cook until tender. Reduce heat to low, and add tomatoes. Cook just until heated.

Combine chicken broth and water in a large Dutch oven; bring to a boil. Add pasta, and cook according to package directions; drain well, reserving ½ cup broth mixture. Place cooked pasta in a large bowl, and toss with reserved broth mixture. Add vegetable mixture, cheese, and pine nuts; toss gently. Yield: 4 servings.

Jane Byington

Fruits of Our Labor
St. Joseph Parish
Lincoln, Nebraska

Spinach-Garlic Pasta

Making homemade pasta requires passion and plenty of time, but it's well worth the effort once you've savored every bite. Try making the dough the day before and refrigerating it overnight before rolling and cutting it.

1 (10-ounce) package fresh spinach
2 cups all-purpose flour, divided
2 large eggs
4 egg yolks
1 tablespoon olive oil or vegetable oil
6 large cloves garlic, crushed and minced
½ teaspoon salt
Garlic-Onion Sauce
½ cup freshly grated Parmesan cheese (optional)

Place spinach in a large saucepan; add water to depth of 2 inches. Bring to a boil; cook just until spinach wilts, stirring occasionally. Drain well; press spinach between paper towels until barely moist. Finely chop spinach, and set aside.

Place 1 cup flour in a large bowl; make a well in center. Combine eggs, egg yolks, oil, garlic, salt, and reserved spinach, stirring until blended; add to flour. Whisk egg mixture with a fork, gradually stirring in flour from bottom of well. Continue stirring, working in remaining flour in bowl. Gradually add some of remaining 1 cup flour if mixture is sticky.

Begin kneading dough by hand on work surface. Continue kneading and dusting with remaining flour until dough is no longer sticky and springs back when pressed in center. Reserve any remaining flour. Cover dough with plastic wrap. Let rest 1 hour or place dough in an airtight container; chill up to 8 hours.

Divide dough into 4 portions, keeping reserved dough covered to prevent drying. Working with 1 portion at a time, pass dough through smooth rollers of pasta machine on widest setting. Brush dough lightly with remaining flour, using a pastry brush; fold in half, and brush both sides with flour. Repeat rolling and brushing procedure until dough becomes smooth and pliable.

Pass dough through rollers 2 through 6, repeating brushing and folding procedure if dough becomes sticky. Brush dough with flour; pass through fettuccine-sized cutting rollers. Hang pasta to dry on a wooden rack for no longer than 30 minutes. Repeat procedure with remaining portions of dough.

Cook pasta in boiling salted water 2 minutes or until al dente; drain. Toss with Garlic-Onion Sauce, and sprinkle with Parmesan cheese, if desired. Yield: 4 cups.

Garlic-Onion Sauce

½ cup butter or margarine
1 tablespoon olive oil
1 large Vidalia or other sweet
  onion, sliced (about 1 pound)
⅓ cup chopped fresh garlic
  (about 12 large cloves)

1 tablespoon honey
¼ cup dry Marsala wine
¼ teaspoon salt

Heat butter and oil in a large skillet over medium heat. Add onion and garlic; cook 5 minutes or until soft. Reduce heat to medium-low; stir in honey. Cook, uncovered, 30 minutes, stirring occasionally. Add wine and salt to skillet, and cook over medium heat 10 minutes. Yield: 1½ cups.

Marsha Farris

Mediterranean Delights
St. Elias Orthodox Theotokos Society/Philoptochos Society
St. Elias Orthodox Church
New Castle, Pennsylvania

Blackened Chicken Fettuccine

1 tablespoon garlic powder
1 tablespoon onion powder
1 tablespoon dried thyme
1 tablespoon dried oregano
1 tablespoon paprika
1 tablespoon dried tarragon
1 tablespoon ground nutmeg
1 teaspoon salt
1 teaspoon ground red pepper
½ teaspoon black pepper
⅔ cup olive oil
½ cup Worcestershire sauce
5 skinned and boned chicken breast halves
¼ cup butter, melted
1 (12-ounce) package dried fettuccine

½ sweet red pepper, cut into thin strips
½ sweet yellow pepper, cut into thin strips
½ green pepper, cut into thin strips
2 stalks celery, chopped
1 medium onion, chopped
2 carrots, scraped and diagonally sliced
3 medium tomatoes, chopped
1 cup dry white wine
¾ cup whipping cream
2 tablespoons water
1 teaspoon cornstarch
Freshly grated Parmesan cheese

Combine first 12 ingredients in a heavy-duty, zip-top plastic bag; add chicken. Seal bag, and marinate in refrigerator 8 hours, turning bag occasionally.

Remove chicken from bag, discarding marinade. Cook chicken in melted butter in a large skillet over medium-high heat 5 minutes on each side or until browned. Remove chicken from skillet, reserving drippings in skillet. Slice chicken diagonally, and set aside.

Cook pasta according to package directions; drain well. Set aside.

Sauté peppers, celery, onion, and carrot in drippings in skillet 6 minutes or until vegetables are crisp-tender. Add tomato, wine, and whipping cream; simmer 5 minutes.

Combine water and cornstarch; stir well. Add to vegetable mixture in skillet. Bring to a boil; boil 1 minute or until thickened, stirring constantly. Remove from heat. Add chicken and pasta, tossing well; sprinkle with Parmesan cheese. Yield: 6 servings.

Linen Napkins to Paper Plates
The Junior Auxiliary of Clarksville, Tennessee

Asparagus and Onion Lasagna

2½ pounds sweet onions,
   thinly sliced (about 6 cups)
½ cup plus 2 tablespoons
   butter, divided
¼ teaspoon salt
¼ teaspoon pepper
½ cup dry white wine
1½ pounds asparagus, cut into
   1-inch pieces
½ cup all-purpose flour

2½ cups milk
¼ teaspoon salt
⅛ teaspoon pepper
1½ cups freshly grated
   Parmesan cheese, divided
1 (8-ounce) package no-boil
   lasagna noodles
2 cups (8 ounces) shredded
   mozzarella cheese

Cook onion in 2 tablespoons melted butter in a large skillet over medium heat 15 minutes or until tender, stirring often. Add ¼ teaspoon salt and ¼ teaspoon pepper; stir well. Add wine, and cook 5 more minutes. Transfer to a bowl.

Cook asparagus in 2 tablespoons melted butter in same skillet over medium heat just until tender. Set aside.

Melt remaining ¼ cup plus 2 tablespoons butter in a heavy saucepan over low heat; add flour, stirring until smooth. Cook 1 minute, stirring constantly. Gradually add milk; cook over medium heat, stirring constantly, until mixture is thickened and bubbly. Stir in ¼ teaspoon salt, ⅛ teaspoon pepper, and 1 cup grated Parmesan cheese.

Spread ½ cup sauce in a greased 13- x 9- x 2-inch baking dish. Layer 4 lasagna noodles, half of cooked onions, half of asparagus, ⅔ cup mozzarella cheese, and 1 cup sauce in prepared dish. Repeat layers; top with 4 lasagna noodles, remaining sauce, remaining mozzarella cheese, and remaining ½ cup Parmesan cheese. Cover and bake at 375° for 25 minutes or until bubbly. Let stand 10 minutes before serving. Yield: 6 to 8 servings.

Capital Celebrations
The Junior League of Washington, DC

Pesto Pasta Rolls

Turn to these ham and cheese pasta rolls for a handy, make-ahead option as a light lunch or as impressive appetizers.

5 lasagna noodles
½ (8-ounce) package cream
   cheese, softened
1 tablespoon water
¼ cup sliced ripe olives
¼ cup finely chopped sweet
   red pepper

¼ cup pesto sauce
10 green leaf lettuce leaves,
   divided
5 to 6 ounces thinly sliced ham

Cook noodles according to package directions; drain.

Combine cream cheese and next 3 ingredients; stir well. Spread mixture evenly over 1 side of each noodle. Spread pesto sauce over cream cheese layer. Trim 5 leaves of lettuce as needed to fit over noodles. Place lettuce leaves over pesto layer. Trim ham as needed to fit over noodles; arrange ham over lettuce. Roll up noodles, jellyroll fashion. Cover and chill 2 hours.

Cut each roll in half crosswise. Secure with wooden picks, if desired. Serve on remaining 5 lettuce leaves. Yield: 5 servings.

Sterling Service
The Dothan Service League
Dothan, Alabama

Pasta with Michigan Morels

8 ounces dried linguine,
   uncooked
2 tablespoons unsalted butter
3 tablespoons chopped shallot
8 ounces fresh morel
   mushrooms, rinsed
1 teaspoon salt
¼ cup whipping cream

2 tablespoons cognac
3 tablespoons freshly grated
   Romano cheese
3 tablespoons chopped fresh
   parsley
¼ teaspoon freshly ground
   pepper

Cook linguine according to package directions; drain and set aside. Meanwhile, melt butter in a large cast-iron skillet over low heat. Add shallot, and cook until tender. Stir in mushrooms and salt; cook 10 minutes, stirring gently. Add whipping cream and cognac to skillet; simmer 5 minutes.

Pour mixture over hot linguine; toss well. Sprinkle with cheese, parsley, and pepper; serve hot. Yield: 4 servings.   Frank Beaver

Michigan Cooks
C.S. Mott Children's Hospital
Ann Arbor, Michigan

Pasta with Tomatoes, Brie, and Basil

This fabulous dish is best served hot and fresh. You can easily halve the recipe if it yields too much for your family. To julienne-slice fresh basil, roll several large leaves together, and thinly slice the roll crosswise.

1 (15-ounce) round Brie	⅛ teaspoon pepper
4 large ripe tomatoes	1½ pounds dried linguine,
½ cup plus 1 tablespoon olive	uncooked
oil, divided	½ cup freshly grated Parmesan
1 cup julienne-sliced fresh basil	cheese
3 cloves garlic, minced	Freshly ground pepper
½ teaspoon salt	

Remove rind from Brie, and cut Brie into ½-inch cubes.

Combine Brie, tomato, ½ cup oil, basil, and next 3 ingredients; toss well. Let stand at room temperature at least 2 hours.

Cook pasta according to package directions, adding remaining 1 tablespoon oil to water. Drain pasta, and toss with fresh tomato sauce. To serve, top each serving with 1 tablespoon Parmesan cheese, and sprinkle with freshly ground pepper. Yield: 8 servings.

Savour St. Louis
Barnes-Jewish Hospital Auxiliary Plaza Chapter
St. Louis, Missouri

Korean Noodles with Vegetables

Made with cellophane noodles, this is one of Korea's best-known dishes. The thin, dry noodles turn translucent upon cooking. The recipe uses dried rather than fresh mushrooms because dried have a more concentrated flavor. As with any stir-fry, be sure to allow plenty of preparation time.

10 medium-size dried shiitake
   mushrooms
1 tablespoon plus 1 teaspoon
   sugar, divided
2 tablespoons soy sauce,
   divided
2 tablespoons plus 1 teaspoon
   dark sesame oil, divided
1 green onion, chopped
1 teaspoon sesame seeds
½ teaspoon minced garlic
¼ teaspoon pepper
1½ tablespoons vegetable oil,
   divided

1 medium onion, cut into thin
   strips (about 1 cup)
½ cup julienne-sliced carrot
½ cup julienne-sliced sweet red
   pepper
½ cup julienne-sliced green
   pepper
1 cup cooked spinach, chopped
   (5 ounces fresh spinach)
¼ teaspoon salt
1 large egg, lightly beaten
8 cups water
5 ounces cellophane noodles,
   uncooked

Soak mushrooms in warm water to cover 15 minutes; drain. Place between paper towels, and squeeze until barely moist. Cut mushrooms into very thin strips.

Combine 1 teaspoon sugar, 1½ teaspoons soy sauce, 1 teaspoon sesame oil, green onion, sesame seeds, garlic, and ¼ teaspoon pepper; add mushrooms, and set aside.

Pour 1 tablespoon vegetable oil into a large nonstick skillet; place over medium-high heat until hot. Add onion and next 4 ingredients. Stir-fry 1 minute. Add salt and mushroom mixture; stir-fry 2 minutes or until onion is tender. Remove from skillet, and set aside.

Heat remaining 1½ teaspoons vegetable oil in a small skillet; add egg. Cook until set; do not stir. Cut egg into ¼-inch strips, and set aside.

Bring 8 cups water to a boil in a large saucepan; add noodles. Remove from heat, and set aside 10 minutes. Drain noodles; rinse well with cold water, and drain again.

Place noodles in a bowl, and add remaining 1 tablespoon sugar, 1½ tablespoons soy sauce, and 2 tablespoons sesame oil.

Add noodles and vegetables to skillet; stir-fry 1 minute. Transfer to a serving platter, and garnish with reserved egg strips. Serve warm or chilled. Yield: 6 servings.

International Home Cooking
The United Nations International School Parents' Association
New York, New York

Herbed Orzo

You can change the identity of this dish by varying the herbs you add. We used basil, oregano, thyme, and rosemary.

1 (16-ounce) package orzo	¼ cup chopped mixed fresh
¼ cup olive oil, divided	herbs
2 shallots, minced	⅓ cup dry white wine
1 tablespoon minced garlic	1 teaspoon salt
6 mushrooms, sliced	¼ teaspoon pepper
1 tomato, diced	

Cook orzo according to package directions; drain well. Toss with 1 tablespoon olive oil, and set aside.

Heat remaining 3 tablespoons olive oil in a large skillet over medium heat. Add shallot, garlic, and mushrooms; cook, stirring constantly, until tender. Add tomato, and cook 1 minute. Add mixed herbs and orzo; mix well. Stir in wine, salt, and pepper. Serve immediately. Yield: 8 servings.

Steve Williams

Gracious Gator Cooks
The Junior League of Gainesville, Florida

Tortellini in Cream Sauce

The cream sauce in this recipe is similar to a carbonara sauce.

2 (9-ounce) packages
  refrigerated tortellini
¼ cup chopped onion
½ cup julienne-sliced ham or
  Canadian bacon
½ cup sliced fresh mushrooms
2 tablespoons butter, melted
2 cups heavy whipping cream

1 cup freshly grated Parmesan
  cheese
¼ teaspoon salt
¼ teaspoon cracked black
  pepper
½ cup frozen English peas,
  thawed
Cracked pepper (optional)

Cook tortellini according to package directions; drain well.

Cook onion, ham, and mushrooms in butter in a large skillet over medium-high heat, stirring constantly, until tender. Add cream, cheese, salt, and ¼ teaspoon pepper; stir well. Add tortellini and peas. Cook over medium heat just until mixture thickens, stirring often. Sprinkle with additional cracked pepper, if desired. Serve immediately. Yield: 6 servings.   Elizabeth J. Early

Madalene Cooks–50 Years of Good Taste
Church of the Madalene
Tulsa, Oklahoma

Warm Ziti Pasta

If Italian cheese blend is not available in your area, use ¼ cup each of shredded mozzarella, provolone, Parmesan, Romano, fontina, and Asiago cheese.

8 ounces ziti pasta,
  uncooked
1 (14.5-ounce) can diced
  tomatoes, undrained
3 tablespoons olive oil
1½ tablespoons balsamic
  vinegar
1 clove garlic, minced
½ cup chopped oil-packed
  dried tomatoes, drained

⅓ cup chopped kalamata olives
½ cup chopped sweet red
  pepper
⅓ cup minced fresh basil
½ teaspoon freshly ground
  pepper
1½ cups shredded Italian 6
  cheese blend (we tested with
  Sargento)

Cook pasta according to package directions. While pasta cooks, combine tomatoes and remaining 9 ingredients in a large bowl; stir well, and set aside. Drain pasta, and combine immediately with tomato mixture; toss gently. Yield: 6 servings.

Shalom on the Range
Shalom Park
Aurora, Colorado

Hoppin' John with a Kick

For extra punch, use 2 pounds of hot sausage in this recipe and serve with additional hot sauce—guaranteed to keep your taste buds hoppin'!

1 (1-pound) package dried black-eyed peas	1 pound ground spicy pork sausage
1½ pounds smoked ham hock pieces	1 pound ground mild pork sausage
9 cups water, divided	1 large onion, chopped
1 teaspoon salt	1 tablespoon hot sauce
2 cups uncooked converted rice	½ teaspoon pepper
	Additional hot sauce (optional)

Sort and wash peas; place in a Dutch oven. Cover with water 2 inches above peas. Let soak at least 8 hours; drain.

Combine peas, ham hock pieces, and 5 cups water in a Dutch oven. Bring to a boil; reduce heat, and simmer, uncovered, 1 hour.

Meanwhile, bring 4 cups water and salt to a boil. Stir in rice; cover, reduce heat, and simmer 20 minutes or until water is absorbed and rice is tender. Remove rice from heat, and keep warm.

Cook sausage and onion in a large skillet, stirring until sausage crumbles; drain.

Remove fat and bone from ham hocks; chop meat. Return meat to peas. Add sausage mixture, rice, hot sauce, and pepper, stirring well. Cook, uncovered, over medium heat 10 minutes or until heated. Serve with additional hot sauce, if desired. Yield: 10 servings.

Tested By Time
Porter Gaud Parents Guild
Charleston, South Carolina

Seafood Risotto

This creamy shrimp and scallop risotto makes a meal with a crisp green salad and crusty bread.

2 tablespoons butter or margarine
3 tablespoons olive oil
½ small purple onion, chopped (about ⅔ cup)
2 cloves garlic, minced
½ pound unpeeled large fresh shrimp, peeled and deveined
½ pound sea scallops

1 cup uncooked Arborio rice
½ cup plus 2 tablespoons dry white wine, divided
5 to 6 cups fish stock, warmed
6 fresh basil leaves, chopped
½ cup half-and-half
½ cup freshly grated Parmesan or Romano cheese

Heat butter and olive oil in a large skillet over medium heat; add onion and garlic. Cook 4 minutes or until tender, stirring often. Add shrimp and scallops; cook 4 to 5 minutes or until almost done, turning often. Remove shrimp and scallops from skillet; set aside, and keep warm.

Add rice to skillet; cook, stirring constantly, 2 minutes. Add ½ cup wine. Cook, stirring constantly, until liquid evaporates. Add fish stock to rice mixture, ½ cup at a time, stirring constantly; allow liquid to be absorbed after each addition before adding more stock. Continue adding stock just until rice is al dente.

Stir in remaining 2 tablespoons wine; cook until absorbed. Stir in basil, half-and-half, Parmesan cheese, and reserved shrimp and scallops. Cook 2 to 3 minutes or until liquid is absorbed. Yield: 3 to 4 servings.

Anne Ryan

Note: In place of fish stock, you can use fish bouillon cubes dissolved in water. We tested with Knorr.

Fishing for Compliments
Shedd Aquarium Society
Chicago, Illinois

Browned Rice Pilaf with Vegetables and Garlic

1 medium onion, chopped
1 tablespoon olive oil
1½ cups uncooked brown rice
8 large cloves garlic, minced
3¾ cups water
1 teaspoon salt
1 cup fresh green beans, cut into 2-inch pieces (about ¼ pound)
1 large yellow squash, cubed
1 cup broccoli flowerets
1 cup fresh or frozen whole kernel corn, thawed
½ cup shredded carrot
⅓ cup chopped sweet red pepper
1 tablespoon sesame seeds, toasted
1 tablespoon reduced-sodium soy sauce

Cook onion in hot oil in a large heavy skillet over medium heat, stirring constantly, until onion is tender. Add rice and garlic; cook 1 minute, stirring constantly. Add water and salt; bring mixture to a boil. Cover, reduce heat, and simmer 45 minutes or until water is almost absorbed and rice is tender; do not stir.

Uncover skillet, and add beans, squash, broccoli, corn, and carrot to rice. Cover and cook 12 minutes or until vegetables are crisp-tender; remove from heat.

Add pepper, sesame seeds, and soy sauce; toss gently. Yield: 3 main-dish servings or 6 side-dish servings.

Perennial Palette
Southborough Gardeners
Southborough, Massachusetts

Wild Rice and Apples

4 cups water
1¼ cups (8 ounces) uncooked
  wild rice
1 teaspoon salt
½ cup chopped onion
½ cup butter, melted and
  divided

1 large Granny Smith apple,
  peeled, cored, and chopped
1 cup soft breadcrumbs
  (homemade)
½ cup soft chopped walnuts
¼ cup fresh orange juice

Bring water to a boil; add rice and salt. Return to a boil; cover, reduce heat, and simmer 50 minutes. Fluff rice with a fork. Simmer, uncovered, 10 minutes; drain any excess liquid.

Sauté onion in 3 tablespoons butter over medium heat until tender. Add onion mixture, remaining 5 tablespoons butter, chopped apple, and remaining 3 ingredients to rice, stirring well. Spoon into a greased 2-quart casserole. Cover and bake at 325° for 35 minutes. Yield: 6 servings.

Eat Your Dessert or You Won't Get Any Broccoli
Sea Pines Montessori School
Hilton Head Island, South Carolina

Cheesy Bulgur and Beans

1 cup bulgur
1 cup boiling water
2 tablespoons butter
1 medium onion, chopped
¾ cup sliced fresh mushrooms
1 (16-ounce) package frozen cut
  green beans
2 cups (8 ounces) shredded
  sharp Cheddar cheese,
  divided

1 (6.2-ounce) can kidney beans,
  rinsed and drained (1 cup)
1 teaspoon salt
⅛ teaspoon garlic powder
⅛ teaspoon pepper
⅛ teaspoon dried thyme

Soak bulgur in boiling water 1 hour; drain.

Melt butter in a large skillet over medium-high heat; add onion and mushrooms, and cook, stirring constantly, 3 minutes or until tender. Add green beans and 1½ cups cheese. Stir in bulgur and kidney beans; add salt and remaining 3 ingredients.

Spoon mixture into a lightly greased 1½-quart baking dish; bake, uncovered, at 375° for 25 minutes. Add remaining ½ cup cheese; bake 5 more minutes or until thoroughly heated. Yield: 6 main-dish or 12 side-dish servings.

The Cookbook of the Museum of Science, Boston
The Volunteer Service League of the Museum of Science, Boston
Boston, Massachusetts

Orange-Pineapple Couscous

1 (11-ounce) can mandarin oranges, undrained
2 cups orange juice
1½ teaspoons ground cumin
1 (10-ounce) package couscous
3 tablespoons olive oil
1 tablespoon reduced-sodium soy sauce
3 tablespoons lime juice
¼ cup chopped fresh cilantro
2 tablespoons chopped fresh basil
3 tablespoons chopped green onions
1½ teaspoons grated fresh ginger
1 (15¼-ounce) can pineapple tidbits in juice, drained
⅓ cup pine nuts, toasted

Drain oranges, reserving liquid. Set oranges aside.

Combine liquid, orange juice, and cumin in a large saucepan; bring to a boil. Stir in couscous. Cover, remove from heat, and let stand 5 minutes. Transfer couscous to a large bowl, and let cool.

Combine oil, soy sauce, and lime juice; stir into couscous. Gently stir in oranges, cilantro, and next 4 ingredients; sprinkle with pine nuts. Yield: 8 servings.

Women Who Can Dish It Out
The Junior League of Springfield, Missouri

Rowland's Blue Cheese Grits

These grits were a favorite in our Test Kitchens, even among those who don't consider themselves fond of blue cheese. A combination of creamy Baby Blue Saga, a soft, mellow cheese, and the firmer regular blue cheese add an interesting texture and flavor to these grits. We suggest serving them at a brunch or as a side dish with pork.

4 cups water
2 cups chicken broth
1 teaspoon salt
1 teaspoon pepper
2 cups uncooked regular grits

¼ cup butter
8 ounces blue cheese
6 ounces Baby Blue Saga cheese

Combine first 4 ingredients in a saucepan; bring to a boil. Stir in grits and butter.

Cook grits according to package directions, stirring occasionally. Remove from heat; stir in cheeses. Serve warm with sliced tomatoes, if desired. Yield: 8 servings.

Southern . . . On Occasion
The Junior League of Cobb-Marietta
Marietta, Georgia

Pies & Pastries

Peach-Raspberry Cobbler, page 239

Cranberry-Apple Custard Pie

Take advantage of the bounty that the fall season delivers, and prepare this pie for dessert.

1 cup graham cracker crumbs
⅓ cup quick-cooking oats, uncooked
½ cup butter or margarine, melted
¼ cup firmly packed brown sugar
Vegetable cooking spray
1 (8-ounce) package cream cheese, softened

1 large egg
¼ cup sugar
2 cups peeled, sliced cooking apple (we tested with Rome)
1 cup finely chopped fresh cranberries
1 tablespoon sugar

Combine first 4 ingredients; reserve ¼ cup crumb mixture. Press remaining crumb mixture in bottom and up sides of a 9-inch pieplate coated with cooking spray; set aside.

Beat cream cheese at medium speed of an electric mixer until creamy. Add egg and ¼ cup sugar; beat until smooth. Pour into prepared crust. Arrange apple slices over cream cheese mixture.

Combine cranberries and 1 tablespoon sugar; toss well. Sprinkle cranberry mixture evenly over apple. Sprinkle reserved ¼ cup crumb mixture over cranberry mixture.

Bake at 350° for 30 minutes or until crust is lightly browned. Let cool on a wire rack. Yield: one 9-inch pie.   Kimberly Kress

Note Worthy Recipes
Wilson Presbyterian Church
Clairton, Pennsylvania

Marsala-Peach Pie

½ cup sugar
2 tablespoons cornstarch
1 envelope unflavored gelatin
½ cup orange juice
½ cup water
1 tablespoon sugar

¼ cup sweet Marsala
6 large peaches, peeled, pitted, and sliced (about 7 cups)
1 baked 9-inch pastry shell
1 cup heavy whipping cream, whipped

Combine first 3 ingredients in a medium saucepan, stirring well with a wire whisk. Gradually stir in orange juice and water; let stand 1 minute. Bring to a boil, stirring constantly; reduce heat to medium-high, and cook, stirring constantly, until mixture thickens. Let cool completely, stirring occasionally.

Meanwhile, sprinkle 1 tablespoon sugar and Marsala over peaches; stir gently, and set aside while gelatin mixture cools.

Combine gelatin mixture and peach mixture, stirring gently; spoon into pastry shell. Cover and chill at least 2 hours.

Spread whipped cream over peach filling just before serving. Yield: one 9-inch pie.

Maureen Tirone

What's Cooking in Hampton
Friends of Hampton Community Library
Allison Park, Pennsylvania

Freda's Pear Pie

1 large egg, lightly beaten	3 cups peeled, chopped fresh
½ cup sugar	pear (we tested with Anjou)
1 (8-ounce) carton sour cream	1 unbaked 9-inch pastry shell
1 tablespoon all-purpose flour	⅔ cup all-purpose flour
1 teaspoon vanilla extract	⅓ cup sugar
⅛ teaspoon salt	¼ cup butter

Combine first 6 ingredients in a medium bowl, stirring until blended; stir in chopped pear. Pour mixture into pastry shell; bake at 350° for 15 minutes.

Meanwhile, combine ⅔ cup flour and ⅓ cup sugar; cut in butter with a pastry blender until mixture is crumbly. Remove pie from oven, and sprinkle with flour mixture. Bake 35 more minutes or until golden. Yield: one 9-inch pie.

Sherrie Rawlings Nagy

United Church of Tekoa Cookbook
United Church of Tekoa
Tekoa, Washington

Whiskey Pie

Blackberry jam is the basis of this pie that is loaded with bourbon. A topping of ice cream or whipping cream pairs well with this finale.

3 large eggs, lightly beaten
1 (12-ounce) jar blackberry jam
¼ cup sugar
¼ cup bourbon
2½ tablespoons butter,
   softened

1 teaspoon vanilla extract
⅛ teaspoon ground mace
1 unbaked 9-inch pastry shell

Combine all ingredients except pastry shell in a medium bowl; stir with a wire whisk until blended. Pour mixture into pastry shell. Bake at 375° for 22 minutes. Cool on a wire rack. Yield: one 9-inch pie.

Praiseworthy
Foundation for Historic Christ Church
Irvington, Virginia

Striped Chocolate-Peanut Butter Pie

Kids of all ages will enjoy the winning combination of chocolate and peanut butter in this creamy pie.

¾ cup creamy peanut butter,
   divided
3 tablespoons butter or
   margarine
1½ cups graham cracker crumbs
1 (3-ounce) package vanilla
   pudding mix

3½ cups milk, divided
1 (3.4-ounce) package chocolate
   pudding mix
1 teaspoon vanilla extract
1 (8-ounce) container frozen
   whipped topping, thawed

Combine ½ cup peanut butter and butter in a small saucepan. Cook over low heat until butter melts and mixture is smooth, stirring occasionally. Stir in graham cracker crumbs. Firmly press mixture in bottom and up sides of a 9-inch pieplate. Chill until firm.

Combine vanilla pudding mix and 1¾ cups milk in a medium saucepan. Bring to a boil over medium heat, stirring constantly. Stir in remaining ¼ cup peanut butter. Pour into prepared crust. Cover and chill until firm.

Combine chocolate pudding mix and remaining 1¾ cups milk in a medium saucepan. Bring to a boil over medium heat, stirring constantly. Stir in vanilla. Pour over peanut butter layer. Cover and chill until firm. Spread whipped topping over chocolate layer before serving. Yield: one 9-inch pie.   Maureen A. Wagner

Recipes from Our Home to Yours
Hospice of North Central Florida
Gainesville, Florida

Turtle Pie

This is a short pie in height but it's tall in flavor. Caramels, chocolate, and pecans add up to a spectacular dessert.

12 **caramels (we tested with Farley's)**
1 **(14-ounce) can sweetened condensed milk, divided**
1 **baked 9-inch pastry shell**
2 **(1-ounce) squares unsweetened chocolate**

¼ **cup butter or margarine**
2 **large eggs, lightly beaten**
2 **tablespoons water**
1 **teaspoon vanilla extract**
⅛ **teaspoon salt**
½ **cup chopped pecans**

Combine caramels and ⅓ cup sweetened condensed milk in a small saucepan. Cook over low heat, stirring constantly, until caramels melt. Spread mixture in bottom of pastry shell; set aside.

Combine chocolate and butter in a medium saucepan. Cook over low heat, stirring constantly, until chocolate and butter melt.

Combine remaining sweetened condensed milk, eggs, water, vanilla, and salt in a large bowl; stir well. Add chocolate mixture; stir well. Pour into prepared crust. Sprinkle with pecans. Bake at 325° for 35 minutes or until set. Let cool completely on a wire rack. Cover and chill. Yield: one 9-inch pie.

The Albany Collection: Treasures and Treasured Recipes
Women's Council of the Albany Institute of History and Art
Albany, New York

Heavenly Lime Pie

This dessert lives up to its name, and it's worth the time investment to grate the rind and squeeze the juice from fresh limes for this recipe. It's easier to grate the rind before juicing the limes.

4 egg yolks
½ cup sugar
⅓ cup fresh lime juice
¼ teaspoon salt
1 cup whipping cream,
  whipped

1 tablespoon grated lime rind
Meringue Shell
Garnishes: additional whipped
  cream and grated lime rind

Beat egg yolks until thick and pale. Combine beaten egg yolks, sugar, lime juice, and salt in a large heavy saucepan. Cook over medium heat, stirring constantly, 3 minutes or until mixture thickens. Remove from heat, and let cool.

Fold whipped cream and 1 tablespoon lime rind into egg yolk mixture. Cover and chill 2 hours.

Spoon filling into Meringue Shell, and chill 20 minutes to 1 hour. (The longer the pie is chilled, the softer the Meringue Shell will become.) Garnish, if desired. Yield: one 9-inch pie.

Meringue Shell

4 egg whites
¼ teaspoon cream of tartar

1 cup sugar

Beat egg whites and cream of tartar at high speed of an electric mixer until foamy. Gradually add 1 cup sugar, 1 tablespoon at a time, beating until stiff peaks form and sugar dissolves (2 to 4 minutes). Spread meringue in bottom and up sides of a lightly buttered 9-inch pieplate. Make a large indentation in center of meringue. Bake at 275° for 1 hour. Turn oven off, and let cool in oven 1 hour (do not open oven door). Remove from oven, and let cool on a wire rack. Yield: one 9-inch shell.

Seaboard to Sideboard
The Junior League of Wilmington, North Carolina

Chocolate-Bottom Custard-Fruit Tart

3 (1-ounce) squares semisweet
  chocolate
3 tablespoons half-and-half
1 baked 9-inch pastry shell
3 egg yolks
⅓ cup sugar
1½ teaspoons unflavored
  gelatin
¾ cup warm milk
1½ tablespoons Grand Marnier
  or other orange-flavored
  liqueur

1½ teaspoons vanilla extract
½ cup whipping cream,
  whipped
3 kiwifruit, peeled and sliced
1 cup sliced fresh strawberries
½ cup fresh blueberries
½ cup fresh raspberries
¼ cup plus 2 tablespoons
  apricot preserves
2 tablespoons kirsch or other
  cherry-flavored brandy
Toasted slivered almonds

Place chocolate in top of a double boiler; cook over hot (not boiling) water until chocolate melts, stirring constantly. Stir in half-and-half; pour into pastry shell. Cover and chill 30 minutes or until set.

Combine egg yolks and sugar in top of double boiler; beat with a wire whisk 5 minutes or until mixture is thick and pale.

Sprinkle gelatin over warm milk; let stand 1 minute. Stir gelatin mixture into egg mixture; cook, stirring constantly, 10 minutes or until thickened. Remove from heat; stir in liqueur and vanilla. Cover and chill custard mixture 20 to 30 minutes or until mixture mounds slightly when dropped from a spoon.

Fold whipped cream into custard mixture; pour into pastry shell. Cover and chill 30 minutes or until set. Arrange kiwifruit, strawberries, blueberries, and raspberries on top of custard.

Combine apricot preserves and kirsch in a small saucepan; cook over medium heat until smooth, stirring constantly. Brush preserves mixture over fruit; sprinkle with almonds. Cover and chill at least 30 minutes before serving. Yield: one 9-inch tart.

Tested by Time
Porter Gaud Parents Guild
Charleston, South Carolina

Coffee-Coconut Tart

Java lovers gave this tart our highest rating not only for the delicious combination of coconut and coffee but also for its picture-perfect presentation.

1 (15-ounce) can cream of coconut, divided
¾ cup all-purpose flour
⅔ cup shredded coconut, toasted and divided
⅓ cup sifted powdered sugar
¼ cup plus 3 tablespoons unsalted butter, cut into pieces
1 teaspoon instant coffee granules
¼ teaspoon salt
Coffee Filling
¾ cup whipping cream
2 tablespoons powdered sugar

Stir cream of coconut with a wire whisk; reserve ¼ cup, and set aside. (Use remaining cream of coconut for Coffee Filling.)

Process flour, ½ cup toasted coconut, ⅓ cup powdered sugar, and next 3 ingredients in a food processor 1 minute or until crumbly. Firmly press dough in bottom and up sides of a 9-inch tart pan with removable bottom; freeze 10 minutes. Pierce crust with a fork; place pan on a baking sheet. Bake at 350° for 25 minutes or until crust is golden. Remove from oven, and cool in pan on a wire rack. Spoon Coffee Filling into prepared crust. Cover and chill 1 hour.

Combine reserved ¼ cup cream of coconut, cream, and 2 tablespoons powdered sugar in a mixing bowl. Beat at high speed of an electric mixer until stiff peaks form. Spoon mixture into a pastry bag fitted with a medium star tip. Pipe mixture over filling. Sprinkle with remaining toasted coconut. Cover; chill 1 hour. Yield: one 9-inch tart.

Coffee Filling

¼ cup sugar
2 tablespoons cornstarch
2 tablespoons instant coffee granules
½ cup plus 2 tablespoons whipping cream
¼ cup plus 2 tablespoons cream of coconut
4 egg yolks, lightly beaten
½ teaspoon vanilla extract

Combine first 3 ingredients in a heavy saucepan; stir with a wire whisk until blended (coffee granules will not completely dissolve).

Gradually stir in whipping cream and ¼ cup plus 2 tablespoons cream of coconut. (Reserve remaining cream of coconut for other uses.) Stir in egg yolks; bring to a boil over medium-high heat, stirring constantly, and cook 3 to 4 minutes or until mixture thickens. Stir in vanilla. Remove from heat, and let cool, stirring occasionally. Yield: 1½ cups.

Victorian Thymes and Pleasures
The Junior League of Williamsport, Pennsylvania

Apricot-Cheese-Rum Tarts

1 (8-ounce) package cream
   cheese, softened
1¼ cups sifted powdered
   sugar, divided
1 teaspoon rum flavoring
1 (17.3-ounce) package frozen
   puff pastry, thawed

½ cup apricot preserves
1 egg yolk, beaten
1 tablespoon milk
Vegetable cooking spray

Beat cream cheese at medium speed of an electric mixer until creamy. Add 1 cup powdered sugar and rum flavoring, beating until smooth.

Cut each sheet of puff pastry into four squares. Spoon cream cheese mixture evenly into center of each square of pastry; top each with 1 tablespoon apricot preserves.

Combine egg yolk and milk in a small bowl; stir well. Brush edges of pastry squares lightly with egg mixture. Fold each square of pastry into a triangle; press edges together with a fork to seal. Place tarts on a baking sheet lightly coated with cooking spray. Brush tarts with remaining egg mixture.

Bake at 400° for 10 to 15 minutes or until puffed and golden. Remove tarts to wire racks to cool; sprinkle with remaining ¼ cup powdered sugar. Yield: 8 tarts.   H.C. Muller

In the Breaking of Bread
Catholic Committee on Scouting and Camp Fire
Lake Charles, Louisiana

Danish Caramel Tarts

Chewy caramel and crunchy almonds make quite a show in these dainty tarts, perfect for easy serving at a dessert buffet.

1½ cups all-purpose flour
1⅓ cups sugar, divided
¼ teaspoon salt
½ cup butter or margarine

1 large egg, beaten
¾ cup whipping cream
¾ cup sliced almonds

Combine flour, ⅓ cup sugar, and salt; cut in butter with a pastry blender until mixture is crumbly. Stir in egg. Press dough with lightly floured fingertips in bottom and ½ inch up sides of 16 ungreased muffin pans. Set aside.

Sprinkle remaining 1 cup sugar in a heavy skillet; cook over medium heat until melted and golden, stirring constantly. Slowly stir in cream; cook, stirring constantly, until smooth (mixture will be lumpy at first). Remove from heat; stir in almonds.

Fill each muffin pan with about 1 tablespoon almond mixture. Bake at 350° for 20 to 25 minutes or until edges are golden. Cool in pans on wire racks (filling will firm as it cools). Yield: 16 tarts.

Sweet Memories
Holy Covenant United Methodist Women
Katy, Texas

Pumpkin-Nut Cups

Pumpkin and pecans pair nicely for fall. Each little dessert cup makes an easy-to-serve alternative to the traditional Thanksgiving pies of the same flavors.

½ cup unsalted butter, softened
1 (3-ounce) package cream cheese, softened
1 cup all-purpose flour
½ cup firmly packed brown sugar
¼ cup canned pumpkin
1 egg yolk
1 tablespoon plus 1 teaspoon unsalted butter, melted

1 tablespoon milk
1 tablespoon light rum
1 teaspoon vanilla extract
⅛ teaspoon ground nutmeg
⅛ teaspoon ground cinnamon
½ cup coarsely chopped pecans
¼ cup firmly packed brown sugar
1 tablespoon unsalted butter, melted

Beat ½ cup butter and cream cheese in a medium bowl at medium speed of an electric mixer until creamy. Stir in flour. Divide dough into 24 (1-inch) balls. Press dough evenly in bottom and up sides of ungreased miniature (1¾-inch) muffin pans. Bake at 325° for 10 minutes.

Meanwhile, combine ½ cup brown sugar and next 8 ingredients; stir well. Spoon pumpkin mixture into warm cups. Combine pecans, ¼ cup brown sugar, and 1 tablespoon melted butter in a small bowl; sprinkle over pumpkin mixture. Bake at 325° for 25 to 30 minutes or until set. Cool in pans on wire racks 10 minutes. Carefully loosen cups, and remove from pans. Serve warm, or cool completely on wire racks. Yield: 2 dozen.

Miriam L. Craig

Our Favorite Recipes
Claremont Society for the Prevention of Cruelty to Animals
Serving Sullivan County
Claremont, New Hampshire

Christmas Tassies

Serve these bite-size cranberry-nut gems when family and friends drop in during the holidays.

½ cup butter or margarine, softened
1 (3-ounce) package cream cheese, softened
1 cup all-purpose flour
Vegetable cooking spray
1 large egg, beaten
¾ cup firmly packed brown sugar

1 tablespoon butter or margarine, melted
1 teaspoon grated orange rind
½ cup chopped fresh cranberries
½ cup chopped pecans

Beat ½ cup butter and cream cheese at medium speed of an electric mixer until creamy. Gradually add flour, beating well. Cover and chill 1 hour.

Shape dough into 24 (1-inch) balls; press balls into miniature (1¾-inch) muffin pans lightly coated with cooking spray. Set aside.

Combine egg and next 3 ingredients; stir in cranberries and pecans. Spoon 1 tablespoon mixture into each shell. Bake at 325° for 25 minutes or until filling is set. Remove from pans immediately, and let cool completely on wire racks. Yield: 2 dozen.

Gracious Goodness Christmas in Charleston
Bishop England High School Endowment Fund
Charleston, South Carolina

Apple Country Turnovers

Cinnamon and sugar cloak the pastry wrapped around the chunky apple filling in these old-fashioned favorites.

1¾ cups all-purpose flour
2 tablespoons whole wheat flour
1 tablespoon brown sugar
1 teaspoon salt
¼ cup cold water
⅔ cup unsalted butter
4 cups peeled and diced Granny Smith apple
1 teaspoon vanilla extract
¼ cup firmly packed brown sugar
¼ cup sugar
1 tablespoon cornstarch
¼ teaspoon ground cinnamon
Vegetable cooking spray
1 egg white, lightly beaten
Additional ground cinnamon
Additional sugar

Combine first 4 ingredients. Combine ⅓ cup flour mixture and cold water to make a paste. Set paste aside.

Cut butter into remaining flour mixture with a pastry blender until mixture is crumbly. Stir paste into mixture to form a dough; divide dough into 8 portions. Roll each portion into an 8-inch circle on a lightly floured surface.

Combine apple and vanilla; toss. Combine ¼ cup brown sugar, ¼ cup sugar, cornstarch, and ¼ teaspoon cinnamon; sprinkle over apple mixture, and toss gently. Spoon mixture evenly onto dough circles. Fold dough over; seal edges with a fork. Prick tops with a fork; place pastries on a baking sheet coated with cooking spray. Brush lightly with egg white; sprinkle with additional cinnamon and sugar. Bake at 425° for 10 minutes. Reduce oven temperature to 350°; bake 20 to 25 more minutes or until golden. Yield: 8 turnovers.   Cheryl Fox

Kenwood Lutheran Church Cookbook
Kenwood Women of the Evangelical Lutheran Church in America
Duluth, Minnesota

Hazelnut Napoleons with Frangelico

A rich hazelnut liqueur-laced custard nestles between 2 layers of flaky pastry in these heavenly desserts. There's even a little custard leftover that's perfect for serving over pound cake, fresh berries, or all by itself.

1 (17.3-ounce) package frozen puff pastry, thawed
2½ cups evaporated milk
1½ cups sugar
¼ cup plus 1 tablespoon all-purpose flour
4 egg yolks, lightly beaten
2 tablespoons butter

½ cup Frangelico or other hazelnut-flavored liqueur
1 teaspoon vanilla extract
2¼ cups sifted powdered sugar
3 tablespoons milk
¼ cup (1½ ounces) semisweet chocolate morsels

Place pastry on a lightly floured surface; cut into 2- x 3-inch rectangles. Transfer half of pastry to an ungreased baking sheet. Bake at 400° for 18 minutes or until pastry is puffed and golden. Gently remove pastry from baking sheet with a spatula, and cool on wire racks. Repeat procedure with remaining pastry.

Combine evaporated milk and next 4 ingredients in a heavy saucepan, stirring with a wire whisk until smooth. Cook over medium heat, stirring constantly, until mixture thickens and begins to bubble. Continue to cook 3 more minutes, stirring constantly. Remove from heat; stir in liqueur and vanilla. Cover and chill at least 1 hour.

Carefully split each pastry in half horizontally, using a serrated knife. Spread each with about 1 tablespoon custard, and replace top of pastry.

Combine powdered sugar and milk, stirring until smooth; spoon glaze over tops of pastries, spreading evenly.

Melt chocolate in microwave oven according to package directions; cool slightly. Spoon chocolate into a pastry bag fitted with a piping tip. Pipe a decorative pattern across top of glaze. Let stand until set. Yield: 3 dozen.

Southern . . . On Occasion
The Junior League of Cobb-Marietta
Marietta, Georgia

Peach-Raspberry Cobbler

Frozen peaches work nicely in this colorful cobbler if fresh ones are out of season.

½ cup sugar
1 tablespoon cornstarch
2 tablespoons water
4 cups peeled and sliced fresh
  peaches
1 teaspoon grated lemon rind

1 teaspoon fresh lemon juice
2 cups fresh raspberries
¼ cup butter
Lattice Crust
1 tablespoon sugar

Combine first 3 ingredients in a medium saucepan, stirring until smooth. Add peaches, lemon rind, and lemon juice. Cook over medium heat, stirring constantly, until mixture thickens and comes to a boil. Boil 1 minute, stirring constantly. Remove from heat. Gently stir in raspberries. Return mixture to a boil, stirring gently. Pour mixture into an ungreased 8-inch square baking dish; dot with butter.

Roll pastry for Lattice Crust to ⅛-inch thickness on a lightly floured surface; cut into ¾-inch strips. Arrange strips in lattice design on top of peach mixture. Trim strips even with edges. Sprinkle with 1 tablespoon sugar. Bake at 425° for 25 to 30 minutes or until golden. Serve warm with ice cream. Yield: 6 servings.

Lattice Crust

1 cup all-purpose flour
½ teaspoon salt
¼ cup plus 2 tablespoons
  shortening

2 tablespoons cold water

Combine flour and salt; cut in shortening with a pastry blender until mixture is crumbly. Sprinkle cold water (1 tablespoon at a time) evenly over surface; stir with a fork until dry ingredients are moistened. Shape into a ball; chill. Yield: pastry for one 8-inch cobbler.

Southern Settings
Decatur General Foundation, Inc.
Decatur, Alabama

Pear Crisp with Lemon Sauce

⅔ cup regular oats, uncooked
⅓ cup all-purpose flour
⅓ cup firmly packed brown
  sugar
¼ teaspoon ground cardamom
¼ cup butter or margarine, cut
  into ½-inch pieces
⅓ cup sliced almonds
5 firm ripe pears, peeled and
  sliced (we tested with Bosc)
1 tablespoon sugar
½ teaspoon grated lemon rind
Lemon Sauce

Combine first 4 ingredients; cut in butter with a pastry blender until mixture is crumbly. Stir in almonds; set aside.

Combine pear slices, 1 tablespoon sugar, and lemon rind. Spoon mixture into a lightly greased 2-quart baking dish. Sprinkle oat mixture evenly over fruit mixture. Bake at 375° for 35 minutes or until golden. Let stand 10 minutes. Serve with warm Lemon Sauce. Yield: 6 servings.

Lemon Sauce

½ cup water
¼ cup sugar
2 teaspoons cornstarch
1 egg yolk, beaten
1 tablespoon butter or
  margarine
¼ teaspoon grated lemon rind
1 tablespoon fresh lemon juice

Combine first 3 ingredients in a medium saucepan, stirring well. Cook over medium heat, stirring constantly, until mixture comes to a boil; boil, stirring constantly, 2 minutes or until mixture thickens. Remove from heat. Gradually stir about one-fourth of hot mixture into egg yolk; add to remaining hot mixture, stirring constantly. Cook over low heat until mixture comes to a boil; boil 1 minute or until thickened. Remove from heat, and stir in butter, lemon rind, and lemon juice. Yield: ⅔ cup.   Mark Benson

St. Paul's 50th Anniversary Cookbook
St. Paul's Lutheran Church
Erie, Pennsylvania

Poultry

Grilled Chicken with Sweet Corn Salsa, page 247

Stuffed Chicken

Chunks of mozzarella cheese are a wonderful surprise in this stuffing.

1 (3½-pound) broiler-fryer
½ (18-ounce) loaf dry Italian
  bread
½ pound sweet Italian link
  sausage, cooked and cut into
  small pieces
1 (2¼-ounce) can sliced ripe
  olives, drained
3 ounces mozzarella cheese,
  cubed

3 tablespoons freshly grated
  Romano cheese
2 tablespoons chopped fresh
  parsley
1 clove garlic, minced
1 tablespoon olive oil, divided
¼ teaspoon salt, divided
¼ teaspoon pepper, divided

Remove giblets and neck from chicken; reserve for another use. Rinse chicken thoroughly under cold water, and pat dry with paper towels.

Soak bread in cold water until saturated; squeeze out water, and finely crumble bread in a large bowl. Add sausage and next 5 ingredients. Add 1 teaspoon olive oil, ⅛ teaspoon salt, and ⅛ teaspoon pepper; stir well.

Spoon stuffing into body cavity of chicken, reserving extra stuffing mixture. Place chicken, breast side up, in a lightly greased roasting pan. Brush chicken with remaining 2 teaspoons olive oil, and sprinkle with remaining ⅛ teaspoon each salt and pepper.

Bake, uncovered, at 350° for 1 hour and 30 minutes or until a meat thermometer inserted in meaty part of thigh registers 180° and stuffing registers 165°. Yield: 4 to 6 servings.   Susan M. Rotella

Note: Extra stuffing can be baked, uncovered, in a lightly greased 8-inch square pan at 350° for 25 minutes.

Tutto Bene
Salvaltore Mancini Lodge #2440
North Providence, Rhode Island

Roasted Chicken with Herb-Lemon Sauce

1 (4-pound) broiler-fryer
4 cloves garlic
1 small lemon, halved
1 small onion, quartered
1 teaspoon dried rosemary
½ teaspoon dried thyme
Vegetable cooking spray
1 cup low-sodium chicken broth (we tested with Campbell's)

2 tablespoons fresh lemon juice
¼ cup water
2 tablespoons dry white wine
1 tablespoon cornstarch
1 tablespoon reduced-sodium soy sauce
¼ teaspoon dried sage

Remove giblets and neck from chicken; reserve for another use. Rinse chicken thoroughly under cold water, and pat dry with paper towels. Place garlic and next 4 ingredients into cavity of chicken. Place chicken, breast side up, on a rack in broiler pan coated with cooking spray. Bake at 400° for 30 minutes.

Combine chicken broth and lemon juice; pour over chicken. Reduce oven temperature to 325°, and bake 1 hour and 15 minutes or until a meat thermometer inserted in meaty part of thigh registers 180°, basting every 15 minutes with pan drippings. Place chicken on a serving platter; cover and let stand 15 minutes before carving.

Meanwhile, pour pan drippings (about ½ cup) into a medium saucepan. Combine water and remaining 4 ingredients in a small bowl; stir well. Stir cornstarch mixture into pan drippings; bring to a boil, stirring constantly. Cook 2 minutes or until thickened, stirring often. Serve sauce over chicken. Yield: 4 to 6 servings.

Women Who Can Dish It Out
The Junior League of Springfield, Missouri

Caribbean Chicken

1 (2½- to 3-pound) broiler-
    fryer, quartered
2 teaspoons salt
1 teaspoon pepper
1 tablespoon olive oil
4 small onions, peeled and
    quartered
3 carrots, scraped and
    quartered
3 medium tomatoes, quartered

½ cup water
2 teaspoons Angostura bitters,
    divided
2 large sweet potatoes, peeled
    and cut into eighths
3 tablespoons butter or
    margarine
½ cup molasses
Garnish: chopped fresh parsley

Sprinkle chicken with salt and pepper; cook in oil in a Dutch oven over medium-high heat until browned, turning once. Remove chicken from pan; set aside, and keep warm. Add onion, carrot, and tomato to pan; cook until lightly browned. Return chicken to pan. Add water and 1 teaspoon bitters; cover and cook over medium-low heat 20 minutes. Uncover and cook 20 more minutes or until chicken is done, stirring occasionally.

Meanwhile, cook sweet potato in boiling water 15 minutes or until tender; drain. Set aside.

Melt butter in a large skillet over medium heat; stir in molasses and remaining 1 teaspoon bitters. Cook until mixture thickens, stirring often. Add sweet potato, and cook until glazed and thoroughly heated, stirring often.

To serve, spread sweet potato on a serving platter. Spoon chicken and vegetables over sweet potatoes. If desired, spoon pan juices over chicken. Garnish, if desired. Yield: 4 servings.

The Many Tastes of Haverstraw Middle School
Home and Career Skills Department, Haverstraw Middle School
Haverstraw, New York

Chicken in Almond Sauce

Ground almonds in the sauce of this fragrant dish represent the Middle Eastern influence in many Spanish dishes.

2¼ cups chicken broth
Pinch of saffron powder
⅓ cup all-purpose flour
1 teaspoon salt
½ teaspoon pepper
1 (3½- to 4-pound) broiler-
    fryer, skinned and cut up
⅓ cup olive oil

2 large cloves garlic
1 medium onion, chopped
1 cup dry sherry
1 bunch parsley, coarsely
    chopped (about 1 cup)
1 bay leaf
2 hard-cooked egg yolks
2 tablespoons ground almonds

Combine chicken broth and saffron in a small saucepan. Cook over medium heat until thoroughly heated, stirring occasionally. Set aside.

Place flour, salt, and pepper in a large heavy-duty, zip-top plastic bag. Place chicken pieces in bag, one at a time, and shake to coat chicken completely. Remove chicken, and cook in hot oil in a large skillet over medium-high heat until browned. Remove chicken from skillet, reserving drippings in skillet; set chicken aside, and keep warm.

Add garlic to drippings in skillet, and cook, stirring constantly, until golden. Remove garlic from skillet, and set aside. Add onion to skillet; cook, stirring constantly, until tender. Return chicken to skillet. Stir in sherry. Bring to a boil; add 2 of the cups reserved broth mixture, parsley, and bay leaf. Cover, reduce heat, and simmer 30 minutes.

Process remaining reserved ¼ cup broth mixture, reserved garlic, egg yolks, and almonds in container of an electric blender 30 seconds or until smooth, stopping once to scrape down sides. Stir yolk mixture into chicken mixture; cook, uncovered, over medium-low heat 20 minutes or until sauce is consistency of thickened cream. Remove and discard bay leaf before serving. Yield: 4 servings.

International Home Cooking
The United Nations International School Parents' Association
New York, New York

Southwest Orange-Chile Chicken With Black Beans

These ingredients simmer into a dark, rich broth perfect for spooning over hot cooked rice served on the side.

3 to 4 pounds assorted chicken pieces, skinned
2 tablespoons olive oil
1 large purple onion, halved and thinly sliced
4 cloves garlic, minced
1½ cups fresh orange juice
¾ cup chicken broth
3 tablespoons hot chile sauce
1 sweet red pepper, cut into strips
2 (15-ounce) cans black beans, drained
1 tablespoon dark rum
¼ teaspoon salt
¼ teaspoon pepper
¼ cup chopped fresh cilantro

Cook chicken in hot oil in a large skillet over medium-high heat until browned, turning once. Remove chicken, reserving drippings in skillet; set chicken aside.

Add onion and garlic to skillet; cook 6 minutes or until tender, stirring often. Return chicken to skillet; add orange juice, broth, and chile sauce. Bring to a boil; cover, reduce heat, and simmer 30 minutes. Add pepper strips; simmer, uncovered, 30 minutes. Add black beans and next 3 ingredients; simmer, uncovered, 15 minutes. Sprinkle with cilantro. Serve immediately. Yield: 4 servings.

Savoring the Southwest Again
Roswell Symphony Guild
Roswell, New Mexico

Grilled Chicken with Sweet Corn Salsa

Corn, jalapeño pepper, and onion make up a jazzy salsa that's served with this golden grilled chicken.

¼ cup peanut oil
2 cloves garlic, minced
2 tablespoons coarse salt or
  1 tablespoon salt
2 tablespoons fresh lime juice
1 teaspoon chili powder

½ teaspoon freshly ground
  pepper
8 bone-in skinned chicken
  breast halves
Sweet Corn Salsa

Combine first 6 ingredients in a large heavy-duty, zip-top plastic bag; add chicken. Seal bag, turning to coat chicken. Marinate in refrigerator 2 hours.

Remove chicken from marinade, discarding marinade.

Grill chicken, covered, over medium-hot coals (350° to 400°) 30 minutes or until done, turning once. Serve with Sweet Corn Salsa. Yield: 8 servings.

Sweet Corn Salsa

2 cups fresh or frozen whole
  kernel corn, thawed
¼ cup rice wine vinegar
1 small jalapeño pepper,
  seeded and minced
2 tablespoons minced purple
  onion
2 tablespoons chopped fresh
  cilantro

½ teaspoon coarse salt or
  ¼ teaspoon salt
⅛ teaspoon freshly ground
  pepper
1 plum tomato, seeded and
  diced (about ¼ cup)
3 tablespoons butter, cut into
  pieces

Combine first 7 ingredients in a skillet; bring to a boil. Reduce heat to medium-high, and cook until liquid has almost evaporated, stirring often. Remove from heat; stir in tomato. Add butter; cook, stirring constantly, until butter melts. Yield: 1½ cups. Sandy Ricker

Our Sunrise Family Cookbook
Sunrise Drive Elementary School
Tucson, Arizona

Oven-Fried Chicken

Vegetable cooking spray
12 bone-in skinned chicken
  breast halves
1 cup Italian-seasoned
  breadcrumbs (store-bought)
1 cup all-purpose flour
1 tablespoon Old Bay seasoning
½ teaspoon Creole seasoning
½ teaspoon garlic powder

½ teaspoon dried thyme
½ teaspoon dried basil
½ teaspoon dried oregano
⅛ teaspoon freshly ground
  black pepper
⅛ teaspoon ground red pepper
1 (8-ounce) carton plain nonfat
  yogurt

Line a very large baking sheet with aluminum foil; coat foil with cooking spray. Set aside.

Place chicken in a large bowl of ice water; set aside.

Combine breadcrumbs and next 9 ingredients in a large zip-top plastic bag; seal and shake well.

Remove chicken from water, and pat dry. Brush 2 chicken breasts with yogurt, and place in bag. Seal and shake to coat chicken completely. Place chicken on prepared baking sheet. Repeat procedure with remaining chicken breast halves and yogurt.

Coat chicken with cooking spray. Bake, uncovered, on bottom rack of oven at 400° for 1 hour or until done. Yield: 12 servings.

A Taste of the Good Life from the Heart of Tennessee
Saint Thomas Heart Institute
Nashville, Tennessee

Grilled Chicken Pesto and Tortellini

1 (7.5-ounce) jar pesto
½ cup mayonnaise
¼ cup finely chopped purple
   onion
2 (9-ounce) packages
   refrigerated tortellini or 1
   (20-ounce) package dried
   tortellini

6 skinned and boned chicken
   breast halves
1 medium-size sweet red
   pepper
1 medium-size sweet yellow
   pepper
1 medium-size green pepper
6 Roma tomatoes

Combine first 3 ingredients in a small bowl; stir well, and set aside.

Cook tortellini according to package directions; drain well. Toss with 1 cup reserved pesto mixture. Set aside.

Baste chicken with remaining pesto mixture; place chicken and peppers on grill rack. Grill, covered, over medium-hot coals (350° to 400°) 10 to 12 minutes or until done, turning chicken once and basting with remaining pesto mixture. Turn peppers every 3 minutes to thoroughly cook each side. Add tomatoes during last 3 minutes of grilling time, turning once.

Thinly slice cooked chicken. Peel peppers, if desired, and cut into thin slices. Cut tomatoes in half lengthwise.

To serve, place tortellini on a large platter; top with sliced chicken. Top chicken with sliced peppers. Arrange tomato around chicken and peppers. Yield: 6 servings.

Sterling Service
The Dothan Service League
Dothan, Alabama

Chicken Fajitas

For added flavor, serve fajitas with grilled onions and peppers and top with salsa and a dollop of sour cream.

8 skinned and boned chicken breast halves
4 cups water
¼ cup grated lime rind
⅔ cup fresh lime juice (about 4 limes)
½ cup dry red wine (optional)
1 large tomato, chopped (about 1⅓ cups)
½ cup chopped onion
2 jalapeño peppers, chopped
1 cup chopped fresh cilantro
1 teaspoon salt
1 teaspoon garlic powder
1 teaspoon pepper
1 teaspoon Worcestershire sauce
12 (6-inch) flour tortillas

Place chicken in a large bowl. Add water and next 11 ingredients. Cover and marinate in refrigerator at least 8 hours, turning chicken occasionally.

Remove chicken from marinade, discarding marinade.

Grill, covered, over medium-hot coals (350° to 400°) 10 to 12 minutes or until done, turning chicken once. Cut chicken into thin strips, and serve on flour tortillas. Yield: 12 servings.

Landmark Entertaining
The Junior League of Abilene, Texas

Walnut-Stuffed Chicken Breasts

8 skinned and boned chicken
 breast halves
1 cup (4 ounces) shredded
 Cheddar cheese
½ cup chopped walnuts
½ cup soft breadcrumbs
 (homemade)
2 tablespoons minced onion
¼ teaspoon pepper
3 tablespoons butter or
 margarine
½ cup all-purpose flour
1 cup chicken broth
½ cup dry white wine
2 tablespoons chopped fresh
 parsley

Place chicken between two sheets of heavy-duty plastic wrap; flatten to ¼-inch thickness, using a meat mallet or rolling pin.

Combine Cheddar cheese and next 4 ingredients; spoon about 1½ tablespoons cheese mixture in center of each chicken breast half. Fold ends over, and secure with wooden picks.

Heat butter in a large skillet over medium-high heat. Dredge each chicken roll in flour; add to skillet, and cook 4 minutes on each side or until lightly browned. Add broth and wine; cover, reduce heat, and simmer 20 minutes or until done.

Transfer chicken to a serving platter, reserving sauce in pan. Remove wooden picks from chicken. Bring sauce to a boil; cook, uncovered, 4 minutes or until reduced to about ½ cup. Stir in parsley. Spoon sauce over chicken. Yield: 8 servings.   Virginia Westwood

Our Heritage Cookbook
First Baptist Church
Billings, Montana

Chicken with Hoisin Sauce

*An Asian-inspired sauce highlights this dish. The sauce nicely comple-
ments a pork tenderloin cut into 1-inch pieces and marinated and
cooked like the chicken breasts.*

4 skinned and boned chicken
   breast halves
6 green onions, cut into ½-inch
   pieces
3 tablespoons soy sauce
1 tablespoon rice wine or
   cooking sherry
1 teaspoon salt

1 teaspoon dark sesame oil
¼ cup peanut oil
5 cloves garlic, minced
1 (1-inch) piece fresh ginger,
   peeled and minced
2 tablespoons hoisin sauce
Hot cooked rice

Cut chicken into 1-inch pieces; place pieces in a large bowl. Add
green onions, soy sauce, rice wine, salt, and sesame oil. Cover and
marinate in refrigerator 30 minutes.

Pour peanut oil around top of a preheated wok or large nonstick
skillet. Add garlic and ginger; stir-fry 10 seconds. Add hoisin sauce,
and stir-fry 30 seconds. Add chicken mixture to wok. Cook 5 minutes
or until chicken is done, stirring occasionally. Serve over rice. Yield: 4
servings.

Connie Fukuda

Bridging the Generations
Japanese American Citizen's League
Bloomington, Minnesota

Mexican Chicken with Orange, Cumin, and Olives

Soak up the extra sauce from this dish with a serving of hot cooked rice.

1 (14.5-ounce) can whole
   tomatoes, undrained
2 tablespoons cornstarch
2 tablespoons olive oil
12 skinned chicken thighs
   (about 4¾ pounds)
2 medium onions, halved
   lengthwise and thinly sliced
2 cloves garlic, minced
1 cup dry red wine
½ cup sliced ripe olives

¼ cup plus 2 tablespoons fresh
   orange juice
¼ cup golden raisins
2 bay leaves
1 tablespoon ground cumin
2 teaspoons grated orange rind
½ teaspoon salt
½ teaspoon ground cinnamon
¼ teaspoon ground red pepper
2 tablespoons chopped fresh
   parsley

Chop and drain tomatoes, reserving juice; set aside. Place ½ cup juice in a 1-cup liquid measure; add cornstarch, and stir until smooth. Set aside.

Heat oil in a large skillet over medium-high heat; add chicken, in batches, and cook 6 minutes, turning once. Remove chicken, and set aside.

Drain skillet; reserving 2 tablespoons drippings in pan. Add onion and garlic to drippings; cook, stirring constantly, until onion is tender. Add wine; bring to a boil, scraping particles that cling to bottom. Add reserved tomato, remaining reserved tomato juice, olives, and next 8 ingredients; stir well. Return chicken to skillet; bring to a boil. Cover, reduce heat, and simmer 30 to 40 minutes or until chicken is done. Remove and discard bay leaves.

Transfer chicken to a large serving platter; set aside, and keep warm. Add reserved cornstarch mixture to mixture in skillet; cook over low heat, stirring constantly, until slightly thickened. Pour sauce over chicken. Sprinkle with parsley. Yield: 6 servings.

Praiseworthy
Foundation for Historic Christ Church
Irvington, Virginia

Chicken and Artichoke Crêpes

Make the crêpes the day before, and store them in the refrigerator to ease preparation. Use leftover crêpes in another recipe or with ice cream and chocolate sauce.

16 Entrée Crêpes
¼ cup plus 1 tablespoon butter or margarine, divided
½ cup minced onion
¼ pound fresh mushrooms, sliced
3 tablespoons all-purpose flour
⅔ cup chicken broth
½ cup half-and-half
2½ cups diced cooked chicken

1 (14-ounce) can artichoke hearts, drained and coarsely chopped
⅓ cup freshly grated Parmesan cheese
1¼ teaspoons minced fresh or dried rosemary
½ teaspoon salt
1 cup (4 ounces) shredded Swiss cheese

Prepare Entrée Crêpes.

Heat 2 tablespoons butter in a large skillet over medium-high heat; add onion and mushrooms. Sauté 4 minutes or until tender. Reduce heat; add remaining 3 tablespoons butter, stirring until melted. Stir in flour; cook 2 minutes or until bubbly.

Gradually add broth and half-and-half, stirring until mixture thickens. Remove from heat; stir in chicken and next 4 ingredients. Spoon about ¼ cup chicken mixture down center of each crêpe; roll up crêpes, and place seam side down in a lightly greased 13- x 9- x 2-inch baking dish.

Bake, uncovered, at 350° for 15 minutes. Sprinkle with Swiss cheese, and bake 5 more minutes or until cheese melts. Yield: 8 servings.

Entrée Crêpes

1 cup all-purpose flour
¼ teaspoon salt
¾ cup water
¾ cup milk

3 large eggs
2 tablespoons butter, melted
Vegetable cooking spray

Combine first 4 ingredients, beating with a wire whisk until smooth. Add eggs, beating well; stir in butter. Cover and chill at least 1 hour.

Coat bottom of a 6-inch crêpe pan or heavy skillet with cooking spray; place over medium heat until hot. Pour 2 tablespoons batter into pan; quickly tilt pan in all directions so batter covers bottom. Cook 1 minute or until crêpe can be shaken loose. Turn crêpe over, and cook 30 seconds. Place crêpe on a cloth towel to cool. Repeat with remaining batter. Stack crêpes between sheets of wax paper; place in an airtight container, and store in refrigerator up to 2 days, if desired. Yield: 24 (6-inch) crêpes. Helen O'Keefe King

Blessings
First Presbyterian Church
Pine Bluff, Arkansas

Chicken Livers and Mushrooms in Madeira Wine Sauce

1 (8-ounce) package sliced fresh mushrooms
2 tablespoons butter, melted
1½ teaspoons salt, divided
¾ teaspoon freshly ground pepper, divided
2 tablespoons finely chopped green onions
1 cup chicken broth
⅓ cup plus 1 tablespoon Madeira wine, divided
2 teaspoons tomato paste
1 teaspoon cornstarch
¾ cup all-purpose flour
2 pounds chicken livers
½ cup vegetable oil, divided
2 tablespoons butter
Hot cooked rice

Cook mushrooms in 2 tablespoons melted butter in a large skillet, stirring constantly, 5 minutes or until tender. Stir in ½ teaspoon salt and ¼ teaspoon pepper. Add green onions, and toss well. Add chicken broth, ⅓ cup wine, and tomato paste; cook 6 minutes.

Combine cornstarch and remaining 1 tablespoon wine; add to mushroom mixture, and cook, stirring constantly, until mixture thickens and boils. Boil 1 minute. Set aside, and keep warm.

Combine flour, remaining 1 teaspoon salt, and remaining ½ teaspoon pepper. Dredge chicken livers in flour mixture. Fry half of livers in a large skillet in ¼ cup oil over medium-high heat 5 minutes or until browned; drain on paper towels. Repeat procedure with remaining ¼ cup oil and livers. Add livers to wine sauce. Stir in 2 tablespoons butter. Cook until butter melts, stirring occasionally. Serve livers over rice. Yield: 4 to 6 servings. Jan Wieland

Southern Born and Bread
The Junior Service League of LaGrange, Georgia

Roast Turkey with Cornbread Dressing

Choose your favorite dressing. The Cornbread Dressing is very moist and soft while the Cornbread Sausage Dressing contains a pound of pork sausage and is drier and spicier. You'll be satisfied either way you choose.

1 (10- to 12-pound) turkey
2 teaspoons salt
2 teaspoons paprika
1½ teaspoons pepper
½ cup vegetable oil

⅓ cup butter, melted
4 cups water
Cornbread Dressing or
   Cornbread Sausage Dressing

Remove giblets and neck from turkey; reserve for another use. Rinse turkey thoroughly under cold water, and pat dry with paper towels. Combine salt, paprika, and pepper; sprinkle body cavity and outside of turkey with salt mixture. Lift wingtips up and over back, and tuck under bird.

Place turkey, breast side up, on a rack in a roasting pan. Combine oil and butter; brush entire bird with oil mixture. Add water to roasting pan, and cover tightly with aluminum foil. Bake at 375° for 2 hours and 45 minutes or until a meat thermometer inserted in meaty part of thigh registers 180°. Let stand 15 minutes before carving. Serve with choice of Cornbread Dressing or Cornbread Sausage Dressing. Yield: 8 servings.

Cornbread Dressing

4 slices white bread, cut into
   ½-inch cubes
4½ cups turkey broth or
   chicken broth

4 cups crumbled cornbread *
3 hard-cooked eggs, chopped
1 cup finely chopped celery
½ cup finely chopped onion

Place white bread cubes on an ungreased baking sheet. Bake at 350° for 12 minutes or until golden. Set aside.

Bring broth to a boil in a medium saucepan. Combine crumbled cornbread and toasted bread cubes in a large bowl; pour broth over cornbread mixture. Let stand 5 minutes. Stir in chopped egg, celery, and onion. Spoon into a greased 11- x 7- x 1½-inch baking dish. Bake, uncovered, at 375° for 45 to 50 minutes or until golden. Yield: 8 servings.

Cornbread Sausage Dressing

4 cups crumbled cornbread *
1 pound ground pork sausage
1 cup chopped onion
1 cup chopped celery

2 (10¾-ounce) cans cream of
chicken soup, undiluted
¾ teaspoon salt
½ teaspoon pepper

Place crumbled cornbread in a large bowl. Set aside.

Brown sausage in a large skillet, stirring until sausage crumbles; drain. Return sausage to skillet, and add onion and celery. Cook over medium-high heat, stirring constantly, until vegetables are tender. Add soup, salt, and pepper, stirring until blended. Add sausage mixture to cornbread, stirring well. Spoon mixture into a greased 11- x 7- x 1½-inch baking dish. Bake, uncovered, at 375° for 20 minutes or until golden. Yield: 8 servings.

Linen Napkins to Paper Plates
The Junior Auxiliary of Clarksville, Tennessee

* To make 4 cups crumbled cornbread, we prepared 1 (5.9-ounce) package self-rising white cornmeal mix by Martha White according to package directions. Cool the cornbread, and crumble enough to measure 4 cups.

Peppered Turkey Breast

Baking in an oven bag keeps this turkey breast moist.

1 (5½-pound) bone-in turkey breast
½ cup pepper
¼ cup salt
¾ cup cider vinegar
¼ cup vegetable oil
3 cloves garlic, minced
1 medium onion, chopped
3 tablespoons chopped fresh parsley
1 (10-ounce) bottle steak sauce (we tested with A-1)
1 tablespoon all-purpose flour
1 turkey-size oven bag

Place turkey breast in a large heavy-duty, zip-top plastic bag or large shallow dish; set aside.

Combine pepper and next 7 ingredients, stirring well; pour over turkey breast, coating thoroughly. Seal or cover, and marinate in refrigerator 8 hours, turning occasionally.

Remove turkey breast from marinade, discarding marinade. Add flour to oven bag, shaking to coat; place in a 13- x 9- x 2-inch baking pan. Add turkey breast to oven bag. Close bag with nylon tie; cut six ½-inch slits in top of bag. Bake at 325° for 1 hour and 35 minutes or until meat thermometer registers 170°. Let stand 15 minutes before carving.

Cut top of oven bag, and remove turkey breast to a serving platter, reserving drippings. Strain drippings, and serve with turkey. Yield: 12 servings.

Julie Jackson

Savory Secrets
Runnels School
Baton Rouge, Louisiana

Turkey Breast with Cranberry-Nut Stuffing

Complete your holiday table with a turkey breast stuffed with seasonal flavors such as cranberries, almonds, and oranges.

½ cup chopped onion
¼ cup slivered almonds
½ cup butter, melted
4 cups herbed bread cubes
1 cup chopped cranberries
3 tablespoons sugar
2 tablespoons grated orange
 rind

½ cup orange juice
1 (5-pound) bone-in turkey
 breast
½ teaspoon salt
¼ teaspoon pepper
¼ cup orange marmalade
1 tablespoon butter
¼ teaspoon ground ginger

Cook onion and almonds in ½ cup melted butter until onion is tender, stirring often. Stir in bread cubes and next 4 ingredients.

Sprinkle turkey cavity with salt and pepper. Tightly pack cavity with 2 cups stuffing. Place remaining stuffing in a greased 1-quart baking dish; cover and chill. Place turkey, skin-side up, on a rack in a roasting pan. Bake, uncovered, at 325° for 1½ hours. Combine marmalade, 1 tablespoon butter, and ginger in a small bowl; brush mixture over turkey breast; bake turkey 30 more minutes or until a meat thermometer inserted in breast registers 170°, basting every 10 miutes with additional marmalade mixture. Bake reserved stuffing, uncovered, during last 30 minutes of baking time. Yield: 12 servings.

Simply Cape Cod
The Sandwich Junior Women's Club
Sandwich, Massachusetts

Jalapeño-Glazed Cornish Hens

3 (1½-pound) Cornish hens,
  split
½ teaspoon salt
¼ teaspoon pepper
1 (10½-ounce) jar hot jalapeño
  jelly
2 teaspoons grated lime rind
⅓ cup fresh lime juice
¼ cup vegetable oil
1 tablespoon chopped fresh
  cilantro

Sprinkle hens with salt and pepper. Place hens, cut side down, in a large shallow dish; set aside.

Melt jelly in a saucepan over low heat; add lime rind and remaining 3 ingredients. Pour mixture over hens in a heavy-duty, zip-top plastic bag. Seal tightly, and marinate in refrigerator 4 to 6 hours, turning occasionally.

Prepare a charcoal fire in one end of grill; let burn 15 to 20 minutes. Drain hens, reserving marinade. Place hens on grill opposite hot coals. Grill, covered, 35 minutes, brushing once with marinade. Grill 45 more minutes or until hens are done. Place remaining marinade in a small saucepan; bring to a boil. Serve with hens. Yield: 6 servings.

Pick of the Crop, Two
North Sunflower Academy PTA
Drew, Mississippi

Grilled Game Hens Merlot

2 (1½-pound) Cornish hens,
  split
¼ cup Merlot
¼ cup fresh lemon juice
2 tablespoons minced fresh
  ginger
1 clove garlic, minced
Glaze

Place hens in a large heavy-duty, zip-top plastic bag or shallow dish; set aside.

Combine Merlot, lemon juice, ginger, and garlic, stirring well; pour over hens, coating thoroughly. Seal or cover, and marinate in refrigerator 8 hours, turning occasionally.

Remove hens from marinade, discarding marinade. Grill hens, covered, over medium-hot coals (350° to 400°) 15 minutes on each side or until hens are done, basting often with Glaze. Yield: 4 servings.

Glaze

½ cup seedless raspberry jam
¼ cup Merlot

2 tablespoons fresh lemon juice
2 tablespoons butter

Bring all ingredients to a boil in a small saucepan over medium heat. Boil 5 minutes or until mixture thickens slightly. Yield: ¾ cup.

Apron Strings: Ties to the Southern Tradition of Cooking
The Junior League of Little Rock, Arkansas

"Down-East" Duck

Use only pure maple syrup, not pancake syrup, in this recipe.

1 (16-ounce) package frozen
  blueberries
1 (14-ounce) whole boned duck
  breast

½ teaspoon salt
½ teaspoon pepper
½ cup brandy
½ cup pure maple syrup

Remove ½ cup blueberries from package; set aside. Thaw remaining blueberries in package according to package directions. Gently squeeze bag to crush berries. Press blueberries through a wire-mesh strainer into a bowl, reserving ½ cup blueberry juice; set aside. Reserve blueberry pulp in strainer and any remaining juice for another use.

Trim excess skin from duck. Cut down middle of breast with kitchen shears to form two breast halves. Season with salt and pepper.

Brown both pieces of duck in a large skillet over medium-high heat. Remove from skillet, and place in a lightly greased 8-inch square pan. Bake, uncovered, at 400° for 20 to 25 minutes or until meat thermometer inserted in the thickest part registers 170°.

Meanwhile, discard drippings from skillet. Add reserved ½ cup blueberries, reserved ½ cup blueberry juice, brandy, and maple syrup to skillet. Cook over medium-high heat 5 minutes or until mixture is reduced by half, stirring occasionally. Slice duck breast halves lengthwise into thin slices. Arrange slices on a serving plate; spoon blueberry sauce over duck. Yield: 1 to 2 servings. Geoffrey Boardman

Rave Reviews
Ogunquit Playhouse
Ogunquit, Maine

Roast Duckling Gourmet with Cointreau Sauce

1 (5-pound) dressed duckling
2 tablespoons lemon juice
Celery leaves
1 medium onion, sliced
1 teaspoon salt, divided
1 teaspoon pepper, divided
1½ cups dry white wine
1 tablespoon honey
2 tablespoons butter or
  margarine
½ cup sliced fresh mushrooms
1 clove garlic, pressed

3 tablespoons all-purpose flour
1 tablespoon grated orange
  rind
½ cup orange juice
½ cup Cointreau or other
  orange-flavored liqueur
¼ cup dry sherry
¼ cup cognac
1 tablespoon currant jelly
Garnishes: sautéed mushroom
  caps, orange slices

Remove giblets and neck from duckling; reserve for another use. Rinse duckling thoroughly under cold water, and pat dry. Rub cavity with lemon juice; place celery leaves and onion inside cavity.

Place duckling, breast side up, on a lightly greased rack in a shallow roasting pan; sprinkle with ½ teaspoon salt and ½ teaspoon pepper. Insert meat thermometer into meaty portion of thigh, making sure it does not touch fat or bone.

Bake, uncovered, at 325° for 30 minutes; pour wine over duckling. Bake 1 hour and 15 minutes more, basting with pan juices every 20 minutes. Brush duckling with honey; bake 15 more minutes or until thermometer registers 180° (do not baste again). Transfer duckling to a serving platter; keep warm.

Pour drippings into a gravy strainer; reserve drippings, and discard fat. Set drippings aside.

Melt butter in roasting pan over medium heat; add mushrooms and garlic. Cook, stirring constantly, 3 minutes or until tender. Stir in flour, using a wire whisk; cook 1 minute. Stir in reserved drippings, orange rind, orange juice, Cointreau, sherry, cognac, and remaining ½ teaspoon salt and ½ teaspoon pepper. Bring just to a simmer; cook until thickened. Stir in currant jelly. Garnish duckling, if desired. Serve duckling with Cointreau Sauce. Yield: 4 servings.

Beneath the Palms
The Brownsville Junior Service League
Brownsville, Texas

Salads

Glazed Pecans and Gorgonzola Salad, page 270

Cranberry-Wine Mold

1 (12-ounce) package fresh
    cranberries
1½ cups sugar
¾ cup dry red wine

2 (3-ounce) packages raspberry-
    flavored gelatin
¾ cup water
1 cup chopped pecans

Combine first 3 ingredients in a large saucepan. Bring to a boil over medium heat; reduce heat, and simmer, uncovered, 5 minutes or until cranberries burst. Remove from heat.

Place gelatin in a medium bowl. Bring water to a boil; add to gelatin, stirring 2 minutes or until gelatin dissolves. Combine gelatin mixture and cranberry mixture in a large bowl, stirring well. Cover and chill until consistency of unbeaten egg white.

Gently fold in pecans. Pour mixture into a lightly oiled 5-cup mold. Cover and chill until firm. Unmold onto a serving plate. Yield: 6 servings.   Rachel Waits

The Fruit of the Spirit
Sumrall United Methodist Women's Circle
Sumrall, Mississippi

Blueberry and Rice Salad

Serve this versatile salad for a brunch or as a dessert.

1 (8-ounce) carton vanilla
    yogurt
¼ cup honey
3 cups chilled cooked rice
1 (8-ounce) can pineapple
    chunks, drained

1 cup fresh blueberries
1 medium banana, sliced
½ cup shredded coconut
1 (2.25-ounce) package
    chopped walnuts (½ cup)

Combine yogurt and honey in a large bowl; stir well. Add rice, stirring until blended. Gently fold in pineapple and next 3 ingredients. Cover and chill thoroughly. Sprinkle with walnuts just before serving. Yield: 5 servings.   Sue Ann Burtman

Our Country Christmas Collection
Skaggs Community Health Center
Branson, Missouri

Carrot-Raisin Salad with Honey-Orange Dressing

¾ cup vegetable oil
⅓ cup honey
3 tablespoons frozen orange
  juice concentrate, thawed
3 tablespoons lemon juice
½ teaspoon dry mustard
¼ teaspoon celery salt
¼ teaspoon paprika
3 cups shredded carrot
2 medium apples, peeled and
  diced (we tested with Gala)
½ cup raisins

Combine first 7 ingredients in a large bowl; stir well with a wire whisk.

Add carrot, apple, and raisins; toss gently to combine. Cover and chill thoroughly. Yield: 6 servings.   Kelley L. Wright

Southern Elegance: A Second Course
The Junior League of Gaston County
Gastonia, North Carolina

Dilled Pea Salad

Tiny English peas are preferred in this recipe. Look for them labeled as such in the freezer section of your supermarket.

2 (10-ounce) packages frozen
  tiny English peas, thawed
1 (8-ounce) carton sour cream
1 tablespoon plus 1 teaspoon
  lemon juice
1 tablespoon sliced green
  onions
2 teaspoons sugar
1 teaspoon chopped fresh dill
½ teaspoon salt
½ teaspoon curry powder
¼ teaspoon pepper
Shredded Cheddar cheese
  (optional)

Combine first 9 ingredients in a large bowl; toss gently. Cover and chill 1 hour. Top with cheese, if desired. Yield: 6 servings.

River City Recipes
Cape Girardeau Senior Center
Cape Girardeau, Missouri

Peanut Potato Salad

This potato salad bursts with flavor with a dressing made of chunky peanut butter and roasted peppers.

3 pounds red potatoes, unpeeled
12 slices bacon, cooked and crumbled
1 medium-size sweet red pepper, chopped
¾ cup chopped celery
4 green onions, chopped
¼ cup chopped fresh cilantro
¼ cup chopped fresh parsley
¾ cup mayonnaise
½ cup chunky peanut butter
3 tablespoons cider vinegar
1 teaspoon salt
¼ teaspoon pepper
1 cup salted roasted Spanish peanuts

Cook potatoes in boiling water to cover 25 minutes or just until tender. Drain well, and let cool slightly. Peel and cube potatoes.

Combine potato, bacon, and next 5 ingredients in a large bowl; toss gently.

Combine mayonnaise, peanut butter, vinegar, salt, and pepper in a small bowl; stir well. Add dressing and peanuts to potato mixture, and toss gently. Serve immediately, or cover and chill. Yield: 10 servings.

Beyond Burlap, Idaho's Famous Potato Recipes
The Junior League of Boise, Idaho

South-of-the-Border Potato Salad

This highly seasoned potato salad will make you think you're south of the border.

2 pounds red potatoes, unpeeled
⅓ cup vegetable oil
⅓ cup white vinegar
1 tablespoon sugar
1½ teaspoons chili powder
1 teaspoon seasoned salt
Dash of hot pepper sauce
1 small onion, coarsely chopped
1 (11-ounce) can Mexican-style corn, drained (we tested with Green Giant Mexicorn)
½ cup shredded carrot
½ cup chopped green pepper
1 (2¼-ounce) can sliced ripe olives, drained

Peel potatoes, if desired; cut into 1-inch pieces. Cook potato in boiling salted water 12 to 14 minutes or until tender; drain well. Place potato in a large bowl.

Combine oil and next 5 ingredients; stir well. Pour dressing over potato, and toss gently to coat. Cover and chill 1 hour. Add onion and remaining ingredients; stir gently. Serve immediately, or cover and chill. Yield: 8 servings.   Ingrid Lipscomb

Praise the Lord and Pass the Gravy
Stanley United Methodist Church
Stanley, Virginia

Grilled Vegetable Salad

⅓ cup white balsamic vinegar
2 tablespoons olive oil
2 shallots, finely chopped
1 teaspoon dried Italian
  seasoning
¼ teaspoon salt
¼ teaspoon pepper
1½ teaspoons molasses

½ pound carrots, scraped
  (about 4 medium)
1 sweet red pepper, seeded
1 sweet yellow pepper, seeded
1 zucchini
1 yellow squash
1 large onion

Combine first 7 ingredients in a large bowl. Cut carrots in half lengthwise. Cut carrot and remaining 5 ingredients into large pieces (about 1½ inches). Add vegetables to vinegar mixture, tossing to coat. Let stand 30 minutes, stirring occasionally.

Drain vegetables, reserving vinegar mixture. Arrange vegetables in a grill basket. Grill, covered, over medium-hot coals (350° to 400°) 15 to 20 minutes, turning once.

Return vegetables to reserved vinegar mixture. Cover and chill at least 8 hours. Yield: 6 servings.   Peggy Monroe

Cougar Bites
Crestline Elementary School
Birmingham, Alabama

Red Cabbage Salad

No grated knuckles from this Asian-inspired slaw. A brief stint in the microwave wilts thinly sliced cabbage perfectly for this colorful marinated salad. It's a great make-ahead dish to accompany grilled chicken.

1 small red cabbage, thinly sliced
¼ cup chopped fresh cilantro
⅓ cup soy sauce
¼ cup lemon juice
2 tablespoons chopped fresh ginger

2 tablespoons peanut oil
2 tablespoons balsamic vinegar
2 tablespoons dark sesame oil
1 teaspoon ground coriander

Place cabbage in a large bowl. Cover tightly with heavy-duty plastic wrap; fold back a small edge of wrap to allow steam to escape. Microwave at HIGH 3 minutes.

Add cilantro and remaining ingredients; toss well. Cover and chill 8 hours. Yield: 8 servings. Francine Christiansen

We Cook Too
Women's Committee, Wadsworth Atheneum
West Hartford, Connecticut

Spectacular Overnight Slaw

We describe this slaw as true to its name! Chilling the slaw overnight allows the flavors to blend, resulting in a very tasty dish.

1 medium cabbage, finely shredded
1 medium-size purple onion, thinly sliced
½ cup chopped green pepper
½ cup chopped sweet red pepper
½ cup sliced pimiento-stuffed olives

½ cup sugar
½ cup vegetable oil
½ cup white wine vinegar
1 teaspoon salt
1 teaspoon celery seeds
1 teaspoon mustard seeds
2 teaspoons Dijon mustard

Combine first 5 ingredients; stir well. Combine sugar and remaining 6 ingredients in a small saucepan; bring to a boil. Boil 1 minute.

Pour dressing over cabbage mixture; toss well. Cover and chill 8 hours. Toss well before serving. Yield: 12 servings.   Jo Jennings

Foods and Flowers
Hermosa Garden Club
Hermosa Beach, California

Mixed Salad with Cranberry Dressing

4 cups torn Bibb lettuce, loosely packed

4 cups torn green leaf lettuce, loosely packed

1 cup torn fresh spinach, loosely packed

2 large oranges, peeled, seeded, and sectioned

1 small purple or sweet onion, thinly sliced

1¼ cups fresh cranberries

⅓ cup sugar

3 tablespoons fresh orange juice

1 tablespoon red wine vinegar

1 tablespoon olive oil

½ teaspoon grated orange rind

Combine first 5 ingredients in a large bowl; cover and chill.

Combine cranberries, sugar, and orange juice in a saucepan; cook over medium heat, stirring constantly, 5 minutes or until cranberries burst and mixture thickens. Remove from heat.

Combine vinegar, oil, and orange rind in a small bowl; add to cranberry mixture, stirring with a wire whisk until blended. Cover and chill. To serve, drizzle dressing over chilled greens mixture. Yield: 8 servings.   William and Libby Graves

Bully's Best Bites
The Junior Auxiliary of Starkville, Mississippi

Glazed Pecans and Gorgonzola Salad

1 large head romaine lettuce, torn
½ cup light olive oil
2 tablespoons lemon juice
1 tablespoon red wine vinegar
½ teaspoon salt
½ teaspoon pepper
6 ounces Gorgonzola cheese, crumbled
Spicy Glazed Pecans

Place lettuce in a large bowl. Combine olive oil and next 4 ingredients in a jar; cover tightly, and shake vigorously. Pour dressing over lettuce, and toss well. Top each salad evenly with Gorgonzola cheese and Spicy Glazed Pecans. Yield: 6 servings.

Spicy Glazed Pecans

2 teaspoons butter or margarine
1 tablespoon sugar
1 teaspoon water
½ teaspoon black pepper
¼ teaspoon salt
⅛ teaspoon ground red pepper
⅔ cup pecan halves

Melt butter in a skillet. Add sugar and next 4 ingredients; stir well. Cook over low heat until mixture bubbles; stir in pecans, and cook, stirring constantly, about 4 minutes or until pecans are well coated and sugar begins to caramelize. Spoon pecans onto an ungreased baking sheet; separate pecans. Cool completely. Yield: ¾ cup.

Classically Kiawah
The Alternatives
Kiawah Island, South Carolina

Layered Mexican Salad

A vinaigrette of lime juice and fresh cilantro tops the colorful layers of this Mexican salad.

2 cups shredded iceberg lettuce
¼ cup chopped green pepper
Black Bean Relish
½ cup frozen whole kernel corn, thawed
1 small avocado, sliced
Lime Vinaigrette

Layer lettuce, green pepper, ¾ cup Black Bean Relish, and corn in a 2-quart clear straight-sided bowl. Arrange remaining Black Bean Relish and avocado slices over top layer. Serve with Lime Vinaigrette. Yield: 4 to 6 servings.

Black Bean Relish

1 (15-ounce) can black beans, rinsed and drained	¼ cup finely chopped purple onion
1 medium tomato, finely chopped	2 tablespoons white wine vinegar
1 serrano chile pepper, seeded and finely chopped	1 tablespoon vegetable oil
½ cup chopped sweet red pepper	¼ teaspoon salt

Combine all ingredients in a large bowl; stir well. Cover and chill 1 hour. Yield: 3 cups.

Lime Vinaigrette

½ teaspoon grated lime rind	1 small clove garlic
2 tablespoons fresh lime juice	¼ teaspoon salt
1 tablespoon minced fresh cilantro	½ cup olive oil

Process first 5 ingredients in a food processor. With processor running, pour oil through food chute in a slow, steady stream; process until blended. Yield: ½ cup. Jim Driggs

A Bite of the Best
Relief Society Church of Jesus Christ of Latter Day Saints
Provo, Utah

Bulgur Salad with Oriental Dressing

This recipe can easily be prepared a day ahead if time is tight.

1 cup water
1 cup bulgur, uncooked
1 cup thinly shredded red
   cabbage
1 cup coarsely grated carrot
1 cup seedless red grapes,
   halved
½ cup chopped sweet red
   pepper

½ cup chopped green onions
½ cup chopped fresh parsley
⅓ cup white wine vinegar
2 tablespoons peanut oil
1 tablespoon soy sauce
1 tablespoon dark sesame oil
1 tablespoon sesame seeds,
   toasted
1 teaspoon Dijon mustard

Bring water to a boil in a medium saucepan; add bulgur. Cover, remove from heat, and let stand 20 minutes.

Place bulgur in a large bowl. Add shredded cabbage and next 5 ingredients; stir well. Combine vinegar and remaining 5 ingredients in a small bowl, stirring with a wire whisk until blended. Pour dressing over bulgur mixture, and stir gently. Serve immediately, or cover and chill. Yield: 4 to 6 servings.

Ivy Marwil

A Taste of Tradition
Temple Emanuel-El
Providence, Rhode Island

Citrus and Spinach Couscous Salad

To coarsely chop spinach, first tightly roll several leaves together, and thinly slice to make ribbons; this technique is called a chiffonade. From this point, just coarsely chop the long strips.

2¼ cups water
1 (10-ounce) package
   couscous
1 teaspoon salt
¼ cup olive oil
2 tablespoons lemon zest
   (grated rind)
3 tablespoons fresh lemon
   juice

½ teaspoon salt
1 teaspoon pepper
3 cups coarsely chopped fresh
   spinach (about 1 bunch)
3 green onions, sliced
½ cup golden raisins

Bring water to a boil in a medium saucepan. Remove from heat, and stir in couscous and 1 teaspoon salt. Cover and let stand 5 minutes. Fluff with a fork; let cool, uncovered.

Combine couscous, olive oil, and next 4 ingredients in a large bowl; toss well. Add spinach, green onions, and raisins; toss well. Serve immediately at room temperature, or cover and chill up to 8 hours. Yield: 8 servings.

Beth Morris

Savory Secrets
P.E.O. Chapter LR
St. Charles, Missouri

Very Wild Rice Salad

4 cups water
1 teaspoon salt
1 (6-ounce) package wild rice (about 1 cup)
½ chopped dried figs (we tested with Calimyrna)
⅓ cup chopped pecans, toasted
⅓ cup chopped cashews, toasted
¼ cup finely chopped green onion tops
2 tablespoons finely chopped celery
2 tablespoons finely chopped purple onion
2 tablespoons raspberry or red wine vinegar
1 tablespoon fresh lemon juice
1 clove garlic, minced
1 teaspoon sugar
1 teaspoon Dijon mustard
¼ cup olive or vegetable oil
Salt and pepper to taste

Bring water and salt to a boil in a medium saucepan. Add rice; cover, reduce heat to medium-low, and simmer 45 minutes or until rice is tender. Drain and place in a medium bowl; let cool. Add figs and next 5 ingredients to rice; toss well.

Process vinegar and next 4 ingredients in container of an electric blender until combined. With blender on high, gradually add oil in a slow, steady stream; blend until thoroughly combined. Pour over rice mixture; mix well. Season with salt and pepper to taste. Cover and chill thoroughly. Yield: 4 servings.

Symphony of Flavors
The Associates of the Redlands Bowl
Redlands, California

Farfalle Pasta Salad with Brie and Tomatoes

1 (16-ounce) package farfalle (bow tie) pasta
1 (15-ounce) round Brie
4 large tomatoes, seeded and diced
1 cup chopped fresh basil
½ cup extra-virgin olive oil
1 teaspoon salt
1 teaspoon minced garlic
½ teaspoon freshly ground pepper

Cook pasta according to package directions; drain. Rinse pasta, and drain again. Cover and chill several hours.

Remove and discard rind from cheese with a vegetable peeler. Cut cheese into 1-inch cubes. Combine cheese, tomato, and remaining 5 ingredients; stir well. Cover and chill several hours. Add pasta, and toss gently. Serve at room temperature. Yield: 8 servings.

Call to Post
Lexington Hearing and Speech Center
Lexington, Kentucky

Cold Marinated Beef Salad

You can cook a sirloin steak just for this hearty salad or slice leftover steak. Either way the salad makes a mouthwatering one-dish meal.

1½ pounds top sirloin steak
2 (8-ounce) packages sliced fresh mushrooms
2 cloves garlic, minced
3 tablespoons lemon juice
½ teaspoon salt
¼ teaspoon pepper
2 tablespoons vegetable oil
¼ cup olive oil
¼ cup red wine vinegar
¼ teaspoon salt
¼ teaspoon dried chervil
¼ teaspoon dried thyme
¼ teaspoon dried basil
⅛ teaspoon pepper
1 pint cherry tomatoes, halved
1 head iceberg lettuce, shredded
½ cup freshly grated Asiago cheese
Garnish: chopped fresh parsley

Place steak on a rack in a broiler pan; broil 3 inches from heat (with electric oven door partially opened) 7 minutes on each side or to desired degree of doneness. Cool and cut into thin strips.

Cook mushrooms and next 4 ingredients in 2 tablespoons vegetable oil in a large skillet over medium heat. Cook until mushrooms are tender, stirring often; set aside.

Combine ¼ cup olive oil and next 6 ingredients in a large bowl, stirring well with a wire whisk. Add beef, mushroom mixture, and tomato. Cover and chill at least 2 hours.

Toss beef mixture lightly to coat; arrange on shredded lettuce on a large serving platter. Sprinkle with cheese. Garnish, if desired. Yield: 6 servings.

Sterling Service
The Dothan Service League
Dothan, Alabama

Greek Chicken Salad

Stuff leftovers in a pita pocket for a light lunch on the go!

3 cups cubed cooked chicken breast (about 3 breast halves)
2 medium cucumbers, peeled, seeded, and sliced
1 (4-ounce) package crumbled feta cheese
1 (2¼-ounce) can sliced ripe olives
¼ cup chopped fresh parsley
1 cup mayonnaise
½ cup plain yogurt
1 tablespoon dried oregano
3 cloves garlic, minced
Spinach or lettuce leaves

Combine first 5 ingredients in a large bowl. Combine mayonnaise and next 3 ingredients; stir well. Stir mayonnaise mixture into chicken mixture, tossing to coat; cover and chill. Serve over spinach leaves. Yield: 5 servings.

Jeanie Brice Geist

Shared Treasures
First Baptist Church
Monroe, Louisiana

Turkey and Roquefort Salad with Cranberry Dressing

We used smoked turkey when testing this salad, and we loved the flavor combination. Leftover roasted turkey works equally well.

3 cups cooked diced turkey breast (about 1¼ pounds)
4 cups torn romaine lettuce, tightly packed
1 cup chopped celery
1 cup seedless red or green grapes, halved

½ cup chopped pecans, toasted
1½ ounces Roquefort cheese, crumbled
Cranberry Dressing

Combine first 5 ingredients in a large bowl; toss well. Sprinkle with cheese. Serve with Cranberry Dressing. Yield: 4 servings.

Cranberry Dressing

1 (8-ounce) can jellied cranberry sauce
¼ cup soy sauce
3 tablespoons fresh lemon juice

3 tablespoons cooking sherry
1 tablespoon vegetable oil
1 clove garlic, minced

Combine all ingredients in a small saucepan. Cook over medium-low heat, stirring constantly, until mixture is smooth and thoroughly heated. Yield: 1⅓ cups.

Victorian Thymes and Pleasures
The Junior League of Williamsport, Pennsylvania

Paella Salad

All you need to do is add crusty bread to this classic Spanish main-dish salad.

3 cups water
1 pound unpeeled medium-size fresh shrimp
1 cup frozen English peas
2¼ cups chicken broth
1 cup uncooked long-grain rice
1 teaspoon crushed saffron threads
½ cup Italian dressing with herbs (we tested with Kraft Tomato and Herb)
6 ounces smoked sausage, sliced
1 cup cubed cooked chicken breast
2 medium tomatoes, peeled, seeded, and chopped
¼ cup chopped green pepper
¼ cup sliced green onions
Lettuce leaves
1 tomato, cut into wedges

Bring water to a boil; add shrimp, and cook 3 to 5 minutes or until shrimp turn pink. Drain well; rinse with cold water. Chill. Peel shrimp, and devein, if desired.

Cook peas according to package directions; drain and set aside.

Combine chicken broth, rice, and saffron in a medium saucepan. Bring to a boil; cover, reduce heat, and simmer 25 minutes or until chicken broth is absorbed and rice is tender. Combine rice and dressing in a large bowl; stir well. Cover and chill 2 hours.

Cook sausage in a large skillet over medium heat until browned; drain well.

Combine rice mixture, shrimp, peas, sausage, chicken, and next 3 ingredients. Cover and chill. To serve, line salad plates with lettuce, and spoon paella onto prepared plates; top each plate evenly with tomato wedges. Yield: 6 servings.

Secrets of Amelia
McArthur Family Branch YMCA
Fernandina Beach, Florida

Chinese Salad

This salad is a great Asian version of an American chef salad.

3 cups water
1 pound unpeeled medium-size fresh shrimp
1 cup mayonnaise
¼ cup soy sauce
¼ cup vegetable oil
¼ cup lemon juice
½ teaspoon Worcestershire sauce
5 cups thinly sliced napa cabbage
1 cup cooked, shredded chicken breast
1 (4-ounce) container fresh bean sprouts

½ (8-ounce) can water chestnuts, drained and diced
4 ounces Swiss cheese, cut into thin strips
4 ounces cooked ham, cut into thin strips
1 (4.25-ounce) can chopped black olives
¼ green pepper, diced
5 leaves romaine lettuce, cut into thin strips
5 green onions, chopped
1 stalk celery, chopped
Chopped cooked bacon
Chow mein noodles

Bring water to a boil; add shrimp, and cook 3 to 5 minutes or until shrimp turn pink. Drain well; rinse with cold water. Chill. Peel shrimp, and devein, if desired. Set aside.

Combine mayonnaise and next 4 ingredients in a small bowl; stir well. Cover and chill dressing.

Combine cabbage and next 10 ingredients in a large bowl; toss gently. Add reserved shrimp. Cover and chill. Add 1 cup dressing, and toss gently; sprinkle with bacon and noodles. Serve with remaining dressing. Yield: 8 servings.

Savour St. Louis
Barnes-Jewish Hospital Auxiliary Plaza Chapter
St. Louis, Missouri

Summer Shrimp and Avocado Salad

3 cups water
1 pound unpeeled medium-size fresh shrimp
1 (14-ounce) can hearts of palm, drained and sliced
⅓ cup vegetable oil
¼ cup minced onion
3 tablespoons red wine vinegar
1 tablespoon lemon juice
1½ teaspoons salt
1 teaspoon prepared mustard
½ teaspoon garlic powder
¼ teaspoon pepper
Mixed baby greens (optional)
Avocado slices (optional)

Bring water to a boil. Add shrimp; cook 3 to 5 minutes or until shrimp turn pink. Drain; rinse with water. Chill. Peel shrimp; devein, if desired. Place shrimp and hearts of palm in a large heavy-duty, zip-top plastic bag. Combine oil and next 7 ingredients; stir well. Pour dressing over shrimp mixture. Seal bag securely; marinate in refrigerator 2 to 3 hours, turning bag occasionally. If desired, serve over mixed greens and avocado slices. Yield: 3 to 4 servings.   Will Hoke

Cougar Bites
Crestline Elementary School
Birmingham, Alabama

Authentic Roquefort Dressing

Don't be alarmed about the generous amount of pepper in this recipe; it stands up nicely to the tangy Roquefort cheese.

1 cup mayonnaise
4 ounces Roquefort cheese, crumbled
½ cup buttermilk
1 tablespoon freshly ground pepper
1 tablespoon minced onion
2 tablespoons dry white wine
1 teaspoon minced garlic
1 teaspoon lemon juice

Combine all ingredients in a small bowl, stirring with a wire whisk until blended. Cover and chill. Serve over salad greens. Yield: 2 cups.

Shalom on the Range
Shalom Park
Aurora, Colorado

Dressing for Coleslaw or Salad

Yes, we indeed used sweetened condensed milk for this recipe. Coupled with the vinegar, it lends a tangy-sweet flavor perfect for dressing up prepackaged slaw mixes.

2 cups mayonnaise
1 (14-ounce) can sweetened
    condensed milk (we tested
    with Eagle Brand)

½ cup sugar
½ cup white vinegar

Combine all ingredients in a medium bowl, stirring with a wire whisk until blended. Cover and chill, if desired. Serve over coleslaw or with salad greens. Yield: 3 cups.   Sheila and Helen Hadaway

Sharing Tasteful Memories
L.A.C.E. (Ladies Aspiring to Christian Excellence) of
First Church of the Nazarene
Longview, Texas

Creamy Italian Dressing

1 cup mayonnaise
½ small onion, quartered
1 tablespoon sugar
2 tablespoons red wine vinegar
¾ teaspoon dried Italian
    seasoning

¼ teaspoon salt
¼ teaspoon garlic salt
⅛ teaspoon pepper

Process all ingredients in container of an electric blender until smooth, stopping once to scrape down sides. Cover and chill. Serve over salad greens. Yield: 1 cup.

Culinary Classics
Hoffman Estates Medical Center Service League
Hoffman Estates, Illinois

Sauces & Condiments

Cranberry Chutney, page 288

Eggnog Sauce

We recommend serving this rich dessert sauce with gingerbread, fruitcake, or plum pudding.

2½ cups milk
½ cup whipping cream
¼ teaspoon rum flavoring

1 (3.4-ounce) package vanilla
   instant pudding mix
⅛ teaspoon ground nutmeg

Combine all ingredients in a medium bowl; beat at medium-low speed of an electric mixer until well blended. Let stand 5 minutes. Serve immediately, or cover and chill. Yield: 3¼ cups.

Historically Heavenly Home Cooking
Corry Area Historical Society
Corry, Pennsylvania

Peppermint Marshmallow Sauce

Spoon this frothy pink peppermint sauce over scoops of fudgy chocolate ice cream to create minty magic.

1 (7-ounce) jar marshmallow
   creme
¼ cup finely crushed hard
   peppermint candy (8 pieces)
¼ cup milk

⅛ teaspoon peppermint
   extract
Red liquid food coloring
   (optional)

Combine first 3 ingredients in a medium saucepan. Cook over low heat, stirring constantly, 5 minutes or until mixture is smooth. Remove from heat.

Stir in peppermint extract and, if desired, food coloring. Cover and chill. Stir gently just before serving. Serve sauce over ice cream. Yield: 1⅔ cups.

I'll Cook When Pigs Fly
The Junior League of Cincinnati, Ohio

Horseradish Sauce

Horseradish adds its unique zip to this versatile meat and vegetable topper. Bread is the secret ingredient that thickens this sauce to perfection.

½ cup whipping cream
2 tablespoons fresh lemon
  juice
2 tablespoons prepared
  horseradish

⅛ to ¼ teaspoon seasoned salt
Dash of ground red pepper
2 slices white bread, crusts
  removed

Combine first 5 ingredients in a small saucepan. Crumble bread, and add to whipping cream mixture. Cook over medium-low heat, stirring constantly, 15 minutes or until smooth and thickened. Serve sauce warm as a topping for beef or steamed vegetables. Yield: about ¾ cup.

Donna Farlow

Carnegie Hall Cookbook
Carnegie Hall, Inc.
Lewisburg, West Virginia

Tarragon Mustard Cream

If you love béarnaise sauce, you'll equally adore this similar cream sauce. Fresh tarragon provides the integral flavor punch.

⅓ cup sour cream
2 tablespoons butter, softened
2 tablespoons Dijon mustard
1 tablespoon red wine vinegar
1 teaspoon tarragon vinegar
¼ teaspoon salt

¼ teaspoon coarsely ground
  black pepper
⅛ teaspoon ground red pepper
½ teaspoon minced fresh
  tarragon

Combine first 8 ingredients in a small saucepan. Cook over low heat, stirring constantly with a wire whisk, until sauce is thoroughly heated (do not boil). Stir in tarragon. Serve warm as a topping for chicken, fish, or asparagus. Yield: ½ cup.

Betty Livingston

Madalene Cooks–50 Years of Good Taste
Church of the Madalene
Tulsa, Oklahoma

Powderpuff Barbeque Sauce

There's nothing soft and gentle about this sassy barbecue sauce. It's thick and spicy and ready to slather over ribs or chicken. If it packs too much heat for your taste, use a milder can of tomatoes with green chiles.

3 (6-ounce) cans tomato paste
1 (10-ounce) can tomatoes with
 green chiles, pureed
1 cup firmly packed brown
 sugar
1 cup cider vinegar
1 cup molasses
1 medium onion, minced

4 cloves garlic, minced
1 tablespoon salt
2 tablespoons chili powder
1 tablespoon pepper
1 tablespoon paprika
1 teaspoon celery seeds
1 teaspoon dry mustard
1 teaspoon hot sauce

Combine all ingredients in a large saucepan; stir well. Bring to a boil; reduce heat, and simmer, uncovered, 1 hour, stirring occasionally. Store any leftover sauce in an airtight container in the refrigerator. Yield: 5 cups.

Janeyce Michel-Cupito

The Kansas City Barbeque Society Cookbook
Kansas City Barbeque Society
Kansas City, Missouri

Chile Verde (Green Chile Sauce)

Be sure to use no-salt-added chicken broth when preparing this chile verde or it will be too salty to enjoy over your favorite Mexican fare.

1 medium onion, chopped
2 cloves garlic, minced
3 tablespoons vegetable oil
3 cups no-salt-added chicken
 broth
2 (11-ounce) cans tomatillos,
 undrained

2 (4-ounce) cans whole green
 chiles, drained and chopped
4 fresh jalapeño peppers,
 seeded and minced
1 tablespoon dried oregano
½ cup chopped fresh cilantro

Cook onion and garlic in hot oil in a Dutch oven over medium heat, stirring constantly, until onion is tender. Add chicken broth and next 4 ingredients. Bring to a boil; reduce heat, and simmer, uncovered, 40 minutes or until vegetables are tender and mixture thickens, stirring occasionally. Stir in cilantro. Serve warm as a topping for pork or Mexican food. Yield: 6 cups.

Foods from the Homelands
Kingsburg Friends of the Library
Kingsburg, California

Pesto Sauce

You can bring out the blender to make this pesto if you don't want to assemble your food processor. Either way, let the blending begin–this pesto is worth the effort.

2 cups tightly packed fresh basil leaves (1½ large bunches)	2 cloves garlic
	½ teaspoon salt
	¼ teaspoon freshly ground pepper
¾ cup olive oil	
2 tablespoons pine nuts	½ cup grated Parmesan cheese

Process first six ingredients in a food processor or blender 2 minutes or until mixture is smooth, stopping twice to scrape down sides. Stir in cheese. Store sauce in an airtight container in refrigerator. Yield: 1¼ cups.

Penny Lindsay

Block-Brantley Family Favorites
Block-Brantley Reunion
San Antonio, Texas

Peach Salsa

Peak of summer peaches show off this salsa at its best, but you can enjoy the fresh fiesta of flavors year-round by substituting frozen peaches in the off-season.

3 cups peeled and diced fresh ripe peaches (about 6 medium)
1 medium cucumber, unpeeled, seeded, and chopped
1 medium-size fresh tomato, seeded and diced
½ cup diced purple onion
1 jalapeño pepper, seeded and minced
1 clove garlic, crushed
2 tablespoons chopped fresh cilantro
2 tablespoons red wine vinegar
1 tablespoon fresh lime juice

Combine all ingredients in a large bowl; stir well. Cover and chill. Serve as a dip for tortilla chips or as a topping for grilled chicken, pork, or fish. Yield: 4 cups.   Jennifer Bowles

Silver Spoons
Kaiser Rehabilitation Center
Tulsa, Oklahoma

Mango and Avocado Salsa

2 large ripe mangos, peeled and chopped
1 large avocado, peeled and chopped
1 cup chopped fresh cilantro
½ medium-size purple onion, finely chopped
2 tablespoons fresh lime juice
½ teaspoon hot sauce
¼ teaspoon salt
⅛ teaspoon pepper

Combine all ingredients in a large bowl; stir gently. If desired, cover and chill. Serve as a dip for tortilla chips or as a topping for fish, chicken, or Mexican food. Yield: 4 cups.   Tammy Gahica

Cookin' in the Canyon
Jarbidge Community Hall
Jarbidge, Nevada

Black-Eyed Pea Salsa

2 (15-ounce) cans black-eyed
  peas, rinsed and drained
2½ cups chopped fresh plum
  tomatoes (about 6 tomatoes)
2½ cups peeled, seeded, and
  chopped cucumber (about 2
  large)
2 teaspoons seeded and
  minced jalapeño pepper

½ cup white wine vinegar
½ cup olive oil
1 clove garlic, minced
1 teaspoon sugar
1 teaspoon salt
1 teaspoon dried basil
½ teaspoon pepper

Combine first 4 ingredients in a large bowl; stir well.

Combine vinegar and remaining 6 ingredients; pour over black-eyed pea mixture, and toss gently to coat. Cover and chill at least 3 hours. Serve as a dip for tortilla chips or as a topping for grilled pork or chicken. Yield: 8 cups.

Down by the Water
The Junior League of Columbia, South Carolina

Cranberry, Ginger, and Orange Relish

Crown tender slices of your Thanksgiving turkey with a spoonful of this crystallized ginger-studded cranberry relish.

1 (12-ounce) package fresh
  cranberries
2 cups sugar
¼ cup chopped crystallized
  ginger

Grated rind of 1 orange
¼ cup fresh orange juice
½ cup chopped walnuts

Combine first 5 ingredients in a saucepan; stir well. Bring to a boil; cover, reduce heat to low, and simmer 15 minutes or until cranberry skins pop. Stir in walnuts. Serve warm, or cover and chill (mixture will thicken as it cools). Serve with turkey. Yield: 3 cups.   Gloria Berlin

Treasured Recipes of Provincetown
Provincetown Council on Aging
Provincetown, Massachusetts

Cranberry Chutney

To create a nonalcoholic version of this spicy chutney, use an additional ¼ cup fresh orange juice in place of the liqueur.

4 cups fresh cranberries
2 Granny Smith apples, peeled and chopped
1 pear, peeled and chopped
1 cup sugar
1 cup golden raisins
1 cup minced onion
½ cup dried apricots, chopped
1 tablespoon grated orange rind
1 teaspoon ground cinnamon
⅛ teaspoon freshly grated nutmeg
½ cup fresh orange juice
¼ cup Grand Marnier or other orange-flavored liqueur

Combine first 10 ingredients in a large saucepan; stir well. Stir in orange juice. Bring to a boil over medium-high heat; reduce heat, and simmer, uncovered, 30 to 45 minutes or to desired consistency, stirring often. Stir in liqueur. Let cool to room temperature (mixture will thicken as it cools.) Cover and chill. Serve with game, turkey, or chicken. Yield: 5 cups.

Renee Bergstrom

The Cookbook Tour
Good Shepherd Lutheran Church
Plainview, Minnesota

Green Tomato Chutney

Perky green tomatoes from your summer's-end garden are gloriously transformed into this sweet yet spicy creation.

3 pounds green tomatoes, unpeeled and chopped (about 5 large)
2 teaspoons salt
1½ cups white vinegar
¾ cup firmly packed brown sugar
¾ cup unpeeled and chopped Golden Delicious apple
¾ cup chopped onion
½ cup chopped prunes
3½ tablespoons dry mustard
½ teaspoon pickling spice
½ teaspoon pepper

Place tomato in a large bowl. Sprinkle with salt; stir well. Cover and chill 8 hours; drain.

Place tomato in a large saucepan; add vinegar and remaining ingredients, and stir well. Bring to a boil; reduce heat, and simmer, uncovered, over very low heat 1 hour and 15 minutes or until tomato and apple are very soft and liquid is slightly reduced.

Pour hot chutney into hot sterilized jars, filling ¼ inch from top. Remove air bubbles; wipe jar rims. Cover at once with metal lids, and screw on bands. Process jars in boiling water bath 5 minutes. Serve with meat or poultry. Yield: 6 half-pints.   Norma Latimer

From ANNA's Kitchen
Adams-Normandie Neighborhood Association (ANNA)
Los Angeles, California

Rhubarb Cherry Jam

This rosy jam is supereasy to make because no processing is needed.
Just spoon it into containers, and then store in the refrigerator.

5 cups chopped fresh rhubarb (1¼ pounds)
5 cups sugar
1 cup water
1 (6-ounce) package cherry-flavored gelatin
1 (21-ounce) can cherry pie filling
¼ teaspoon almond extract

Combine first 3 ingredients in a large saucepan. Bring to a boil; reduce heat, and simmer, uncovered, 15 minutes. Add gelatin. Cook, stirring constantly, until gelatin dissolves. Remove from heat, and stir in pie filling and almond extract.

Spoon into sterilized containers; let cool. Store in refrigerator up to 1 month. Yield: 7 cups.   Peggy Sayles and Jean Jarnagin

The Great Delights Cookbook
Genoa Serbart United Methodist Churches
Genoa, Colorado

Kumquat Marmalade

The tiniest of citrus sensations, the kumquat resembles a very small orange. While the edible rind is sweet, the flesh remains tart, which creates a delightfully different taste experience.

2 pounds fresh ripe kumquats	1 (1¾-ounce) package
6 cups water	powdered pectin
½ cup lemon juice	9½ cups sugar

Thinly slice kumquats, and remove seeds.

Combine kumquats, 6 cups water, and lemon juice in a large Dutch oven; bring to a boil. Reduce heat, and simmer, uncovered, 20 minutes, stirring often. Measure cooked mixture carefully; add additional water to make mixture equal 7 cups. Return mixture to pan; stir in pectin. Bring to a boil, stirring constantly. Add sugar, and return to a boil, stirring constantly. Boil 4 minutes, stirring constantly. Skim off foam with a metal spoon.

Pour hot mixture into hot sterilized jars, filling ¼ inch from top. Remove air bubbles; wipe jar rims. Cover at once with metal lids, and screw on bands. Process jars in boiling water bath 5 minutes. Yield: 7 half-pints.

Foods from the Homelands
Kingsburg Friends of the Library
Kingsburg, California

Peanut-Honey Butter

¼ cup butter or margarine, softened	¼ cup creamy peanut butter
	¼ cup honey

Beat butter and peanut butter at medium speed of an electric mixer until creamy. Slowly add honey while beating at high speed 5 minutes or until fluffy. Serve with sliced apples or pears, or on toast, bagels, or graham crackers. Store in an airtight container in refrigerator. Yield: ½ cup.

Heather Hillman

Just Desserts
Amsterdam Free Library
Amsterdam, New York

Soups & Stews

Cioppino, page 304

Cantaloupe Soup

Take out your prettiest soup bowls and ladle for this juicy melon concoction. Float fresh mint leaves on each serving to add fragrance and flavor to this sweet dessert soup.

1 medium-size ripe cantaloupe, cubed
3 cups vanilla ice cream, softened
¼ cup honey

½ (6-ounce) can frozen orange juice concentrate
1½ cups ginger ale, chilled
Garnish: fresh mint leaves

Process first 4 ingredients in a large food processor until smooth; cover and chill at least 30 minutes. Gently stir in ginger ale just before serving. To serve, ladle soup into individual bowls. Garnish, if desired. Serve immediately. Yield: 8½ cups.   Jean Aldag

Cook Bookery
The University of Illinois College of Medicine at Peoria
Peoria, Illinois

Grand Marnier-Strawberry Soup

The first step of this recipe requires a standing period to create what's known as crème fraîche. You'll want to take note that it's worth the wait. The mixture has a tangy flavor and velvety texture that heightens the sweetness of the fresh strawberries in the soup.

1 cup whipping cream
2 tablespoons buttermilk
6 cups fresh strawberries, divided

1½ cups fresh orange juice
¼ cup Grand Marnier or other orange-flavored liqueur
3 tablespoons sugar

Combine whipping cream and buttermilk in a small saucepan; heat to 110°. Transfer to a small glass bowl; stir well. Cover and let stand at room temperature 6 to 12 hours or until thickened.
Reserve 6 strawberries for garnish; slice remaining strawberries.
Process half each of cream mixture, sliced strawberries, orange juice, liqueur, and sugar in container of an electric blender until smooth; pour into a bowl. Repeat procedure with remaining half of ingredients; stir well. Cover and chill 1 hour.

To serve, ladle soup into individual bowls; garnish with reserved strawberries. Yield: 6 cups.   Leslie Frederick

The Parkway Palate
San Joaquin River Parkway & Conservation Trust
Fresno, California

Chilled Avocado Soup

5 ripe avocados, coarsely
  chopped (about 5 cups)
¼ cup plus 2 tablespoons fresh
  lime juice
1 clove garlic, minced
2 cups chicken broth or stock,
  divided
4 cups buttermilk
1½ cups plain yogurt

1¼ teaspoons salt
1 teaspoon chili powder
1 teaspoon ground cumin
⅛ teaspoon ground red pepper
⅛ teaspoon dried mint flakes
3 cucumbers, peeled, seeded,
  and chopped (about 4 cups)
¼ cup chopped fresh cilantro

Process avocado, lime juice, garlic, and ⅓ cup chicken broth in container of an electric blender until smooth, stopping once to scrape down sides. Pour into a large bowl; stir in remaining 1⅔ cups broth, buttermilk, and yogurt, using a wire whisk. Stir in salt and next 4 ingredients; stir in cucumber. Serve at room temperature, or cover and chill. When ready to serve, ladle soup into individual bowls; sprinkle each serving with cilantro. Yield: 13 cups.

Made in the Shade
The Junior League of Greater Fort Lauderdale, Florida

Black Bean Gazpacho

No cooking is required to create this satisfying soup fit for hot summer days. Black beans and ham add boldness and body to this spicy vegetable medley.

3 cups peeled, seeded, and chopped fresh tomato
½ cup unpeeled chopped and seeded cucumber
½ cup chopped yellow squash or zucchini
½ cup chopped green pepper or sweet yellow pepper
¼ cup thinly sliced green onions
1 (15-ounce) can black beans, rinsed and drained

1 (11.5-ounce) can spicy vegetable juice or vegetable juice (about 1½ cups)
2 tablespoons Italian salad dressing
¼ teaspoon salt
1 cup cubed cooked ham (optional)
½ teaspoon hot sauce (optional)

Combine first 9 ingredients in a large bowl; stir gently. If desired, stir in ham and hot sauce. Cover and chill gazpacho at least 2 hours. Yield: 7 cups.

Sunny Mays Schust

The Hallelujah Courses
Mayo United Methodist Church
Edgewater, Maryland

Oriental Cucumber Soup

1 tablespoon cornstarch
2 tablespoons soy sauce
1 tablespoon dry sherry
½ pound lean pork, finely shredded
2 tablespoons vegetable oil
6 cups chicken broth

2 green onions, thinly sliced
1 medium cucumber, peeled, seeded, and chopped
½ teaspoon salt
¼ to ½ teaspoon ground white pepper

Combine first 3 ingredients in a large bowl, stirring with a wire whisk until smooth. Add pork, stirring gently to coat. Brown pork in hot oil in a large Dutch oven over medium-high heat 5 minutes, stirring constantly. Add broth; bring to a boil. Reduce heat, and simmer, uncovered, 10 minutes. Add green onions and remaining ingredients; bring to a boil. Reduce heat, and simmer, uncovered, 5 minutes. Serve immediately. Yield: 7 cups.

Call to Post
Lexington Hearing and Speech Center
Lexington, Kentucky

Roasted Red Pepper Soup

Top each serving of this brilliant red pepper soup with a dollop of sour cream; then fancy it up with a sprinkling of freshly grated lemon rind and chopped fresh parsley.

4 large sweet red peppers	¼ teaspoon salt
1 tablespoon olive oil	⅛ teaspoon curry powder
1 large onion, chopped	Garnishes: sour cream, grated
6 cups chicken broth	lemon rind, chopped fresh
2 medium carrots, scraped and diced	parsley
1 medium potato, peeled and diced	

Cut peppers in half crosswise; discard seeds and membranes. Place peppers, skin side up, on a baking sheet; flatten with palm of hand. Broil peppers 3 inches from heat (with electric oven door partially opened) 15 minutes or until charred. Place peppers in a heavy-duty, zip-top plastic bag; seal and let stand 10 minutes to loosen skins. Peel peppers, and discard skins. Chop peppers; set aside.

Heat oil in a large saucepan over medium-high heat. Add onion, and cook, stirring constantly, until tender. Add broth, carrot, and potato. Bring to a boil; cover, reduce heat, and simmer 20 minutes or until vegetables are tender. Add reserved red pepper, salt, and curry powder; simmer, uncovered, 5 minutes.

Process soup in batches in container of an electric blender until smooth. To serve, ladle soup into individual bowls. Garnish, if desired. Yield: 9 cups.

Merle Turner

Great Expectations
Assistance League of Southeastern Michigan
Rochester Hills, Michigan

Zucchini and Pasta Soup with Pistou

Pistou is France's answer to Italy's popular sauce, pesto. Fresh basil leaves provide the pungent and aromatic base. The classic sauce robustly flavors and garnishes this chunky vegetable soup.

1 cup peeled, cubed potato
1½ teaspoons salt
1 teaspoon pepper
8 cups water
2 large leeks, chopped (about 1½ cups)
2 large carrots, scraped and chopped (about 1½ cups)
1 medium onion, chopped
1 tablespoon butter or margarine, melted
1 tablespoon olive oil
½ pound green beans, trimmed and cut into 1-inch pieces (2 cups)

2 cups sliced zucchini (about 8 ounces)
1½ cups chopped fresh tomato (about 8 ounces)
¼ cup tightly packed torn fresh spinach
1 (15-ounce) can chick-peas (garbanzo beans), drained
½ cup elbow macaroni, uncooked
Pistou

Combine first 4 ingredients in a large Dutch oven. Bring to a boil; reduce heat, and simmer, uncovered, 30 minutes.

Remove and discard roots, tough outer leaves, and green tops from leeks. Coarsely chop remaining white portion of leeks. Cook leek, carrot, and onion in melted butter and olive oil in a large skillet over medium-high heat, stirring constantly, until vegetables are tender.

Add leek mixture to potato mixture. Add green beans and next 5 ingredients. Bring to a boil; reduce heat, and simmer, uncovered, 20 minutes or until vegetables are tender. Stir in ¼ cup Pistou. To serve, ladle soup into individual bowls. Top each serving with about 1 teaspoon Pistou. Yield: 12 cups.

Pistou

1 cup tightly packed fresh basil leaves
¼ cup olive oil

3 cloves garlic
⅓ cup freshly grated Parmesan cheese

Process fresh basil leaves, olive oil, and garlic cloves in a food processor until smooth. Stir in freshly grated Parmesan cheese. Yield ½ cup.   Prue Rosenthal

Michigan Cooks
C.S. Mott Children's Hospital
Ann Arbor, Michigan

Portuguese Sopas

Serve steaming bowlfuls of this hearty cabbage mix with substantial slices of crusty French bread.

1 (3-pound) chuck roast, cubed	1 teaspoon salt
1 (8-ounce) can tomato sauce	2 teaspoons ground cumin
1 cup fresh mint leaves	2 teaspoons ground allspice
1 cup dry red wine	1 teaspoon ground cloves
1 large onion, sliced	½ teaspoon pepper
3 bay leaves	1 medium cabbage, quartered
1 clove garlic, chopped	
2 tablespoons ground cinnamon	

Combine first 13 ingredients in a large Dutch oven; add water to cover. Bring to a boil; reduce heat to medium, and cook, uncovered, 4 hours, adding additional water to cover, if necessary. Add cabbage, and cook 15 more minutes or until cabbage is tender. Remove and discard bay leaves. Yield: 16 cups.

Out of the Ordinary
The Hingham Historical Society
Hingham, Massachusetts

Steak and Mushroom Soup

1¼ pounds sirloin steak, cut
    into 1-inch cubes
Steak Marinade
3 tablespoons all-purpose flour
3 tablespoons olive oil, divided
3 tablespoons butter, divided
1 medium onion, chopped
2 small carrots, scraped and
    minced
2 small stalks celery, minced
2 (8-ounce) packages sliced
    fresh mushrooms

2 medium onions, thinly sliced
5 cups beef broth (we tested
    with Swanson's)
1½ teaspoons salt
1 teaspoon freshly ground
    pepper
1 large bay leaf
6 cups tightly packed escarole,
    torn into bite-size pieces
    (about 1 pound)

Place steak in a heavy-duty, zip-top plastic bag; add Steak Marinade. Seal bag securely, and marinate in refrigerator 1 hour, turning once.

Remove steak from bag, and drain. Dredge meat in flour. Brown in 1½ tablespoons oil and 1½ tablespoons butter in a large Dutch oven over medium heat, stirring occasionally. Remove meat, and set aside.

Add remaining 1½ tablespoons oil and 1½ tablespoons butter to Dutch oven. Stir in chopped onion, carrot, and celery. Cook over medium-high heat, stirring constantly, until tender. Add mushrooms, and cook 3 minutes, stirring often. Add steak, sliced onion, beef broth, and next 3 ingredients. Bring to a boil; reduce heat, and simmer, uncovered, 15 minutes. Stir in escarole, and simmer 10 minutes (do not overcook). Discard bay leaf. Yield: 12 cups.

Steak Marinade

⅔ cup safflower oil
1 tablespoon dark brown sugar
2 tablespoons lemon juice

2 tablespoons soy sauce
1 teaspoon Dijon mustard
1 large clove garlic, minced

Combine all ingredients, stirring well with a wire whisk. Yield: about 1 cup.

Simply Divine
Second-Ponce de Leon Baptist Church
Atlanta, Georgia

Italian Sausage and Tortellini Soup

Herbs abound in this flavorful soup. Cut the amount of herbs in half or substitute fresh if you want a more subtle version of this sausage-tortellini showstopper.

1 pound mild Italian link
   sausage
1 medium-size green pepper,
   chopped
1 cup chopped onion
2 large cloves garlic, minced
5 cups beef broth
2 cups chopped fresh tomato
1 (8-ounce) can tomato sauce
1 large zucchini, sliced

1 large carrot, scraped and
   thinly sliced
½ cup dry red wine
2 tablespoons dried basil
2 tablespoons dried oregano
1 (9-ounce) package
   refrigerated cheese tortellini,
   uncooked
Freshly grated Parmesan
   cheese

Brown sausage in a Dutch oven over medium-high heat. Drain, reserving 1 tablespoon drippings in pan. Slice sausage, and set aside.

Add green pepper, onion, and garlic to drippings in pan; cook, stirring constantly, 5 minutes or until vegetables are tender. Add reserved sausage, beef broth, and next 7 ingredients, stirring well. Bring to a boil; cover, reduce heat, and simmer 40 minutes. Gently stir in tortellini. Bring to a boil; reduce heat, and simmer, uncovered, 5 minutes or until tortellini is done.

To serve, ladle soup into individual soup bowls. Sprinkle each serving with cheese. Yield: 9 cups.

Past to Present: A Pictorial Cookbook
Washington School Restoration Committee
Oakland, Oregon

Harbourtown Scallop Soup with Chardonnay and Saffron

3 medium leeks
3 tablespoons unsalted butter, divided
1 sweet red pepper, thinly sliced
4 cups fish stock
1 cup Chardonnay or other dry white wine
1 cup whipping cream
½ teaspoon salt
¼ teaspoon pepper
Pinch of saffron threads
¼ pound fresh mushrooms, sliced
¾ pound swordfish steaks, cut into bite-size pieces
¾ pound bay scallops
Garnish: chopped fresh parsley

Remove roots, tough outer leaves, and tops from leeks, leaving 2 inches of dark leaves. Wash thoroughly; finely chop. Melt 2 tablespoons butter in a skillet over medium heat; add leek. Cook, stirring constantly, 5 minutes or until tender. Add sliced red pepper; cook 2 more minutes. Set aside.

Combine fish stock and wine in a 4-quart Dutch oven; bring to a boil. Cook, uncovered, 10 minutes or until reduced to about 4 cups. Add cream; cook 10 more minutes. Stir in salt, pepper, saffron, and reserved leek mixture; set aside.

Heat remaining 1 tablespoon butter in a skillet over medium heat; add mushrooms. Cook, stirring constantly, 3 minutes or just until tender; set aside.

Bring fish stock mixture to a simmer; add swordfish. Cook, uncovered, 3 minutes. Add scallops; cook 3 more minutes. Stir in reserved mushrooms. Garnish, if desired. Yield: 6½ cups.

Note: In place of fish stock, you can use fish bouillon cubes dissolved in water according to package directions.

Eat Your Dessert or You Won't Get Any Broccoli
Sea Pines Montessori School
Hilton Head Island, South Carolina

Sicilian Seafood Chowder

This hearty chowder is packed with clams, shrimp, and scallops. Get a jump start on tomorrow night's dinner by chopping the vegetables and peeling the shrimp the night before.

3 tablespoons olive oil
½ cup chopped onion
½ cup chopped celery
½ cup chopped green pepper
3 large cloves garlic, minced
½ teaspoon dried basil
½ teaspoon dried thyme
½ teaspoon pepper
¼ teaspoon dried oregano
¼ teaspoon dried crushed red pepper

1 (6-ounce) can chopped clams, undrained
2 (8-ounce) bottles clam juice
1 (15-ounce) can tomato sauce
⅓ cup uncooked orzo
½ pound unpeeled fresh medium-size shrimp, peeled and deveined
½ pound sea scallops
1 tablespoon chopped fresh parsley

Heat olive oil in a large saucepan over medium-high heat; add onion, celery, and green pepper. Sauté 7 minutes or until mixture is tender. Add garlic and next 5 ingredients; cook 2 minutes.

Drain chopped clams, reserving liquid; set clams aside. Stir reserved clam liquid, clam juice, and tomato sauce into vegetable mixture; bring to a boil. Reduce heat, and simmer, uncovered, 30 minutes or until slightly thickened, stirring occasionally.

Cook orzo according to package directions; drain. Rinse with cold water; drain well, and set aside.

Add shrimp and scallops to chowder; cook 3 minutes or until shrimp turn pink and scallops are white. Stir in orzo, reserved chopped clams, and parsley; cook until chowder is thoroughly heated. Yield: 6 cups.

Emalou Grable

Victorian Secrets
The Chiselers, Inc.
Tampa, Florida

Fabulous Chili

An entire bottle of chili powder adds spicy appeal to this family pleaser.

4 stalks celery with leaves, chopped
3 green onions, chopped
2 cloves garlic, minced
1 large onion, chopped
1 medium-size green pepper, chopped
1 tablespoon vegetable oil
2 pounds ground chuck

2 cups water
1 (15-ounce) can tomato sauce
1 (6-ounce) can tomato paste
1 (1¼-ounce) bottle chili powder
1 teaspoon salt
¼ teaspoon pepper
1 (16-ounce) can kidney beans, undrained

Cook first 5 ingredients in oil in a large Dutch oven over medium-high heat, stirring constantly, until vegetables are tender. Remove vegetables from pan, and set aside.

Brown ground chuck in Dutch oven, stirring until it crumbles; drain well. Return vegetables to pan; add water and next 5 ingredients, stirring well. Bring to a boil; reduce heat, and simmer, uncovered, 25 minutes. Add beans, and cook 15 more minutes or to desired consistency. Yield: 10 cups.

Casey Payne

Cougar Bites
Crestline Elementary School
Birmingham, Alabama

Turkey and Wild Rice Chili

1 tablespoon vegetable oil
1 medium onion, chopped
1 clove garlic, minced
1¼ pounds skinned and boned turkey breast, cut into ½-inch pieces
2 cups cooked wild rice
1 (15.8-ounce) can Great Northern beans, drained
1 (11-ounce) can white whole kernel corn, drained
1 (10½-ounce) can reduced-sodium chicken broth
2 (4.5-ounce) cans diced green chiles, undrained
1 teaspoon salt
1 teaspoon ground cumin
2 teaspoons chili powder
⅛ teaspoon hot sauce
Shredded Monterey Jack cheese
Sour cream
Garnish: chopped fresh parsley or cilantro

Heat oil in a Dutch oven over medium heat; add onion and garlic, and cook, stirring constantly, until vegetables are tender. Add turkey and next 8 ingredients. Bring to a boil; cover, reduce heat, and simmer 30 minutes or until turkey is done. Stir in hot sauce.

To serve, ladle chili into individual bowls, and top with cheese and sour cream. Garnish, if desired. Yield: 8 cups.

Gracious Gator Cooks
The Junior League of Gainesville, Florida

Cioppino

San Francisco's immigrants from Italy are said to have created this seafood lovers' fantasy of a stew. It can be made ahead up to the point of adding the fresh seafood. The abundant yield assures a satisfying supper for all. Serve the stew in big bowls accompanied by chunks of crusty sourdough bread.

24 fresh littleneck clams
2 large onions, chopped
2 green peppers, chopped
4 cloves garlic, minced
¼ cup olive oil
¼ cup butter
½ pound fresh mushrooms, quartered
1 (28-ounce) can Italian-style tomatoes, undrained and chopped
1 (15-ounce) can tomato sauce
2 cups dry red wine
1 bay leaf

2 teaspoons salt
1 teaspoon pepper
1 teaspoon dried basil
1 teaspoon dried oregano
½ teaspoon hot sauce
2 pounds grouper or snapper fillets, cut into bite-size pieces
1 pound large fresh shrimp, peeled and deveined
½ pound sea scallops
½ pound fresh lump crabmeat, drained

Scrub clams thoroughly; discard any opened, cracked, or heavy clams (they're filled with sand); set clean clams aside.

Cook onion, green pepper, and garlic in oil and butter in a large stockpot over medium-high heat 5 minutes or just until vegetables are tender. Add mushrooms, and cook 5 minutes. Add tomatoes and next 8 ingredients; bring to a boil. Cover, reduce heat, and simmer 1 hour.

Add reserved clams; cover and simmer 3 minutes. Add grouper, shrimp, and scallops; cover and simmer 3 more minutes or until clams open and shrimp turn pink. Gently stir in crabmeat, and cook just until crabmeat is heated (do not overcook). Remove and discard bay leaf. Yield: 19 cups.

Note: To make ahead, let the vegetable mixture cool after it cooks 1 hour; cover and chill. Reheat just to a simmer before adding seafood.

Symphony of Flavors
The Associates of the Redlands Bowl
Redlands, California

Green Chile Pork Stew

To carry out the Spanish theme of this stew, serve warm flour tortillas alongside.

2 pounds boneless pork loin roast, cut into 1-inch cubes
1 tablespoon vegetable oil
4 cups chicken broth, divided
3 (15-ounce) cans whole kernel corn, drained
3 (4.5-ounce) cans diced green chiles, undrained
2 medium potatoes, peeled and diced
2 stalks celery, diced
1 teaspoon salt
1 teaspoon dried oregano
2 teaspoons ground cumin
3 tablespoons all-purpose flour

Brown pork in hot oil in a large Dutch oven. Add 3½ cups broth, corn, and next 6 ingredients; stir well. Bring to a boil; cover, reduce heat, and simmer 1 hour or until meat is tender.

Combine remaining ½ cup broth and flour; stir until blended. Stir into pork mixture. Bring to a boil; cook, stirring constantly, until mixture is thickened and bubbly. Yield: 10 cups.   Rhonda Howard

Our Favorite Recipes
Lutheran Church of the Good Shepherd
Billings, Montana

Hunter's Stew

Apples, carrots, and prunes add a gentle sweetness to this rich and smoky venison stew.

1 medium onion, sliced
2 cloves garlic, minced
¼ cup vegetable oil
1 pound venison stew meat
¼ cup all-purpose flour
2 tablespoons sweet Hungarian paprika
2 (14½-ounce) cans beef broth
¼ pound smoked ham, cut into 1-inch pieces
¼ pound smoked sausage, cut into 1-inch pieces
½ cup water
2 tablespoons tomato paste
1 teaspoon salt
1 teaspoon dried marjoram

1 teaspoon dried parsley flakes
¼ teaspoon black pepper
⅛ teaspoon ground red pepper
1 (2-pound) cabbage, chopped (about 9 cups)
2 Golden Delicious apples, unpeeled and chopped (about 3 cups)
2 medium carrots, scraped and thinly sliced (about 1½ cups)
8 pitted prunes, coarsely chopped
3 fresh tomatoes, peeled and coarsely chopped
⅓ cup dry red wine
Pinch of sugar

Cook sliced onion and minced garlic in hot oil in a 6-quart Dutch oven over medium-high heat 3 minutes, stirring constantly. Remove vegetables from pan, reserving drippings in pan; set vegetables aside.

Brown venison in pan drippings. Return onion and garlic to pan. Sprinkle flour over meat mixture, and stir to moisten. Add paprika, and cook 1 minute, stirring constantly. Gradually stir in broth, and add next 9 ingredients. Bring to a boil; cover, reduce heat, and simmer 45 minutes or until meat is tender, stirring occasionally.

Add cabbage and next 3 ingredients; stir well. Bring to a boil; reduce heat, and simmer, uncovered, 20 minutes. Stir in tomato, wine, and sugar. Bring to a boil; reduce heat, and simmer, uncovered, 10 more minutes. Yield: 14½ cups.   Maxim Dem´Chak

Past Receipts, Present Recipes
Cumberland County Historical Society
Carlisle, Pennsylvania

Vegetables

Sugar Snap Peas in Toasted Sesame Vinaigrette, page 313

Asparagus Gratin

Pair this elegant asparagus side dish with your best basic chicken recipe to elevate your entrée to impressive new heights.

3 pounds fresh asparagus
½ cup dry white wine
1 cup sliced green onions
½ cup butter, melted
2 tablespoons chopped sweet
   red pepper

½ teaspoon salt
½ teaspoon dried thyme
½ teaspoon dried rosemary
2 tablespoons freshly grated
   Parmesan cheese

Snap off tough ends of asparagus. Remove scales from stalks with a vegetable peeler, if desired. Arrange asparagus in a steamer basket over boiling water. Cover and steam, in batches, if necessary, 4 to 6 minutes or until crisp-tender. Drain. Place asparagus in a lightly greased 11- x 7- x 1½-inch baking dish. Pour wine over asparagus.

Cook green onions in butter in a medium skillet over medium-high heat, stirring constantly, until tender. Add pepper and next 3 ingredients. Pour over asparagus mixture. Sprinkle with Parmesan cheese. Bake, uncovered, at 350° for 5 minutes or until cheese melts. Yield: 10 to 12 servings.

Mary Hutz

What's Cooking in Hampton
Friends of Hampton Community Library
Allison Park, Pennsylvania

Black Beans, Corn, and Tomatoes

Serve this make-ahead side dish with your favorite grilled meat or by itself as a hearty vegetable salad.

⅓ cup vegetable oil
¼ cup fresh lemon juice
1½ teaspoons salt
1 teaspoon Worcestershire
   sauce
½ teaspoon dry mustard
½ teaspoon celery salt
¼ teaspoon ground white pepper
¼ teaspoon ground red pepper

¼ teaspoon ground black
   pepper
3 cups chopped fresh tomato
1 (15-ounce) can black beans,
   drained
1 (11-ounce) can white corn,
   drained
1 cup chopped green onions
⅓ cup chopped fresh cilantro

Combine first 9 ingredients in a small bowl, and stir well. Cover and chill.

Combine tomato and remaining 4 ingredients in a large bowl; toss gently. Pour lemon juice mixture over vegetables, tossing well. Cover and chill 8 to 10 hours, stirring occasionally. Stir before serving. Yield: 6 servings.

Texas Ties
The Junior League of North Harris County
Spring, Texas

Absolutely Best Baked Beans

Our triple bean bonanza is beefed up with ground chuck and crumbled bacon. The sweet kisses of sugars and ketchup add balance to this hearty mix.

½ **pound ground chuck**
½ **cup sugar**
½ **cup firmly packed brown sugar**
½ **cup chopped onion**
½ **cup ketchup**
1 **(16-ounce) can kidney beans, rinsed and drained**

1 **(15¼-ounce) can baby lima beans, drained**
1 **(15-ounce) can pork and beans**
½ **pound bacon, cooked and crumbled**

Brown meat in a large skillet, stirring until it crumbles; drain well.

Combine meat, sugars, and next 5 ingredients in a lightly greased 11- x 7- x 1½-inch baking dish. Cover bean mixture, and bake at 350° for 1 hour. Sprinkle beans with crumbled bacon just before serving. Yield:5 servings.

Georgia Link

The Great Delights Cookbook
Genoa Serbart United Methodist Churches
Genoa, Colorado

Sprouts Supreme

These supreme sprouts will make converts out of nonbrussels sprouts eaters.

1 pound fresh brussels sprouts
1 teaspoon sugar
1 (10¾-ounce) can cream of chicken soup, undiluted
1 (8-ounce) can sliced water chestnuts, drained
1 cup mayonnaise
2 tablespoons fresh lemon juice
1 tablespoon grated fresh onion
½ teaspoon ground nutmeg
½ teaspoon dried dillweed
¼ teaspoon salt
¼ teaspoon garlic powder
¼ teaspoon dried tarragon
¼ teaspoon pepper
Dash of hot sauce
1½ cups crushed round buttery crackers (about 35 crackers)
⅓ cup grated Parmesan cheese
⅛ teaspoon garlic powder
¼ cup butter or margarine, melted

Wash brussels sprouts; remove discolored leaves. Cut off stem ends, and cut a shallow X in the bottom of each sprout. Place brussels sprouts and sugar in a saucepan; add water to cover. Bring to a boil; cover, reduce heat, and simmer 8 to 10 minutes or until almost tender. Drain and transfer to a buttered 11- x 7- x 1½-inch baking dish.

Meanwhile, combine soup and next 11 ingredients in a medium bowl; stir well. Spoon sauce over sprouts in dish.

Combine cracker crumbs, Parmesan cheese, and ⅛ teaspoon garlic powder; add melted butter, stirring well. Sprinkle over sauce. Bake, uncovered, at 350° for 20 minutes or until bubbly. Yield: 8 servings.

I'll Cook When Pigs Fly
The Junior League of Cincinnati, Ohio

Cauliflower Suisse

1 medium cauliflower (about 2 pounds), cut into flowerets
½ cup sour cream
½ cup (2 ounces) shredded Swiss cheese
½ cup (2 ounces) shredded Monterey Jack cheese
¼ cup mayonnaise
½ cup soft breadcrumbs (homemade)
2 tablespoons butter or margarine, melted
4 slices bacon, cooked and crumbled

Cook cauliflower in boiling water to cover 8 minutes; drain. Place cauliflower in an ungreased 11- x 7- x 1½-inch baking dish; set aside.

Combine sour cream and next 3 ingredients in a small heavy saucepan; cook over low heat, stirring constantly, 16 minutes or until smooth. Spoon cheese sauce over cauliflower.

Combine breadcrumbs and melted butter; sprinkle breadcrumbs evenly over cheese sauce. Sprinkle crumbled bacon evenly over breadcrumbs. Bake, uncovered, at 350° for 30 minutes or until casserole is lightly browned. Yield: 4 servings.   Fern Warnecke

Recipes for Champions
Shebas of Khiva Temple Oriental Band
Amarillo, Texas

Grilled Wild Mushrooms

If you're partial to shiitake mushrooms, substitute large fresh shiitakes for the portobellos.

4 large portobello mushrooms (about 1 pound)	½ teaspoon salt
½ cup butter, melted	¼ teaspoon freshly ground pepper
¼ cup chopped fresh parsley	Vegetable cooking spray
3 cloves garlic, minced	

Remove and discard stems from mushrooms; set mushrooms aside. Combine butter and next 4 ingredients in a small bowl, stirring well. Brush tops of mushrooms with butter mixture.

Coat grill rack with cooking spray; place on grill over medium-hot coals (350° to 400°). Place mushrooms on rack, top side down, and grill, covered, 4 minutes. Turn mushrooms; brush with remaining butter mixture, and grill, covered, 4 minutes or just until tender. Yield: 4 servings.

Texas Ties
The Junior League of North Harris County
Spring, Texas

Onion Shortcake

1 large sweet onion, chopped (about 3 cups)
¼ cup butter, melted
1 (8½-ounce) package corn muffin mix (we tested with Jiffy)
1 cup canned cream-style corn
½ cup milk

1 large egg, lightly beaten
⅛ teaspoon hot sauce
1 (8-ounce) carton sour cream
1 cup (4 ounces) shredded sharp Cheddar cheese, divided
¼ teaspoon salt
¼ teaspoon dried dillweed

Cook onion in butter in a large skillet over medium-high heat, stirring constantly, until tender. Set aside.

Combine muffin mix and next 4 ingredients. Pour batter into a buttered 8-inch square pan.

Combine onion mixture, sour cream, ½ cup shredded cheese, salt, and dillweed. Spread over batter in pan. Sprinkle with remaining ½ cup cheese. Bake, uncovered, at 425° for 20 to 25 minutes or until set. Cut shortcake into squares, and serve immediately. Yield: 6 to 8 servings.

Sue Schultz

Great Expectations
The Assistance League of Southeastern Michigan
Rochester Hills, Michigan

Honey-Orange Parsnips

These honeyed parsnips are bathed in a citrus glaze thanks to fresh orange juice and grated rind.

1 cup water
1 pound parsnips, peeled and sliced
3 tablespoons butter or margarine

1 tablespoon honey
1 teaspoon grated orange rind
1 tablespoon fresh orange juice

Bring water to a boil in a medium saucepan. Add parsnips; cover and cook 8 minutes or just until tender. Drain. Return parsnips to pan; add butter and remaining ingredients, stirring gently until butter melts. Place pan over medium heat, and cook, uncovered, 1 to 2 minutes or until parsnips are glazed, stirring occasionally. Yield: 3 to 4 servings.

Historically Heavenly Home Cooking
Corry Area Historical Society
Corry, Pennsylvania

Sugar Snap Peas in Toasted Sesame Vinaigrette

Sugar Snaps not in season? Use frozen Sugar Snap peas that have been thawed on paper towels. There's no need to cook the frozen variety before continuing with the recipe.

¼ cup sesame seeds
1 small clove garlic, crushed
1 tablespoon fresh lemon juice
1 teaspoon Dijon mustard
¼ teaspoon salt
¼ teaspoon pepper

1 tablespoon red wine vinegar
2 tablespoons olive oil
1 teaspoon dark sesame oil
1 pound fresh Sugar Snap peas, trimmed

Cook sesame seeds in a skillet over medium heat 3 minutes or until toasted; remove from skillet, and let cool.

Combine garlic and next 4 ingredients in a large bowl. Stir in vinegar. Add oils, stirring well with a wire whisk.

Cook peas in a saucepan in a small amount of boiling water 30 seconds or to desired degree of doneness. Drain and rinse under cold water to stop the cooking process. Add peas and sesame seeds to garlic mixture; toss well to coat. Serve at room temperature, or cover and chill. Yield: 4 to 6 servings.

Seaboard to Sideboard
The Junior League of Wilmington, North Carolina

Florentine Stuffed Red Bell Peppers

¼ cup minced onion
1 clove garlic, minced
1 tablespoon plus 1 teaspoon olive oil
1 (10-ounce) package frozen chopped spinach, thawed
1 teaspoon salt
1 teaspoon dried thyme
½ teaspoon pepper
¼ teaspoon ground nutmeg

4 cups (16 ounces) shredded Swiss cheese
½ cup half-and-half
½ cup vegetable broth
3 tablespoons dry sherry
4 cups cooked orzo
8 medium-size sweet red peppers, cut in half lengthwise

Cook onion and garlic in hot oil in a large skillet over medium-high heat, stirring constantly, until tender. Add spinach and next 4 ingredients. Reduce heat to medium, and cook, uncovered, 1 minute. Add cheese and next 3 ingredients. Cook, stirring constantly, until cheese melts. Stir in orzo.

Spoon ½ cup orzo mixture into each pepper half, and place on an ungreased baking sheet. Bake, uncovered, at 350° for 30 minutes or until thoroughly heated. Yield: 16 servings.   Dina Driggs

A Bite of the Best
Relief Society Church of Jesus Christ of Latter Day Saints
Provo, Utah

Potato and Feta Cheese Soufflé

2¼ pounds red potatoes (about 4 medium), peeled and cut into eighths
4 large eggs, separated
¾ cup half-and-half
1 small onion, minced
1 stalk celery, finely chopped

3 tablespoons butter or margarine, melted
1 (4-ounce) package crumbled feta cheese
½ teaspoon salt
½ teaspoon freshly ground pepper

Cook potato in salted water to cover 20 minutes or until tender. Drain; cool slightly. Place potato in a large mixing bowl; mash well. Add egg yolks and half-and-half. Beat mixture at medium-low speed of an electric mixer just until smooth; set aside.

Cook onion and celery in melted butter in a medium skillet over medium-high heat, stirring constantly, until tender. Add onion and celery mixture, feta cheese, salt, and pepper to potato mixture; stir well.

Beat egg whites at high speed until stiff but not dry; gently fold into potato mixture. Pour potato mixture into a buttered 1½-quart soufflé dish. Bake, uncovered, at 400° for 35 to 40 minutes or until puffed and golden. Serve immediately. Yield: 6 servings.

Carolina Sunshine, Then & Now
The Charity League of Charlotte, North Carolina

Triple-Cheese Potatoes

1½ pounds baking potatoes, peeled and quartered (about 3 medium)
½ cup hot milk
2 tablespoons butter or margarine
1 egg yolk
1 teaspoon dried Italian seasoning
½ teaspoon salt
½ teaspoon pepper
¼ cup fine, dry breadcrumbs (store-bought)
1 cup (4 ounces) shredded mozzarella cheese
1 cup (4 ounces) shredded provolone cheese
½ cup grated Parmesan cheese

Cook potato in boiling water to cover 20 minutes or until tender; drain well. Return potato to pan. Add milk and next 5 ingredients. Mash well with a potato masher; set aside.

Sprinkle breadcrumbs in bottom of a greased 8-inch square baking dish. Combine mozzarella cheese and provolone cheese; set aside.

Carefully spread half of potato mixture in prepared dish; sprinkle with half of cheese mixture. Repeat layers. Top with Parmesan cheese. Bake, uncovered, at 375° for 25 minutes or until top is golden. Yield: 6 servings.

Beyond Burlap, Idaho's Famous Potato Recipes
The Junior League of Boise, Idaho

Tennessee Sippin' Yams

Yams and sweet potatoes are often confused with one another. Yet, technically they aren't the same. Yams are sweeter and moister, and they aren't widely sold in the U.S.

4 pounds sweet potatoes,
  peeled, cooked, and mashed
½ cup butter, melted
⅓ cup firmly packed brown
  sugar
⅓ cup orange juice

¼ cup whiskey
¾ teaspoon salt
½ teaspoon ground allspice
Pecan Crumble
Whiskey Sauce

Combine first 7 ingredients in a large bowl; stir well. Spoon mixture into a greased 2½-quart casserole. Sprinkle evenly with Pecan Crumble. Bake, uncovered, at 350° for 45 minutes or until lightly browned and bubbly around the edges. Serve with warm Whiskey Sauce. Yield: 13 servings.

Pecan Crumble

1 cup firmly packed brown
  sugar
1 cup chopped pecans
½ cup all-purpose flour

1 cup grated coconut
  (optional)
⅓ cup butter

Combine first 3 ingredients; add coconut, if desired. Cut in butter with a pastry blender until mixture is crumbly. Yield: 4 cups.

Whiskey Sauce

⅔ cup firmly packed brown
  sugar
⅓ cup light corn syrup
¼ cup water

¼ cup butter
⅛ teaspoon ground mace
½ cup whiskey

Combine first 5 ingredients in top of a double boiler; bring water to a boil. Reduce heat to medium; cook until thickened, stirring often. Remove from heat; stir in whiskey. Yield: 1½ cups.   Sadie LeSueur

Linen Napkins to Paper Plates
The Junior Auxiliary of Clarksville, Tennessee

Spaghetti Squash

1 (3-pound) spaghetti squash
1 medium onion, chopped
1 clove garlic, minced
2 tablespoons vegetable oil
1 cup chopped fresh Swiss chard
3 large eggs, lightly beaten
1 cup plus 2 tablespoons fine, dry breadcrumbs, divided (store-bought)

½ cup freshly grated Parmesan cheese
1½ teaspoons salt
1 teaspoon dried parsley flakes
1 teaspoon dried Italian seasoning
¼ teaspoon pepper
Vegetable cooking spray

Cut squash in half lengthwise; discard seeds.

Place squash, cut side up, in a Dutch oven; cover with water. Bring to a boil; cover, reduce heat, and simmer 20 minutes or until tender. Using a fork, remove spaghetti-like strands, leaving 2 (¼-inch-thick) shells; set shells aside. Place strands in a large bowl; set aside.

Cook onion and garlic in hot oil in a large skillet over medium-high heat, stirring constantly, 3 minutes or until onion is tender.

Combine squash and Swiss chard. Add to onion mixture; cook, uncovered, 3 to 5 minutes or until Swiss chard is wilted and tender. Add eggs, 1 cup breadcumbs, and next 5 ingredients.

Place reserved squash shells into an ungreased 13- x 9- x 2-inch baking dish. Spoon squash mixture evenly into shells. Sprinkle with remaining 2 tablespoons breadcrumbs. Coat breadcrumbs with cooking spray. Bake, uncovered, at 350° for 45 minutes. Yield: 4 to 6 servings.

Mary J. Dussault

Green Thumbs in the Kitchen
Green Thumb, Inc.
Arlington, Virginia

Acorn Squash Toss

Leaving the skin on the acorn squash not only adds to the flavor of this dish but also makes preparation quick.

1 acorn squash (about 1½ pounds)
1 tablespoon olive oil
1 tablespoon butter or margarine

1 clove garlic, minced
2 tablespoons soy sauce
¼ teaspoon salt
2 teaspoons sesame seeds, toasted

Cut squash in half, and remove seeds. Cut squash into 1-inch pieces.

Arrange squash in a steamer basket over boiling water. Cover and steam 10 to 12 minutes or to desired tenderness. Set aside.

Heat olive oil and butter in a large skillet over medium-high heat until butter melts; add garlic. Cook, stirring constantly, until garlic begins to brown. Add squash, soy sauce, and salt, tossing gently. Sprinkle with sesame seeds. Serve immediately. Yield: 4 servings.

Secrets of Amelia
McArthur Family Branch YMCA
Fernandina Beach, Florida

Zucchini Rounds

Fritter fans will fawn over this vegetable version. Shreds of zucchini and smoky bits of bacon are the stars.

6 to 8 slices bacon, chopped
2 medium zucchini
⅓ cup biscuit mix
¼ cup grated Parmesan cheese
¼ cup finely chopped onion

¼ teaspoon garlic powder
⅛ teaspoon pepper
2 large eggs, lightly beaten
3 tablespoons butter, divided

Cook bacon in a large skillet until crisp; remove bacon from skillet, and set bacon aside.

Shred enough zucchini to measure 2 cups; set aside. Reserve remaining zucchini for another use.

Combine reserved bacon, biscuit mix, and next 4 ingredients; stir well. Add eggs, stirring just until dry ingredients are moistened. Fold in zucchini.

Melt 2 tablespoons butter in a large skillet over medium heat. Using half of zucchini mixture, spoon 2 tablespoons mixture for each fritter into skillet. Cook about 2 to 3 minutes on each side or until browned.

Repeat procedure with remaining butter and zucchini mixture. Serve immediately. Yield: 4 servings (12 fritters).

First Baptist Church Centennial Cookbook
First Baptist Church
Cushing, Oklahoma

Oven-Roasted Ratatouille

2 **medium zucchini, coarsely chopped (about 2 cups)**
1 **small eggplant, coarsely chopped (about 3 cups)**
2 **teaspoons salt**
1 **pound cherry tomatoes**
1 **sweet red pepper, cut into 1-inch pieces**
1 **sweet yellow pepper, cut into 1-inch pieces**
1 **medium onion, cut into 1-inch pieces**
1 **cup lightly packed torn fresh basil leaves (about 1 bunch)**
2 **large cloves garlic, minced**
½ **teaspoon pepper**
3 **tablespoons olive oil**

Place zucchini and eggplant in a colander; sprinkle with salt. Cover with a small plate, and let stand at room temperature 1 hour. Pat dry with paper towels.

Arrange zucchini, eggplant, tomatoes, and next 3 ingredients in a single layer on an ungreased 15- x 10- x 1½-inch jellyroll pan. Sprinkle with basil, garlic, and pepper. Drizzle with oil. Bake, uncovered, at 400° for 40 minutes. Serve immediately. Yield: 6 to 8 servings.

Have You Heard . . . A Tasteful Medley of Memphis
Subsidium, Inc.
Memphis, Tennessee

Acknowledgments

Each of the community cookbooks listed is represented by recipes appearing in *America's Best Recipes*. Unless otherwise noted, the copyright is held by the sponsoring organization whose mailing address is included.

7 Alarm Cuisine, East Mountain Volunteer Fire Department, Rte. 2, Box 162, Gladewater, TX 75647

25 Years of Food, Fun & Friendship, Clifton Community Woman's Club, P.O. Box 105, Clifton, VA 20124

75 Years and Still Cooking, Lakeside Presbyterian Church, 7343 Hermitage Rd., Richmond, VA 23228

The Albany Collection: Treasures and Treasured Recipes, Women's Council of the Albany Institute of History and Art, 125 Washington Ave., Albany, NY 12210

Ambrosia, Junior Auxiliary of Vicksburg, P.O. Box 86, Vicksburg, MS 39180

Apron Strings: Ties to the Southern Tradition of Cooking, Junior League of Little Rock, Inc., 3600 Cantrell Rd., Ste. 102, Little Rock, AR 72202

The Art of Cooking, Muscle Shoals District Service League, P.O. Box 793, Sheffield, AL 35660

Back to the Table, Episcopal Church Women—Christ Church, P.O. Box 25778, Raleigh, NC 27611-5778

Barnard's 'Beary' Best Cookbook, Barnard United Methodist Youth Department, Main St., Box 86, Barnard, KS 67418

Bartlett Memorial Hospital's 25th Anniversary Cookbook, Bartlett Memorial Hospital, 3260 Hospital Dr., Juneau, AK 99801

Beneath the Palms, Brownsville Junior Service League, Inc., 5062 Lakeway Dr., Brownsville, TX 78520

Best and Blessed, Sweet Spirit Singers, 135 Main St., Liberty, MS 39645

Beyond Burlap, Idaho's Famous Potato Recipes, Junior League of Boise, Inc., 5266 W. Franklin Rd., Boise, ID 83705

Beyond Chicken Soup, Jewish Home of Rochester Auxiliary, 2021 Wintin Rd. S., Rochester, NY 14618

A Bite of the Best, Relief Society Church of Jesus Christ of Latter Day Saints, 3687 N. Littlerock Dr., Provo, UT 84604

Blessings, First Presbyterian Church, 717 W. 32nd, Pine Bluff, AR 71603

Block-Brantley Family Favorites, Block-Brantley Reunion, c/o Irma Lee Picketts, 1107 Thorain, San Antonio, TX 78201

Bread from the Brook, The Church at Brook Hills, 3145 Brook Highland Pkwy., Birmingham, AL 35242

Bridging the Generations, Japanese American Citizen's League, 2256 Overlook Dr., Bloomington, MN 55431-3957

Bully's Best Bites, Junior Auxiliary of Starkville, Inc., P. O. Box 941, Starkville, MS 39760

Call to Post, Lexington Hearing and Speech Center, 635 Iron Works Pike, Lexington, KY 40511

Canton McKinley Bulldogs Pup's Pantry, McKinley Booster Club, 3490 Cardiff NW, Canton, OH 44708

A Capital Affair, Junior League of Harrisburg, Inc., 3211 N. Front St., Ste. 301, Harrisburg, PA 17110

Capital Celebrations, Junior League of Washington, 3039 M St. NW, Washington, DC 20007

Carnegie Hall Cookbook, Carnegie Hall, Inc., 105 Church St., Lewisburg, WV 24901

Carolina Cuisine: Nothin' Could Be Finer, Junior Charity League of Marlboro County, Inc., 100 Fayetteville Ave., Bennettsville, SC 29512

Carolina Sunshine, Then & Now, Charity League of Charlotte, P.O. Box 12495, Charlotte, NC 28220

Chautauqua Porches–A Centennial Cookbook, Colorado Chautauqua Cottagers, Inc., % Valerie Hess, Colorado Chautauqua, Cottage #10, Boulder, CO 80302

Classic Italian Cooking, Italian American Society of San Marco Island, 366 Wales Ct., Marco Island, FL 34145

Classically Kiawah, The Alternatives, 10 Rhetts Bluff, Kiawah Island, SC 29455

Cook Bookery, The University of Illinois College of Medicine at Peoria, One Illini Dr., Peoria, IL 61605

The Cookbook of the Museum of Science, Boston, The Volunteer Service League of the Museum of Science, Boston, Science Park, Boston, MA 02114-1099

The Cookbook Tour, Good Shepherd Lutheran Church, P.O. Box 355 Hwy. 42, Plainview, MN 55964

A Cookery & Memories from Old Bourne, The Bourne Society for Historic Preservation, 22 Sandwich Rd., Bourne, MA 02532

Cooking from the Heart, Girl Scout Troop 669, 4319 Newton St., Metairie, LA 70001

Cooking from the Heart, Pleasant View Mennonite Church, 58529 CR 23, Goshen, IN 46528

Cooking with Pride, Madison Park/Camelview PTO, 1431 East Campbell, Phoenix, AZ 85014

Cookin' in the Canyon, Jarbidge Community Hall, P.O. Box 260081, Jarbidge, NV 89826

The Cook's Canvas, St. John's Museum of Art, 114 Orange St., Wilmington, NC 28401

Cougar Bites, Crestline Elementary School, 3785 Jackson Blvd., Birmingham, AL 35213

Crossroads Cookbook, New Albany-Plain Township Historical Society, 107 E. Granville St., P.O. Box 219, New Albany, OH 43054

Culinary Classics, Hoffman Estates Medical Center Service League, 1555 N. Barrington Rd., Hoffman Estates, IL 60194

Culinary Tastes of Blue Mountain Cooks, Grand Terrace Branch Library: Friends, 22795 Barton Rd., Grand Terrace, CA 92313

Doggone Good Cookin', Support Dogs, Inc., 9510 Page Ave., St. Louis, MO 63132

Down by the Water, Junior League of Columbia, Inc., 2926 Devine St., Columbia, SC 29205

Eat Your Dessert or You Won't Get Any Broccoli, Sea Pines Montessori School, 9 Fox Grape Rd., Hilton Head Island, SC 29928

Expressions, National League of American Pen Women, Chester County, 2300 W. Chester Rd., Coatesville, PA 19320

Fire Gals' Hot Pans Cookbook, Garrison Emergency Services Auxiliary, 203 E. Main St., P.O. Box 146, Garrison, IA 52229

First Baptist Church Centennial Cookbook, First Baptist Church, Moses at Little, P.O. Box 187, Cushing, OK 74023

Fishing for Compliments, Shedd Aquarium Society, 1200 S. Lake Shore Dr., Chicago, IL 60605

Flavors of Falmouth, Falmouth Historical Society, 55-65 Palmer Ave., Falmouth, MA 02541

The Flavors of Mackinac, Mackinac Island Medical Center, P.O. Box 536, Market St., Mackinac Island, MI 49757

Food Fabulous Food, Women's Board to Cooper Hospital/University Medical Center, One Cooper Plaza, Camden, NJ 08103

Food for the Soul, Matt Talbot Kitchen, 1911 R St., Lincoln, NE 68501

Food for Thought, Friends of Centerville Public Library, 67 Long Pond Cir., Centerville, MA 02632

Foods and Flowers, Hermosa Garden Club, P. O. Box 782, Hermosa Beach, CA 90254

Foods from the Homelands, Kingsburg Friends of the Library, 1445 Marion St., Kingsburg, CA 93631

From ANNA's Kitchen, Adams-Normandie Neighborhood Association (ANNA), P.O. Box 15153, Los Angeles, CA 90015-0153

From Home Plate to Home Cooking, Atlanta Braves, 755 Hank Aaron Dr., Atlanta, GA 30315

The Fruit of the Spirit, Sumrall United Methodist Women's Circle, P.O. Box 276, Sumrall, MS 39482

Fruits of Our Labor, St. Joseph Parish, 7607 Trendwood Dr., Lincoln, NE 68506

A Gardener Cooks, Danbury Garden Club, 21 Summit St., New Milford, CT 06776

Generations of Good Food, Jeannette Public Library, Sixth and Magee Sts., Jeannette, PA 15644

Gracious Gator Cooks, Junior League of Gainesville, 430-A N. Main St., Gainesville, FL 32605

Gracious Goodness Christmas in Charleston, Bishop England High School Endowment Fund, 203 Calhoun St., Charleston, SC 29401-3522

The Great Delights Cookbook, Genoa Serbart United Methodist Churches, 211 Main St., Genoa, CO 80818

Great Expectations, Assistance League of Southeastern Michigan, 3128 Walton Blvd., Ste. 247, Rochester Hills, MI 48309

Great Lake Effects, Junior League of Buffalo, Inc., 45 Elmwood Ave., Buffalo, NY 14201

Green Thumbs in the Kitchen, Green Thumb, Inc., 2000 N. 14th St. #800, Arlington, VA 22201

The Hallelujah Courses, Mayo United Methodist Church, 1005 Old Turkey Point Rd., Edgewater, MD 21037

Have You Heard . . . A Tasteful Medley of Memphis, Subsidium, Inc., 4711 Spottswood, Memphis, TN 38117

Hearthside: A Country Community Cookbook, Christ Community Church, P.O. Box 391, Weare, NH 03281

Historically Heavenly Home Cooking, Corry Area Historical Society, P.O. Box 107, Corry, PA 16407

I'll Cook When Pigs Fly, Junior League of Cincinnati, 3500 Columbia Pkwy., Cincinnati, OH 45226

International Home Cooking, The United Nations International School Parents' Association, 24-50 Franklin D. Roosevelt Dr., New York, NY 10010

In the Breaking of Bread, Catholic Committee on Scouting and Camp Fire, P.O. Box 1826, Lake Charles, LA 70602

Iowa: A Taste of Home, Iowa 4-H Foundation, 32 Curtiss Hall-Iowa State University, Ames, IA 50011

Just Desserts, Amsterdam Free Library, 28 Church St., Amsterdam, NY 12010

The Kansas City Barbeque Society Cookbook, Kansas City Barbeque Society, 11514 Hickman Mills Dr., Kansas City, MO 64134

Katonah Cooks!, Katonah Village Improvement Society, Katonah Village Library, Katonah, NY 10536

Kenwood Lutheran Church Cookbook, Kenwood Women of the Evangelical Lutheran Church in America, 324 W. Cleveland St., Duluth, MN 55811

Kitchen Keepsakes, United Methodist Church Women, 801 N. Bell St., Beloit, KS 67420

Landmark Entertaining, Junior League of Abilene, 774 Butternut St., Abilene, TX 79602

Let's Get Cooking, Monvale Health Resources Auxiliary, Country Club Rd., Monongahela, PA 15063

Linen Napkins to Paper Plates, Junior Auxiliary of Clarksville, Inc., P.O. Box 30, Clarksville, TN 37041

Love for Others, Our Shepherd Lutheran Church, 2225 E. 14 Mile Rd., Birmingham, MI 48009

Madalene Cooks–50 Years of Good Taste, Church of the Madalene, 3304 N. 3rd St., Broken Arrow, OK 74012

Made in the Shade, Junior League of Greater Fort Lauderdale, 704 SE 1st St., Fort Lauderdale, FL 33301

The Many Tastes of Haverstraw Middle School, Home and Career Skills Department, Haverstraw Middle School, 16 Grant St., Haverstraw, NY 10927

Mediterranean Delights, St. Elias Orthodox Theotokos Society/Philoptochos Society St. Elias Orthodox Church, 915 Lynn St., New Castle, PA 16101

Meet Me in the Kitchen, Northside Church of Christ, 2500 Parrish St., Waco, TX 76705

Michigan Cooks, C.S. Mott Children's Hospital, 1500 E. Medical Center Dr., D5202, Ann Arbor, MI 48109-0718

Moments, Memories & Manna, Restoration Village, 2215 Little Flock Dr., Rogers, AR 72756

The Monarch's Feast, Mary Munford PTA, 211 Westmoreland Rd., Richmond, VA 23227

Morrisonville's 125th Anniversary Cookbook, Morrisonville Historical Society & Museum, % Dorothy Bullard, 611 Dcy St., P.O. Box 227, Morrisonville, IL 62546-0227

Newport Cooks & Collects, Preservation Society of Newport County, 424 Bellevue Ave., Newport, RI 02840

Noel Bluffin' We're Still Cookin', Noel Area Chamber of Commerce, 108 S. Railroad, P.O. Box 173, Noel, MO 64854

Notable Feasts, Friends of the Cape Cod Symphony Orchestra, 712-A Main St., Yarmouth Port, MA 02675

Note Worthy Recipes, Wilson Presbyterian Church, 400 N. 4th St. and Locust, Clairton, PA 15025

Nun Better: Tastes and Tales from Around a Cajun Table, St. Cecilia School, 302 W. Main St., Broussard, LA 70518

Our Country Christmas Collection, Skaggs Community Health Center, 251 Skaggs Rd., Branson, MO 65615

Our Family's Favorite Recipes, University Family Fellowship, 1125 Stanford Way, Sparks, NV 89431

Our Favorite Recipes, Claremont Society for the Prevention of Cruelty to Animals Serving Sullivan County, Inc., Rte. 3 Box 337, Claremont, NH 03743

Our Favorite Recipes, Lutheran Church of the Good Shepherd, 1108 24th St. W., Billings, MT 59102

Our Heritage Cookbook, First Baptist Church, 218 N. 34th, Billings, MT 59101

Our Savior's Lutheran Church 75th Anniversary Cookbook, Our Saviour's Lutheran Church, 318 E. 6th St., Casper, WY 82604

Our Sunrise Family Cookbook, Sunrise Drive Elementary School, 5301 E. Sunrise Dr., Tucson, AZ 85718

Out of the Ordinary, The Hingham Historical Society, P.O. Box 434, Hingham, MA 02043

The Parkway Palate, San Joaquin River Parkway & Conservation Trust, 1550 E. Shaw Ave., Ste. 114, Fresno, CA 93710

Party Pleasers, GFWC Philomathic Club, 1101 E. Plato Rd., Duncan, OK 73533

Past Receipts, Present Recipes, Cumberland County Historical Society, 21 N. Pitt St., Carlisle, PA 17013

Past to Present: A Pictorial Cookbook, Washington School Restoration Committee, P.O. Box 587, Oakland, OR 97462

Perennial Palette, Southborough Gardeners, P.O. Box 184, Southborough, MA 01772

Pick of the Crop, Two, North Sunflower Academy PTA, 148 Academy Rd., Drew, MS 38737

Plummer House Museum, Traill County Historical Society, 308 Caledonia Ave. W., Hillsboro, ND 58045

'Pon Top Edisto, Trinity Episcopal Church, 1589 Hwy. 174, P.O. Box 425, Edisto Island, SC 29438

Praise the Lord and Pass the Gravy, Stanley United Methodist Church, W. Main St., Stanley, VA 22851

Praiseworthy, Foundation for Historic Christ Church, P.O. Box 24, Irvington, VA 22480

Project Open Hand Cookbook, Project Open Hand Atlanta, 176 Ottley Dr., NE, Atlanta, GA 30342

Quad City Cookin', Queen of Heaven Circle of OLV Ladies Council, 4105 N. Division, Davenport, IA 52806

Rave Reviews, Ogunquit Playhouse, Route One North, Ogunquit, ME 03907

Recipes & Remembrances, Frank P. Tillman Elementary PTO, 230 Quan Ave., Kirkwood, MO 63122

Recipes and Remembrances, Otsego County Historical Society, 320 W. Main St., Gaylord, MI 49735

Recipes for Champions, Shebas of Khiva Temple Oriental Band, 5804 Briar St., Amarillo, TX 79109-6238

Recipes for Reading, New Hampshire Council on Literacy, P.O. Box 395, Concord, NH 03302-0395

Recipes from Our Home to Yours, Hospice of North Central Florida, 4200 NW 90th Blvd., Gainesville, FL 32606-3809

Recipes from the Flock, Mandarin Senior Citizens Center, 3848 Hartley Rd., Jacksonville, FL 32257

Renaissance of Recipes, Iao Intermediate School Renaissance Ke 'ala hou, 1910 Kaohu St., Wailuku, HI 96793

River City Recipes, Cape Girardeau Senior Center, 921 North Clark St., Cape Girardeau, MO 63701

Savoring Cape Cod, Massachusetts Audubon Society's Wellfleet Bay Wildlife Sanctuary, P.O. Box 236, 291 State Hwy. Rte. 6, South Wellfleet, MA 02663

Savoring the Southwest Again, Roswell Symphony Guild, P.O. Box 3078, Roswell, NM 88202

Savory Secrets, P.E.O. Chapter LR, c/o Jean Szoko, 22 Lake Forest Dr., St. Charles, MO 63301

Savory Secrets, Runnels School, 17255 S. Harrell's Ferry Rd., Baton Rouge, LA 70816

Savour St. Louis, Barnes-Jewish Hospital Auxiliary Plaza Chapter, One Barnes-Jewish Hospital Plaza, St. Louis, MO 63110

Scent from P.E.O. Sisterhood, Philanthropic Educational Organization, Chapter AG, 109 Forest Hill Way, Newcastle, WY 82701

Seaboard to Sideboard, Junior League of Wilmington, 3803 Wrightsville Ave., Downey Branch Office Park, Unit 9, Wilmington, NC 28403

Secrets of Amelia, McArthur Family Branch YMCA, 1915 Citrona Dr., Fernandina Beach, FL 32034

Shalom on the Range, Shalom Park, 14800 E. Belleview Dr., Aurora, CO 80015

Shared Treasures, First Baptist Church, 201 St. John, Monroe, LA 71201

Sharing Tasteful Memories, L.A.C.E. (Ladies Aspiring to Christian Excellence) of First Church of the Nazarene, 2601 H. G. Mosley Blvd., Longview, TX 75605

Silver Spoons, Kaiser Rehabilitation Center, 1125 South Trenton, Tulsa, OK 74120

Simply Cape Cod, Sandwich Junior Women's Club, P.O. Box 757, Sandwich, MA 02563

Simply Divine, Second-Ponce de Leon Baptist Church, 2715 Peachtree Rd., Atlanta, GA 30327

Somethin's Cookin' with Married Young Adults, Houston's First Baptist Church, 7401 Katy Freeway, Houston, TX 77024

Somethin' to Smile About, St. Martin, Iberia, Lafayette Community Action Agency, 501 St. John St., Lafayette, LA 70501

Southern Born and Bread, Junior Service League of LaGrange, P.O. Box 2195, LaGrange, GA 30241

Southern Elegance: A Second Course, Junior League of Gaston County, 2950 South Union Rd., Ste. A, Gastonia, NC 28054

Southern . . . On Occasion, Junior League of Cobb-Marietta, Inc., One Depot St., Ste. 300, Marietta, GA 30060

Southern Settings, Decatur General Foundation, Inc., 1201 7th St., SE, Decatur, AL 35601

Special Selections of Ocala, Ocala Royal Dames for Cancer Research, Inc., P.O. Box 6163, Ocala, FL 34478

Spice It Up!, Baton Rouge Branch of American Association of University Women, 10345 Barbara St., Baton Rouge, LA 70815

St. Andrew's Foods for the Multitudes and Smaller Groups, St. Andrew's Episcopal Church, 373 E. Carr Ave., P.O. Box 507, Cripple Creek, CO 80813

St. Ansgar Heritage Cookbook, St. Ansgar Heritage Association, P.O. Box 214, St. Ansgar, IA 50472

St. Paul's 50th Anniversary Cookbook, St. Paul's Lutheran Church, 3108 Sterretania Rd., Erie, PA 16506

Star-Spangled Recipes, American Legion Auxiliary, Department of West Virginia, 109 E. Shaver St., Belmont, OH 43718-0104

Sterling Service, Dothan Service League, 460 W. Main St., Ste. 3, Dothan, AL 36301

Swap Around Recipes, Delmarva Square Dance Federation, 28165 Bishop's Ct., Salisbury, MD 21801-0800

Sweet Memories, Holy Covenant United Methodist Women, 22111 Morton Ranch Rd., Katy, TX 77449

Symphony of Flavors, The Associates of the Redlands Bowl, P. O. Box 492, Redlands, CA 92373

A Taste of the Good Life from the Heart of Tennessee, Saint Thomas Heart Institute, 4220 Harding Rd., Nashville, TN 37205

A Taste of Tradition, Temple Emanu-El, 99 Taft Ave., Providence, RI 02906

The Tastes and Tales of Moiliili, Moiliili Community Center, 2535 S. King St., Honolulu, HI 96826

Tasty Temptations, Our Lady of the Mountains Church, 1425 Yagui St., Sierra Vista, AZ 85635

Tested by Time, Porter Gaud Parents Guild, P.O. Box 30431, Charleston, SC 29417

Texas Ties, Junior League of North Harris County, Inc., 5555 Fellowship Ln., Spring, TX 77379

Treasured Recipes of Provincetown, Provincetown Council on Aging, Grace Gouveia Bldg., 26 Alden St., Provincetown, MA 02657

Tutto Bene, Salvatore Mancini Lodge #2440, 49 Belcourt Ave., North Providence, RI 02911

United Church of Tekoa Cookbook, United Church of Tekoa, 301 S. Crosby St., Tekoa, WA 99033

Vermont Children's Aid Society Cookbook, Vermont Children's Aid Society, 79 Weaver St., Winooski, VT 05404

Victorian Secrets, The Chiselers, Inc., P.O. Box 14494, Tampa, FL 33690-4494

Victorian Thymes and Pleasures, Junior League of Williamsport, Inc., 340 Hughes St., Ste. 105, Williamsport, PA 17701

We Cook Too, Women's Committee, Wadsworth Atheneum, 66 Middlebrook Rd., West Hartford, CT 06119

What's Cooking in Hampton, Friends of Hampton Community Library, 4960 Rte. 8, Shopper's Plaza, Allison Park, PA 15101

When Kiwanis Cooks, Wisconsin-Upper Michigan District of Kiwanis International, P.O. Box 33, Plover, WI 54467

White Clay Creek Presbyterian Church 275th Anniversary Cookbook, White Clay Creek Presbyterian Church, 15 Polly Drummond Hill Rd., Newark, DE 19711

Women Who Can Dish It Out, Junior League of Springfield, Inc., 2574 E. Bennett, Springfield, MO 65804

Your Community Cookbook Could Win an Award

The McIlhenny Company of Avery Island, Louisiana, generates a great deal of enthusiasm among service organizations nationwide by sponsoring the Tabasco® Community Cookbook Awards Competition each fall on the family homestead and company headquarters in Avery Island. All community cookbooks published within the last two years are invited to participate in the prestigious awards competition.

The editors salute the winners of the 1999 Tabasco® Community Cookbook Awards competition, many of which have recipes featured in this volume of *America's Best Recipes*. To mark the 10th anniversary of the cookbook awards, the McIlhenny Company awarded a total of $10,000 to the winning entries of the 1999 awards competition. The first place winner received $3,500, followed by $2,000 for second place, and $1,000 for third. Each regional winner was given $500, and special merit winners received $100. The sponsoring organizations of the winning cookbooks, in turn, donated the prize money to charities of their choice.

The 1999 Tabasco® Community Cookbook Awards winners were:

- **First Place Winner:** *De Nuestra Mesa,* New Hope Charities, West Palm Beach, FL
- **Second Place Winner:** *Bravo!,* University Musical Society, Ann Arbor, MI
- **Third Place Winner:** *Yuletide on Hilton Head,* Yuletide Publishing Committee, Inc., Hilton Head Island, SC
- **New England:** *No winner*
- **Mid-Atlantic:** *The Heart of Pittsburgh,* Sacred Heart Elementary School Parent Teacher Guild, Pittsburgh, PA
- **South:** *Seaboard to Sideboard,* Junior League of Wilmington, NC
- **Midwest:** *Cooking Up Memories,* The Tazewell County Genealogical and Historical Society, Pekin, IL
- **Southwest:** *The Dining Car,* The Denison Service League, Inc., Denison, TX
- **West:** *Flavors of Hawaii,* Child & Family Service, Honolulu, HI
- **Special Mention:** *Sounds Delicious,* Atlanta Symphony Associates, Atlanta, GA
- **Special Mention:** *A Sunsational Encore,* Junior League of Greater Orlando, FL
- **Walter S. McIlhenny Hall of Fame 1999:** *Little Rock Cooks,* Junior League of Little Rock, Inc., Little Rock, AR
- **Walter S. McIlhenny Hall of Fame 1999:** *Recipe Jubilee,* Junior League of Mobile, AL
- **Walter S. McIlhenny Hall of Fame 1999:** *Simply Simpático,* Junior League of Albuquerque, NM
- **Walter S. McIlhenny Hall of Fame 1999:** *Deep in the Heart,* Dallas Junior Forum, Inc., Richardson, TX
- **Walter S. McIlhenny Hall of Fame 1999:** *Stop and Smell the Rosemary,* Junior League of Houston, Inc., Houston, TX

For information on the Tabasco® Community Cookbook Awards or for an awards entry form send a self-addressed stamped #10 (legal size) envelope to
Tabasco Community Cookbook Awards
℅ Hunter & Associates, Inc.
41 Madison Ave.
New York, NY 10010-2202

For a free booklet about producing a community cookbook send a self-addressed stamped #10 (legal size) envelope to
Compiling Culinary History
℅ Hunter & Associates, Inc.
41 Madison Ave.
New York, NY 10010-2202

Index